BUILDING CHARACTER

BUILDING CHARACTER

Figure I.1. Frontispiece for *Ausgeführte Bauten und Entwürfe*, by Frank Lloyd Wright, ca. 1911–1912, Harry Ransom Center, University of Texas at Austin.

INTRODUCTION

The Racialization of Architectural Character in the Long Nineteenth Century

The appreciation of beauty on the part of primitive peoples, Mongolian, Indian, Arab, Egyptian, Greek and Goth, was unerring. Because of this their work is coming home to us to-day in another truer Renaissance, to open our eyes that we may cut away the dead wood and brush aside the accumulated rubbish of centuries of false education. This Renaissance means a return to simple conventions in harmony with nature. Primarily it is a simplifying process. Then, having learned the spiritual lesson that the East has power to teach the West, we may build upon this basis the more highly developed forms our more highly developed life will need.

—**Frank Lloyd Wright,**
Ausgeführte Bauten und Entwürfe

FRANK LLOYD WRIGHT HAS BECOME a representative figure of the Western paradigm of architectural organicism that proliferated in the United States during the long nineteenth century. This transatlantic philosophy of design was disseminated through the architectural writings and experimental buildings of European and North American innovators including Eugène Emmanuel Viollet-le-Duc in France; Gottfried Semper in Germany; and Henry Hobson Richardson, Frank Furness, and Wright's mentor, Louis Sullivan, in the United States. In 1911 Wright used a period of personal and professional reassessment to summarize his philosophy of style for European audiences in the German-language monograph *Ausgeführte Bauten und Entwürfe* (fig. I.1). In the introduction to this text, he uses narrative descriptions of nature to outline the metaphorical principles of design behind his architectural style for modern America: the Prairie Style. While his prose is rife with vivid references to living organisms—including the floral imagery that was a common trope of

Sullivan's architectural writings—he does not ground his architectural style in a direct imitation of the external features of plants or animals. For Wright, a mimetic approach was the "dead wood" of Renaissance theory that prevented Americans from formulating their own national building style. He believed an alternative approach was necessary for the renewal of contemporary artistic culture. In lieu of a mimetic model of nature, he chose to abstract the rules nature uses to create life in a system of design that was capable of "growing" the primary features of his architecture from the fundamental "conditions of life and work" in democratic America.[1] While the architectural forms he created did not immediately look like any recognizable living organism, he believed they behaved as living organisms did by using a central idea or concept to functionally and aesthetically integrate the individual parts of the project into a consolidated whole. Wright's Prairie Style of architecture continues an important disciplinary tradition in the West of metaphorically relating the principles of nature to the arts in order to establish the autochthonous building styles that clarified and aesthetically embodied the life of the nation.

In a significant passage in the introduction to *Ausgeführte Bauten und Entwürfe,* Wright explicitly uses the concept of character to denote the ways that a building's material features embody the social, cultural, and political traits of the people it serves. In contrast to an iconographical representation of cultural identity, Wright uses *character* to denote the meanings an architectural environment accrues when its spatial, structural, and material features emerge seamlessly from the patterns of everyday life. As a result of the close relationship between the historical conditions of emergence and the material constitution of this form, the resulting architectural style is perceived to be uniquely expressive of the social conditions of its origin. Supplementing his study of nature on the family farm in Wisconsin with the retrospective gaze of the historian, Wright constructs a comparative list of the relative beauties of primitive building forms as proof that all of the vernacular styles of history are regulated by a common set of universal principles that continue to order architectural forms in the present. He even wonders at the feeling of Italianness he experiences when interacting with the premodern architectures of Florence and the Veneto, a site on his first tour of Europe, as encouragement for his own search for an autochthonous building style for America. The only change that he admits to this historical tradition is the increasing need to secularize the spiritual content of architectural forms to match the secular character of modern society.

By the end of his introduction Wright claims to have developed an authentically expressive architectural character for the modern world in his Prairie Style. Many of his critics have agreed. A long line of Wright interpreters praise the Prairie Style for challenging the interior customs of decorum that subtend the partitioned domestic interiors of Victorian architectures to better support the customs and rituals that were introduced by life on the open prairie.[2] Taking a cue from Wright's *Autobiography,* this scholarly tradition interprets the low-hanging eaves, the horizontal brick banding, and the concrete stylobate of this style as a literal deconstruction of the "closed boxes" that were a common feature of Victorian styles. It is probably more correct to say that Wright effectively synthesizes two seemingly oppositional elements of midwestern culture. As C. Robert Haywood reminds us in his book *Victorian West,* the infrastructural development of the frontier was based on a delicate balance between the cattle ranches that provided the economic substructure for local trade and the aesthetic trappings of middle-class Victorian culture that elevated these towns into new urban centers of commerce and social distinction.[3] By the interwar and postwar periods the Prairie Style had proliferated beyond the geographical confines of the prairie, which transformed this regional building style into a national sign for modern domestic life.

This brief recounting of Wright's comparative history of primitive culture exemplifies an enduring myth of the transatlantic paradigm of architectural organicism. This myth originates with the belief that every society in the premodern world develops a distinct architectural character or style that embodies their unique way of life. This credo reaches back to Vitruvius's *Ten Books of Architecture,* but was updated in the nineteenth century by a complementary set of scientific models for historical study that rationalized disciplinary debates. In Western Europe, the political debates of newly emerging nation-states prompted a frenzied search for the historical origins of European cultures. Nearly every sector of society looked to modern ethnographic histories to trace contemporary national trends back to the remote past and thus distinguish the major powers of the Continent. Viollet-le-Duc and Semper famously employed ethnographical frameworks for their histories of architecture, with the latter going so far as to identify his approach as a practical branch of anthropology for the design professions. As architectural organicism migrated to the United States, modern architects built upon these European origin myths by engaging in the parallel study of world cultures that were brought together by the democratic experiment. Taking the scientific basis of comparative ethnographical histories of architecture as a given, these designers focused on the material cultures of peoples directly related to the semantic associations of architectural programs accruing within their immediate contexts in the New World. The most famous examples of this disciplinary tradition are Sullivan and Wright's celebrations of the material cultures that coexisted in the American Midwest, including the Byzantine references of the Chicago Style and the Japanese precedents of the Prairie Style. While architectural historians have recovered the diverse cultural references that these American innovators used to create an American architecture, not enough have explicitly considered the potential role that Western civilizational frameworks, and especially white nativist discourses, must have exerted on these design movements.

If we stop to consider the hegemonic effects of whiteness on the architectural style debates, then it becomes reasonable to ask how the creation of an autochthonous national style of building reflects nativist interpretations of national character. When this question has been considered in relation to representative figures in the past such as Wright, many of the answers have applied an anachronistic multicultural framework to interpreting his architectural legacy. Much of this scholarship views his textual references to Japanese, Native American, and pre-Columbian cultures as evidence of Wright's progressive attitude toward the growing diversity of the American body politic. But even if we believe that his references to non-Western material cultures and his strident faith in American individualism were progressive for their time, we also know that his Prairie Style was built for an elite audience that could afford servants and, in many cases, were beneficiaries of the white hegemonic ideal of American citizenship operating at that time. This conservative vision of American character may have also influenced Wright's thinking and his architectural production. It makes sense for the architectural historian to at least consider the potential influence that hegemonic definitions of national character might have had on the modern architects' management of modern architectural styles.

The romantic mythologies of the American frontier that underwrote the most popular definitions of American character in the nineteenth century almost exclusively focused upon clarifying the shifting boundaries of whiteness that were being pluralized by the democratic experiment. As waves of European immigrants settled and intermarried in the United States, contentious debates emerged regarding the prevailing national character that resulted from this amalgamation of cultural stock. What were the essential characteristics of the American race, and which peoples best represented the potential of this stock? The political discourse of manifest destiny further racialized period debates on American character, but this time for both white and nonwhite populations. Politicians, preachers, businessmen, and frontier settlers of all stripes depicted the settlement of the New World as a righteous war between the civilized agents of Western civilization and the primitive savages of the East.

Only when we examine the cultural politics of national building styles for the ways they reflect the racial assumptions of this period can we begin to take note of the nativist tones of certain passages in Wright's writings. For example, if we return to his introduction to *Ausgeführte Bauten und Entwürfe*, Wright's admission to gleaning a "spiritual lesson that the East has power to teach the West" is paired with a mandate of aesthetic destruction that paves the way for an authentic future modern style: "His machine, the tool in which his opportunity lies, can only *murder the traditional forms of other peoples and earlier times.* He

Figure I.2. Léon Cogniet, *l'expédition d'Egypte sous les ordres de Bonaparte*, 1835.

must find new forms, new industrial ideals, or stultify both opportunity and forms."[4] This destructive modality for cultural production is a prescient parallel to the political oppressions that nonwhite peoples suffered in the historical fulfillment of manifest destiny—from Native American tribes, African American slaves, and Mexican migrants to the Chinese laborers who laid the railroads that established the first intercontinental railroad in the United States. Wright's mandate for aesthetic destruction treads the same ground that the political strategies of European colonialism set in its settlement of colonies in America if not before. Napoleon Bonaparte's colonization of Africa is famous for its retinue of scientific advisors that established a clear pattern for politically exploiting the artistic knowledge of the other (fig. I.2). These political implications are also present in Semper's artistic interest in the native Māori tribes of New Zealand, a territory that German chancellors later sought to colonize during their brief foray into colonialism in Africa, Asia, and the South Seas.

Within the geographical context of the United States, and especially within the midwestern territories that were previously held by native peoples, modern architectural styles and theories of national character became mutually supportive paradigms for delineating the social boundaries of the nation-state. The romantic mythologies of the American frontier that provided a clear reference point for Wright's Prairie Style was in conversation with hegemonic interpretations of American character that privileged the social, political, and cultural perspectives of European colonial settlers and successive generations of Euro-American citizens. The mere recognition of this relationship better prepares us to identify the specific function of racial discourses in modern architectural debates more broadly. As the historian Anders Stephanson notes in his seminal study of manifest destiny in American studies, the ruminations on white racial character in debates on American citizenship directly enabled white frontiersmen to naturalize their occupations of the west.[5] Sometimes these efforts were levied to wrest claims of land ownership from nonwhite native peoples, but at other times they were used to more clearly define which racial and ethnic groups from Europe were most worthy of determining the central elements of American democracy. Even when nonwhite peoples were recognized as contributing to the development of American life, they labored under the prejudice that they could never fully assimilate the Anglo-American values that dominated the political imagination. Recent publications in American studies demonstrate the inherent racial charge of period definitions for American character, especially in the efforts of competing racial groups to concretize and secure their rights as citizens of the United States.[6] A similar effort needs to be undertaken in architectural history to understand how design factors in enabling and disabling certain populations to secure the American dream (or the dreams of other nation-states that purported to represent the values of Western civilization in the nineteenth century).

Our current examination of the racial politics that conditioned the transatlantic dissemination of architectural organicism begins by asking a few pointed questions of the political function of national architectural styles. What definitions of national character did modern architects use to establish their autochthonous styles of building in the past? And what racial, ethnic, and cultural characters were most privileged by these disciplinary debates? This book poses these questions to the range of architectural strategies that were used to produce national architectural styles within the paradigm of architectural organicism, from the pioneering concepts of French structural rationalism and German tectonic theory to the nationalist associations of the Chicago Style, the Prairie Style, and the International Style. Using the concept of character as an interpretive lens, this study identifies the racial content that has not yet been examined within the modern architectural style debates. This content includes the racial logic that is structurally endemic to scientifically rationalized discourses of architectural style, as well as the specifically racist associations that architectural styles accrued as a result of their discrete political contexts.

My explicit reference to Wright's architectural theory thus far has only been a convenient prompt to begin a critical conversation about the historical integrations of race and style theory that have proliferated within all branches of architectural organicism. The social and political contexts of the nineteenth century effectively foreclosed progressive conceptions of an integrated citizenry that provided equal social status and legal protections for the white and nonwhite peoples cohabiting within Continental and North American territories. This polemic primes us to develop a more principled interpretation of the racial assumptions perpetuated by the organic architectural traditions that were inaugurated to help formulate the mythological boundaries of our national pasts.

Race, the Human Body, and Architectural Organicism

The cultural associations of national building styles found in nineteenth-century architectural treatises are indicative of a deeper critical tendency within architectural organicism that treats race and style as two parallel empirical expressions of natural law. This scientific mode of analyzing the past mythologizes the power of vernacular buildings to operate as transparent signs of cultural identity and emblematic containers for the constituent elements of one's social habitus.[7] The modern architect's belief that certain design solutions more authentically reflect the state of local culture than others is an important supposition to critique, since every design of a time period is, by definition, conditioned in one way or another by the social, political, or economic contexts of its making. So, what is it precisely that grounds the perception that certain building forms have more rigorously mirrored the prevailing customs of a particular social and cultural context? What conceptual principles provided an architect with the aesthetic sensibility required to first interpret and then regulate the aesthetic appearances of national architectural styles?

By the turn of the century a number of humanist scholars experimented with employing the comparative methodologies of the social sciences to deduce the invisible laws of order that regulated the evolution of architectural styles over time. Of the many works included in this tradition, we could cite Johann Gottfried Herder's *Ideen zur Philosophie der Geschichte der Menschheit* (1784); James Cowles Prichard's *The Natural History of Man* (1844); Owen Jones's *The Grammar of Ornament* (1856); Hippolyte Taine's *Philosophie de l'art* (1865); and Sir Banister Fletcher's *A History of Architecture* (1896), to name just a few. These texts collectively propagate the idea that premodern vernacular building styles automatically emerged when a local people learned to apply raw materials toward a functional problem in a straightforward or pragmatic way.

This interpretation echoes the ecological principles of racial variation put forward in the natural sciences, which alternately credited a number of seen and unseen biological mechanisms for the apparent variation of human culture around the world. Subsequent investigations in the burgeoning field of racial anthropology examined the cultural implications of biological laws of development on human settlement patterns and artistic customs. The most influential standards used typological theories to substantiate the taxonomic categories of human differences that were invented by botanists and zoologists in the eighteenth century. Modern architectural critics extended this scientific view of nature into architectural discourses in order to revitalize the spiritual and aesthetic instincts they believed were especially powerful at the beginnings of human culture but had become muted by the rationalist biases of the Enlightenment. Jean-Jacques Rousseau's positive estimations of the primitive world, emblematically represented by his rhetorical figure of the noble savage, is only the most recognizable variation of this line of thinking. The primitive instinct for artistic form was seen as a social palliative for the cultural plights of modern man, who was in great need of a common social principle to bind him to his fellow man within the emerging nation-state.

Within the field of race science, biologists, anthropologists, and sociologists used the term *race* to describe a wide range of phenomena in nature, from the breeding properties of language groups and the physical appearance of organic specimens to the cultural products generated by a common group of people. The analytical value of the race concept strategically shifted in the late eighteenth century from taxonomic to typological criteria as scientists revised the meaning of species criteria in the natural and life sciences. Georges Buffon introduced internal physiological criteria for categorizing race types; namely, the sexual selection of animal species, which complicated the physical or taxonomic criteria that Linnaeus had decided upon nearly half a century earlier. Races were now defined by the organic principles of growth regulating physical appearances instead of just a similarity of appearances. This embodied criterion extended the critical importance of the race concept even to ephemeral phenomena such as language. The German linguists Friedrich Max Müller and Franz Bopp famously used the term *race* to categorize the different language groups that evolved from the first spoken language of European man, what they called the Indo-European language. At this time Müller and Bopp were adamant that the racial typologies for acquired skills such as language did not always cleanly correlate with the physical categories that biologists used to distinguish human differences. Yet languages appeared to exhibit the same organic principles of development as biological race types as phylogeny, or the grammatical structure of mother tongues and sister languages, by passing on a fixed set of recognizable traits from one generation to the next that could be traced back to a common origin (fig. I.3). These relationships were visually communicated through extensive tree diagrams that would find discrete parallels in architectural history.

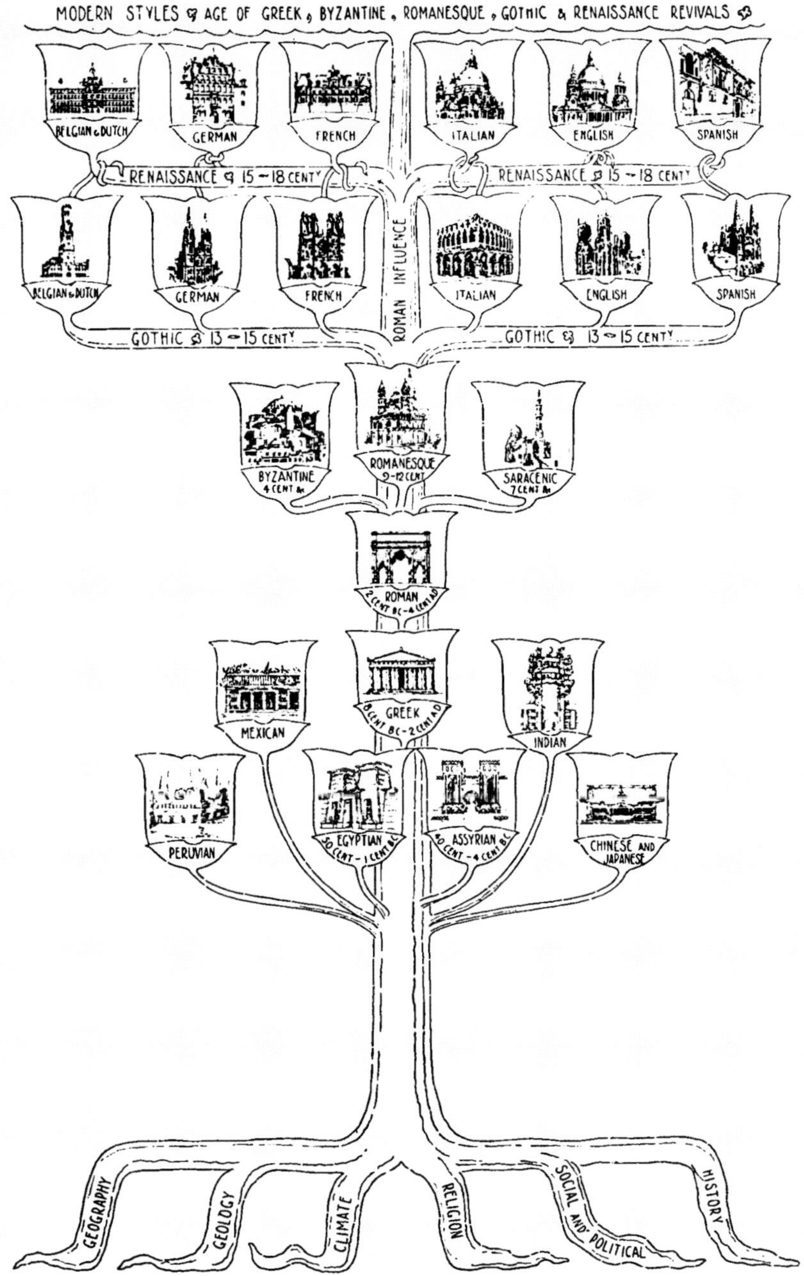

THE TREE OF ARCHITECTURE,

Showing the main growth or evolution of the various styles.

The Tree must be taken as suggestive only, for minor influences cannot be indicated in a diagram of this kind.

Figure I.3. Sir Banister Fletcher, "The Tree of Architecture," from *A History of Architecture on the Comparative Method* (1896).

In response to the social challenges of nation building, modern architects sought new ways of creating national architectural styles that could match the perceived transparency of historical vernacular forms and thus bind national culture. The scientific explanations for race types and cultural differences fundamentally challenged divine metaphors of the human body in neoclassical theories, which implicitly transformed the critical role of character judgments in the modern architectural style debates. Biological models of physiological development provided a privileged model for humanist conceptions of architectural invention that continued to reference the metaphorical figure of the human body to interpret architectural character in the present. By the end of the eighteenth century, scholars of natural history, philosophy, and art began to integrate physiological criteria for organic development such as skull shape, facial profile, skin color, and hair texture into their philosophical accounts for the invisible causes of human character. These efforts established a wide range of standards for representing the inner qualities of racial and ethnic groups in the imitative arts of painting and sculpture and they produced new rules for visualizing racial and national characters in the nonimitative art of architecture. The close disciplinary relationship between the fields of biology and anthropology also contributed to the interchangeability of *race* and *nation* as analytical terms for *community* that exceeded the limits of kinship relations and tribal laws. Georg Wilhelm Friedrich Hegel's *Phenomenology of the Spirit* (1807) and Arthur de Gobineau's *The Inequality of the Human Races* (1853) are just two of the most infamous examples of universal histories of Europe to employ racialized models of national development. Both authors used labels such as "the German race" or "the American race" to communicate the idea that national characters had become just as fixed as biological traits and were just as geographically and historically traceable. Subsequently, nineteenth-century practitioners of physiognomy, craniometrics, and phrenology employed ethnographical techniques of observation for identifying the constituent elements of national character within a population.

By the dawn of the twentieth century North American social workers were entrusted to socially engineer national character through the medical sterilization projects that attempted to eradicate so-called aberrant groups in society, from single mothers and political radicals to convicted criminals, using sanctioned state and federal funds. I argue that the medicalized treatment of the human body enculturated modern architects to expect new definitions for human character to have visual and political effects. The transatlantic theories of organic architecture examined below demonstrate the critical importance of the race concept in enabling modern architects to manage the visual expression of architectural character in seminal points of nation building. I argue that the racial interpretation of human character introduced new concepts of embodiment and corporeality that implicitly revised the human-body metaphors of neoclassical architectural theory that previously served as inspirations for architectural design. This reading recovers the critical importance of race science in the historical transformation of Vitruvian architecture theory that were necessary for placing the humanist architectural traditions of the past on firmer ground in the present.

The explicit use of human-body metaphors in architectural design has a long history. As Caroline van Eck notes in *Organicism in Nineteenth-Century Architecture*, anthropomorphic metaphors for design date back to at least the first century in Vitruvius's *Ten Books of Architecture*, if not earlier in now lost Greek and Etruscan writings referred to by other theorists. Leonardo da Vinci's "Vitruvian Man" famously illustrates the belief in an unseen but all-powerful divinity that guarantees the laws of nature, and in turn the divine proportions of the human body that provided the aesthetic foundation for classical and neoclassical architectural styles. This antique tradition did in fact wane in the eighteenth and nineteenth century as historical knowledge of the past expanded. While postwar scholars have outlined the general influence of archaeology and anthropology on pluralizing the historical sources for eclecticism and revivalism in architectural debates, none have specifically located the constitutive role of the race concept in sustaining the conceptual importance of the human body as a relevant metaphor for design.[8] Modern scientific explanations for human development inherently challenged the divine models of nature found in Roman treatises. While figures such as Wright claimed to have replaced the conceptual tools of Renaissance knowledge, they continued to see themselves as proponents of a humanist tradition in architecture. If we are to take this continuity seriously, then we must examine the conceptual bases upon which this tradition was perpetuated in the nineteenth century.

In this study, I argue that one of the most important and overlooked factors of the nineteenth-century humanist tradition in architecture is the influence of scientific conceptions of racial character on the continued disciplinary interest in the human body. A tide of new empirical models for physical development recast the importance of the human-body metaphor in architectural design. I explore the ways that the race concept suggested both physical and ephemeral modes of embodiment in architectural design. Race became a privileged concept in the paradigm of architectural organicism because it was perceived to be an empirical character of organic life that exhibited a wide range of representative qualities for human life: it was correlated to the inherent qualities of human thought and psychology; it became a fixed category in the study of human language groups; biologists applied it as a physical typology within the natural sciences; and ethnographers employed it as a term for categorizing the

ORGANS OF SPEECH. 121

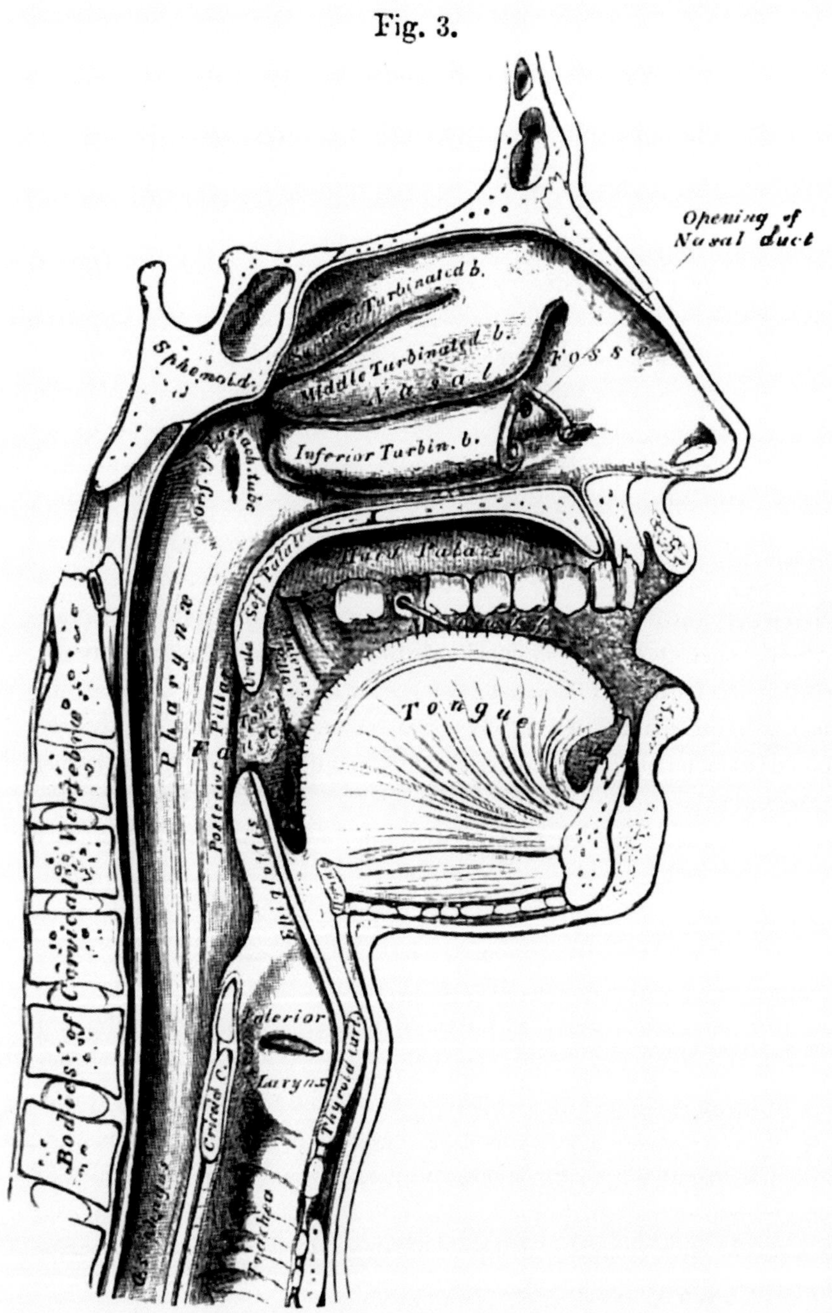

Figure I.4. Friedrich Max Müller, "Organs of Speech," in *The Science of Language*, vol. 2 (London: Longmans, Green, 1871), 121.

cultural differences of primitive peoples (fig. I.4). The birth of the Aryan migration myth is particularly telling in this context, as theorists in linguistics, as noted above, directly related their race categories to the human body's capacity to produce speech in the 1840s. Yet it was not until these inner workings of the body were directly overlaid with the strict typological categories of biology and ethnography in the 1850s and 1860s that the modern conception of the Aryan race was truly born. Contemporary Indo-European studies still continues to struggle with the cultural biases this disciplinary history suggests regarding the ethnographical character of the primitive race that supposedly migrated from the steppe mountains in the past.[9]

Within the realm of architectural theory, race types became a privileged empirical representation of nature's capacity for stylizing organic form, precisely because it placed the human being back at the center of humanistic discourses. Because of the nonvisual criteria that was often associated with the race idea in the nineteenth century, the conceptual realignment of neoclassical human-body metaphors within architectural organicism could proceed without the need for explicit visual references to the human body. Modern architects learned instead to personify the inert building materials of design as creating a metaphorical organic body in its own right. This enervated mass of material could now autonomously adapt the characters required to fit a regional context—the characters that were previously transferred to the building through a mimetic imitation of the human form (fig. I.5). In architectural writings of the nineteenth century, one is more apt to find explicit references to the embodied character of building materials, the personification of building forms, or the corporeal integration of architectural elements into an organic whole than any explicit references to the human body metaphors of neoclassical theories.

Despite this shift in descriptive tactics, however, these tendencies provide explicit clues to the avenues through which modern architects learned to borrow the methodological and representational standards of the natural sciences. From the time that Rudolph Virchow applied the statistical standards of Adolphe Quetelet's nominal study of human character to specific race types, the abstract mathematical representation of cultural differences had become a routine feature of nineteenth-century science.[10] Instead of interpreting the paradigm of architectural organicism as marking a precipitous break with the human-body metaphors of neoclassical theory, this study examines the racialized human-body metaphors that were an implicit element of the scientific rationalization of architectural character. My approach establishes an alternative intellectual history for the architectural style debates that recovers the continued relevance of the human body within disciplinary debates that continued to preserve a humanist tradition of architectural design.

Figure I.5. Bruno Taut, *Die Stadtkrone* (The city crown), 1919.

The five architects examined in this study—Eugène Emmanuel Viollet-le-Duc, Gottfried Semper, Louis Sullivan, Frank Lloyd Wright, and William Lescaze—collectively defined architectural characters as a transparent reflection of the inner character of a national subject, sometimes the user of a building and sometimes the designer. This critical assumption makes it possible for us to infer a wide range of human-body metaphors that were necessary to transform neoclassical theories into a new methodological basis for architectural invention. Within the transatlantic political contexts of the nineteenth century, the racialization of architectural character directly enabled the modern architect to develop more regionally specific representations of the modern nation-state.

An important goal of this study is to outline the critical influence of race science on modern architectural theories and national architectural styles of the nineteenth century. These developments are examined within the transatlantic political contexts that gave birth to the European imperialisms and US settler colonialisms of this period. This book develops a nuanced interpretation of the critical importance of the race concept in personifying the notions of architectural character operating within the paradigm of architectural organicism—for good or ill—to explain the practical methods designers used to manage architecture as a socially expressive art form. I chose the paradigm of architectural organicism for analysis because its leading theorists explicitly used scientific models of nature to update the metaphorical references that were necessary to reform the procedures of architectural invention. The relationship between race and style is most clearly demonstrated by the explicit citations that modern architects made to scientific theories of racial development to legitimize their evolutionary interpretations of cultural history. My examination of the disciplinary importance of the race concept builds upon the work of Martin Berger and Dianne Harris, which has examined the critical effects of white racial discourses on viewer interpretations of architectural spaces, both in the fine arts and in architecture, landscape architecture, and urban design. My research complements their accounts of the invisible ways that racial ideologies condition the visual interpretation of social norms by locating the formalist principles of design and the concepts of material embodiment that modern architects discovered in their study of the race concept.

In this book, I contextualize the hermeneutical function of the race concept in modern architectural theory by relating it to the principles of formal development it was associated with in scientific discourses. When proponents of architectural organicism defined style as the external expression of the underlying conditions of construction, the physical appearances of elements such as ornament, physical cladding, and colored surfaces were perceived to be surface registrations of the underlying ideas or cultural practices of premodern peoples. As modern ethnographical histories colored the meaning of these underlying conditions, these embodied characteristics increasingly became invested with more explicit racial associations in more nuanced and unpredictable ways. Using the scientific interpretation of racial character as a guide, I examine the implicit theoretical revisions to neoclassical human-body metaphors that were necessary to formulate the principles of French structural rationalism, German tectonic theory, the Chicago school of architecture, the Prairie Style, and the polemical definition of the International Style inaugurated at the Museum of Modern Art in 1932. Modern architects in Europe and the United States maintained the conceptual parallels that were established between the categories of race and style in the natural sciences in their textual correlation of racial and architectural characters in the invention of national architectural styles.

In the case studies I examine, each historical figure directly cites the developmental principles of ethnography, ethnology, sociology, or criminal anthropology to inflect racial interpretations of human character into architectural discourses. The cultural and nationalist overtones of Wright's readings of native character referenced in the epigraph are just one example of the sort of discourses that shaped the Euro-American paradigm of architectural organicism. Beginning with Viollet-le-Duc in France and Semper in Germany, this book reconstructs the ethnographical models of architectural history that later influenced Sullivan's and Wright's organic architecture theories in North America. This intellectual history for architectural organicism foregrounds the modern architect's theoretical debt to the race concept as a result of the changing scientific contexts of the nineteenth century. Even when these architectural theorists do not explicitly use a visual representation of the human body in their writings, their visual representation of race types alongside those of vernacular building styles maintain the metaphorical parallel between nature and art that was central to the humanist architectural traditions of neoclassicism.

A study of the race concept in modern architectural debates also provides architectural historians with a useful lens for evaluating the subsequent racialization of International Style architectures that embodied national characters without making use of historical ornament. By the first two decades of the twentieth century, critics in the International Style debates challenged previous nationalist interpretations of architectural style for an outlook that seemed better suited to accommodate the emerging international avant-garde. Lescaze, a Swiss émigré to the United States, became a representative figure of this style in North America upon his inclusion in the Museum of Modern Art's 1932 exhibition on International Style. Despite his inclusion in this exhibit, Lescaze resisted Philip Johnson and Henry-Russell Hitchcock's formalist definition of the International Style by continuing the social and cultural commitments of European avant-gardes in the United States. His dogged advocacy for public housing in the New York City Housing Authority (NYCHA) also continued several critical projects of nineteenth-century architectural organicism, including the notion that the visual aesthetic of social housing communicates an organic ideal for mass culture in contemporary society. Lescaze demanded that, just like the organic architectures of Wright and Sullivan earlier in the century, his public housing transparently reflect the needs of its users while providing a physical context for enculturating local subjects into a hegemonic national culture. His efforts to popularize public housing in 1930s New York finally found mature physical expression in his design for Williamsburg Houses, which established a new urban type for this building typology in the NYCHA into the 1940s and 1950s.

Though he has never been explicitly associated with the ideas of nineteenth-century architectural organicism, I interpret Lescaze's public housing designs for the ways they nationalize the International Style for use as a tool for building up American citizenship. Williamsburg Houses ideologically bridges the pure aesthetic criteria that Johnson and Hitchcock believed constituted a universal style of building and the communal criteria that the social theorists Lewis Mumford, Catherine Bauer, and Clarence Stein believed were necessary for a public architecture to organically emerge from its social context in the twentieth century as it had in the past. Mumford and Bauer's writings especially interpreted the humble brick surfaces of Lescaze's new urban type as an organic expression of the mass sociality then emerging in the modern world. As a representative type of American New Deal architecture, Williamsburg Houses constitutes an interesting example of the late influence of architectural organicism in the International Style debates of the twentieth century.

There were at least two complementary ways that scientific discourses on human character enabled the conceptual integration of race and style theory within the paradigm of architectural organicism—the one theoretical and the other material. In terms of modern architectural theory, scientific explanations for racial character transformed the critical importance of anthropomorphic metaphors for design by reinterpreting design as a simulated process of historical selection of vernacular type forms. Organic models of development were an important tutor for modern architects because they introduced typological interpretations of form that paralleled the empirical criterion of the natural sciences. The critical importance of racial typologies in the natural sciences mirrored the analytical value of vernacular typologies in architectural discourses, but especially in ethnographically inflected cultural histories where the material and expressive cultures of primitive peoples were used as a proxy for representing the cultural differences of premodern peoples. Within this intellectual context, modern architects' early desires to create a science of architectural design introduced the possibility of racializing the notion of architectural character in the European discourses on style. The practical function of type thinking was applied in architectural organicism through the credo that "architecture should imitate the methods rather than the forms of nature, in order to create the illusion of life."[11] The conceptual parallels between racial typologies and vernacular typologies legitimized the authenticity of modern building designs by setting new scientific criteria for assessing how well buildings reflected the principles of nature.

In addition to ethnographical histories that reinterpreted the meaning of premodern aesthetic motifs, evolutionary models of historical change also personified the morphological transformations of architectural styles over time. In a sense, the building seemed to be self-aware in its search for a physical form that was both functionally fit and aesthetically pleasing to its local population. The composition of inert building materials into recognizable styles of architecture, usually interpreted through engineering principles of statics in construction in earlier phases of cultural history, was seemingly as steady, concrete, and predictable as the morphological transformation of organic types in nature. Goethe's theory of *Urpflanze* (the metaform for all plant life), Darwin's theory of natural selection, Bopp's organic theory of language, and Jacob Moleschott's dietary regulations of human character all pointed toward universal laws for refining cultural forms. In the wake of strict materialist interpretations of nature, it became the job of the modern architect to shape architectural materials in accordance with these natural laws, to mirror the organic production of regional types that reflected the needs of and perhaps even conditioned the future form of regional populations. Only a rational and naturalistic process of design could produce the required methodologies for producing an authentic modern style, especially as the fall of Vitruvianism introduced confusion over what historical styles were still appropriate for use in the present.

Within this context racial interpretations of human character served as a heuristic category of interpreting architectural styles. The organic language found in modern architectural debates of the second half of the nineteenth century reveals the collective tendency of European architectural critics to depict the morphological transformations of vernacular building typologies in teleological terms, thus metaphorically investing them with an autonomous will or morphological faculty. The architectural concept of embodiment was further personified by the tacit associations of racial and national character in the sciences: architectural ornament and skin color were perceived to be parallel surface registrations of the invisible forces that shaped matter behind the scenes. The revival of stylistic motifs from architectural history constituted an explicit material strategy for recovering the lost aesthetic instinct of premodern racial and ethnic groups for use in the present. Such revivals attempted to renew the daily patterns of the immediate ancestors of contemporary nation-states by repeating the spatial and structural type forms of vernacular precedents uncovered in ethnographic and ethnological studies of the period. Modern architects used such strategies of design to ensure that the social protocols of the contemporary citizen would overlap with those of their ancestors—a material reinforcement of the national mythologies invented for unifying the masses and enculturating loyal modern subjects. If we can agree with Benedict Anderson that national myths are purposeful fictions created to indoctrinate the citizen-subject and shape the public sphere, then national architectural styles were an instrumental material form of shaping the cultural regimes for ordering the nation-state.[12]

As analogical bodies, organic architectures emulate the deep structural principles of nature that stylized the physical appearances of race types in the generative principles used to construct regional architectural characters. As rationally constituted spatial, structural, and ornamental constructs, organic architectures afforded the leadership of developing nation-states with material contexts to renew the life patterns of their cultural ancestors. In both modalities—as embodied fragments of the past and organically responsive contexts in the present—the spatial and structural elements of architecture did more than hold up ornamental signs of national identity; they provided material proof of the renewed cultural legacies that architecture provides to accommodate the needs of contemporary culture. I outline in this book the ways that the transatlantic debates in architectural organicism privileged the physical embodiment and visual representation of the shifting boundaries of whiteness in modern architectural discourses. While I do not believe that the racial themes of architectural organicism are inherently white, I demonstrate the modern architect's consistent experimentation with regulating the public perception of whiteness in the public sphere. I argue that the case studies reviewed here constitute a historical tradition of white cultural nationalism in Europe and the United States that was sustained through a conscious desire to transform Western civilization as it marched across the globe. Locating the critical importance of racial discourses in architectural organicism does not taint its legacy or its revival in the present; it only enables contemporary designers to better understand how race and architecture meet one another in cultural debates. Perhaps this knowledge will enable us all to be more nimble and responsible in treating architecture as a social art.

The Scope of the Book

In part I of this book I examine the white cultural nationalisms associated with Alpine architectures uncovered in nineteenth-century Europe. The regional building styles of primitive mountain cultures were associated with scientific theories of a pure-blooded race of Aryan men who lived atop the Alps stretching across the entire length of premodern Europe. This fabled white Adam established a new origin point for tracing the historical evolution of national characters in modern Europe. Eighteenth-century scholars in linguistics and philology claimed that Aryanism dated back to primitive tribes of Hindus migrating westward from the steppes of India to various territories in Europe. Linguists analyzed what they perceived to be the organic behavior of Indo-European grammar to reconstruct the archetypal languages that emerged before the proliferation of agrarian culture. By the last three decades of the nineteenth century, biological and ethnographical theories of Aryanism supplemented language theories with visual illustrations of the material cultures of Aryan man—from his clothing and tools to his domestic and religious structures—providing a comprehensive matrix of material and expressive cultural artifacts of this lost culture.

This intellectual context paved the way for French and German architectural theorists to reconstruct the morphological transformations of primitive domestic and religious structures into the civic architectures of their times. Aryanism was a distinct feature of modern architectural debates that instrumentalized the cultural histories of ethnography to categorize the different types of racial characters emerging between the competing nation-states of continental Europe. I explore the power of Aryan myths associated with the French and German Alps during the nineteenth century. In the French case, Protestant theorists traced the historical origins of republican political ideals back to remote Aryans, while in the German case the existence of a common historical origin for the surviving fragments of the Ottoman Empire provided hope that the confusing pluralities of the contemporary nation state could be overcome by a principled return to the past.

The first two chapters of this book outline the theoretical transformations of Vitruvian anthropomorphism that were established by the scientific references of Viollet-le-Duc's theory of structural rationalism and Semper's conception of tectonic theory. The explicit citations of Aryan migration theory and illustrations of primitive wooden structures found in the Alps demonstrate the analytical value of ethnography in the architectural style debates.

Chapter 1 examines the writings and architecture of the French architect Eugène Emmanuel Viollet-le-Duc. For Viollet-le-Duc, the Aryan migration theories of the 1850s and 1860s established an exciting new historical origin for his unconventional historical interpretations of the religious and domestic typologies of the past. After publishing many books on the history of medieval France, including his multivolume *Dictionnaire raisonné de l'architecture française*, he published a popular work titled *Histoire de l'habitation humaine* that outlined a cultural history of domesticity from the ancient world to the Renaissance. *Histoire* combined the illustration of human race types with that of vernacular building types to demonstrate the common "organic" principles of cultural evolution.

In honor of his Aryan ancestors, Viollet-le-Duc designed and constructed a modernized version of the wooden Swiss chalet for his personal use in Lausanne, Switzerland, the location of his late commissioned cartographic studies of the French Alps. The design, which he called La Vedette, reconstituted the overall massing of the chalet type using a new masonry frame. The primitive roots of this aesthetic were revealed by the pictorial representation of the migration routes of his Aryan ancestors in a panoramic mural completed in the first-floor salon of his home. The architectural strategies Viollet employed to revive the old migration patterns of Aryan man and domestic patterns of French medieval life emulated his evolutionary interpretation of cultural history, which he believed influenced the design of all things in the present, for only a theory of living matter could produce a living architectural tradition.

The complexities of German nationalism were likewise managed by creative applications of character judgments in the architectural style debates. Chapter 2 examines the writings of the 1860s, before Germany became a unified nation-state. During this period, Germany consisted of a federation of independent kingdoms and principalities separated by a host of distinct language groups, religious customs, and political ideologies. The economic influence of its Zollverein, or toll-free customs area, which was established to promote free trade among its member states, was not a sufficient political framework to establish a unified hub for governing Germans.

This fraught political context provides the backdrop for Dresden architect Gottfried Semper's ethnographical interpretation of architectural history. Semper believed that a scientific study of the past might offer him an empirical avenue for discovering the common roots of German culture, one that was capable of connecting both the Prussian-controlled Protestant north and the Catholic kingdoms of the Austro-Hungarian south. Emulating the comparative methodologies of ethnography and ethnology, Semper treated architectural design as a practical arm of racial anthropology that taught architects to reconstitute the artistic type-forms of the past in modern materials. His architectural style was marked by a principled revival of the monumental forms of the Roman Empire, which I interpret as an aesthetic revival of German national character as it existed under a strong historical empire. His Roman revivalist building style also cemented new political ties by enabling secularized German-speaking Jews to assimilate within the elite ranks of the nation-state.

Semper also inflected the mythologies of Aryanism in his search for primitive type-forms in architectural history. Following the finds of the Greek revivalist architect Leo von Klenze, Semper claimed that the Bavarian-Tyrolean hut was an autochthonous type of Alpine housing that served premodern Germans during their vast migrations from the Alps to the plains below. His fascination with the origins of German culture provided the grounds for appreciating non-German material cultures, including those discovered during the nation's brief experiment with colonialism. Semper's citation of the material culture of South Sea Islanders anticipated the later subjugation of Māori tribes in colonial territories after the decline of democracy in Weimar Germany.

In part II of this book I examine the racial discourses associated with the transatlantic disseminations of architectural organicism in North America at the turn of the century. American theorists believed that an autochthonous style of building was sure to arise with the gradual refinement of the democratic experiment. However, pressing questions emerged from social theorists regarding the potential longevity of European racial character in the New World. While some believed that modern Europeans would literally degenerate under the harsh conditions of the American prairie, others hoped that this geography might give rise to an entirely new form of national identity that would extend the reach of Western civilization across the Atlantic. Would the American race be defined by the best racial stock of Europe, segregated in distinct enclaves in its new woodlands and outstretched plains, or would patterns of racial amalgamations produce a new American race without precedent in the Old World? European ethnographers and political theorists analyzed the state of affairs through the state of contemporary arts and letters, which served as a visual sign of the health and vibrancy of this new nation. Several American innovators labored in adapting the principles of European architectural organicism to fit their situation in the United States. The political shift in the United States toward the ethnicization of white racial identity was manifest in the architectural style debates by a material transition from the privileged ornamentation of structure in national building styles to the racialization of interior spatial and structural components veiled behind the monolithic planar finishes of the International Style. In the course of this transition, the aesthetic values of nineteenth-century architectural organicism survived to complicate the synthetic pan-European interpretation of the international avant-garde popularized by Johnson and Hitchcock in the 1932 exhibition at the Museum of Modern Art (MoMA).

Chapter 3 traces the transatlantic dissemination of French and German theories of architectural organicism to North America via professional émigrés and authoritative translations of European writings beginning in the mid-1850s and early 1860s. These sources exerted an indelible influence on the materialization of self-described American architectural styles. Yet the distinct political context of the New World provided some unique challenges to translators of European architectural theory. The mix of racial and national origins caused by intermarriage in the United States established a new type of postcolonial identity that was constituted by an amalgamation of distinct European characters. American architects employed a range of aesthetic strategies that expressed what they perceived to be the unique state of American character.

The Irish American architect Louis Sullivan pioneered what I describe as a physiognomic approach to architectural style that uses carved floral ornamentation to visually index the embodied spatial and structural properties of democratic spaces. Sullivan's interpretations of American character were inevitably influenced by the racial politics of his era, which luminaries such as Ralph Waldo Emerson and Walt Whitman credited to the Anglo-Saxon roots of American democracy. The political self-determinism demonstrated by New England's early settlers was theoretically open to all of its citizens, although in practice it was reserved for the subjects who were deemed capable of assimilating the English political heritage that enabled them to successfully manage these responsibilities. Within the context of the expanding American republic, the racial and political criteria used to determine the vicissitudes of American character elevated certain social groups into leadership positions within the modern political elite. Realizing the social stakes of white racial identity, Sullivan used his autobiography to distance himself from his father's Irish heritage in order to qualify himself as the premier architect of his generation.

This prejudice against Irish character persists in Sullivan's negative depiction of Old World immigrants and nonwhite peoples whose characteristics strayed too far from the Anglo-American ideal. Despite the exclusive categories of Sullivan's architecture theory, however, his Jewish clients and the subsequent occupation of his buildings by African Americans posthumously expanded his notion of the body politic by physically reforming the most restrictive formal elements of Sullivan's architectural style. The formal additions and renovations of this space were prompted by the new spatial protocols that were a symptom of the political struggles of America's most marginalized communities. A close examination of Sullivan's architectural oeuvre should sensitize architectural historians to the ways that the historical uses of monumental spaces challenge the critical assumptions of the architect, sometimes to the advantage of his or her architectural theories.

Taken together, the case studies of the first three chapters demonstrate a deep and continuous romantic tendency within architectural organicism to create modern architectural styles that transparently reflect the inner characters of a dominant racial genius within the nation state. Even as twentieth-century theorists dispensed with the natural metaphors of the nineteenth century to pursue the machine metaphors of the International Style debates, the racial connotations of the term *organic* continued to align the properties of race and style in the material and spatial elements of modern architecture as American power expanded around the world. The racial charge of modern architectural styles was partially manifest in a struggle between the nationalist and internationalist themes of exhibits at MoMA during the interwar and postwar periods. The 1932 exhibit on the International Style, titled *Modern Architecture: International Exhibition*, polemically opened the way for the popularization of International Style architectures in the United States. While the European pedigree of the International Style initially served as an obstacle for American decisionmakers' acceptance of it, the curators, Johnson and Hitchcock, worked tirelessly during the 1940s and 1950s to isolate the idiomatic elements of this style that would best fit the intellectual and institutional contexts of the United States. Yet it was not entirely clear whether the presiding character of this movement was to be American or international in focus. A brief look at the early exhibitions of the Department of Architecture at MoMA reveals the conflicted identities associated with this movement as its curators alternated between crediting the transmissibility to its international tendencies and its development as a unique form of American modernism.

Such tensions were visually manifest in early International Style projects such as Lescaze's aesthetic solution for Williamsburg Houses, the first publicly funded housing project in New York City. Lescaze, who was celebrated for his design of the Philadelphia Savings Fund Society building in Philadelphia, achieved an aesthetic unity between social housing in Europe and the United States in his design for Williamsburg Houses in New York City, which effectively Americanized the whitewashed modernist aesthetic pioneered at MoMA in 1932. Despite the strict design protocols outlined by the federal department of housing, Lescaze maintained a visual tension between the brick detailing that Mumford and Bauer describe as an "organic" material expression of the communal character of mass culture in the twentieth century and the concrete shelving of its structural frame that was more prominent in middle-class housing experiments overseas. Both of these material qualities came together to from the requisite platonic volumes mandated by the International Style show. By not completely sacrificing the architectural detailing of nineteenth-century social housing projects in his design, the hybrid style of Lescaze's project continued to provide a human scale for modern housing that indexed the progressive legacy of earlier social movements.

Lescaze's formal attempt to Americanize International Style public housing was negatively affected by the racial discourses of his time. As I suggest in chapter 4, race and style were brought together by virtue of two distinct institutional forces: the segregation policies of most federal and state housing departments in the United States and the European pedigree of the International Style show that gestured toward the white ethnic diaspora in New York City. While the segregation policies of public housing did not cause the pan-European pedigree of the MoMA show, and vice versa, the combined racial charge of these institutional contexts affected the Americanization of working-class white and black residents in oppositional ways: while it consolidated the cultural diversity found within working-class white immigrants of the interwar period by acculturating them to the social standards of middle-class whites, working-class blacks were shut off from the economic gains achieved by racially integrated unionization efforts that were open before the birth of public housing.

The racial character of public housing across the United States colluded to permanently taint the popular reception of Lescaze's organic representation of working-class culture. Instead of becoming an emblem for social uplift among the working classes collectively, Williamsburg Houses became a sign of the positive racial character of working-class whites, as new immigrants and members of the "submerged middle class" moved on from public housing to suburban bungalows. By contrast, the institutional exclusion of black workers from the social and economic gains of the postwar period transformed public housing into a visual sign for the permanent unfitness of working-class blacks as a group. The downward social and economic trajectory for black residents living in modernist public housing units took even clearer visual form once the artistic prestige of designing these structures declined within the avant-garde in the 1940s and 1950s. I argue that the deteriorating material conditions of public housing that were retroactively linked with the perpetual otherness and poverty of black residents were structurally conditioned by the racial pedigree of the International Style exhibit at MoMA. This situation was exacerbated by the decision of public housing advocates to focus on class over race in their efforts to build support for local construction efforts in the United States.

Beginning with the canonical *Modern Architecture: International Exhibition* of 1932, in the conclusion I revisit the racial connotation of "organic" language and practices in curatorial themes of modern architecture exhibits at the MoMA. A close reading of the American themes of these exhibits demonstrates the historical continuity of racial interpretations of international style architectures of the interwar and postwar periods. Philip Goodwin and Elizabeth Mock's 1945 exhibit *Built in USA: 1932–1944* is read as an explicit referendum on the formalist criteria that Johnson and Hitchcock used in 1932 to define the International Style. Mock establishes a domestic lineage for American modernism that predates the European invasions of the 1930s. This alternative narrative credits Wright's organic architecture with continuing the nationalist trajectory of earlier practitioners, including that of his mentor, Sullivan.

This book provides a brief overview of the ways Wright's *An Autobiography* emulates the racial themes of Sullivan's *Autobiography of an Idea*: both architects subscribe to a romantic vision of the American frontier that casts a pessimistic view on the inherent potentials of first-generation white immigrants and nonwhite peoples at the turn of the century. A close reading of Wright's text also reveals the profound whiteness of his agrarian conception of the Prairie Style, which anticipates the racially segregated character of his designs for the domestic interior, as well as colors his emulation of Japanese, Chinese, and Mayan material culture in his architectural ornament. I have selected the design of the Imperial Hotel in Tokyo as a fruitful case study for examining this phenomenon.

In the conclusion, I examine the racial interpretations of American character that are manifest by the organic language of the International Style debates. While these architectural critics did not always make direct references to the generative principles of the natural sciences, they did attribute a set of essential characteristics to the American practitioners who completed the most iconic projects of the postwar period. One of the professional types that Johnson and Hitchcock invented to distinguish American designers from their competitors in the international avant-garde was the figure of the "businessman-architect," who was responsible for shaping the corporate and political architectural programs that marked the rise of American internationalism. I examine the ways that this social type recalls the racial tropes of American pragmatism in the late nineteenth century, which attributed positive values to the Protestant work ethic and humble demeanor of the white working classes. This line of thinking is manifest in Hitchcock's essay for the *Built in USA: Post-war Architecture* exhibit, where he cites Wallace K. Harrison as a representative of this new breed of American practitioner. While the physical appearance of Harrison's architecture does not diverge from Johnson and Hitchcock's formalist conception of the International Style, the architectural character of this project is ultimately credited to the synthetic design process responsible for its making.

Several architectural critics and journalists described Harrison's deliberative approach to the design for the United Nations complex as an "organic" integration of competing aesthetic ideas. This notion of organicism—a synthetic integration of various elements into a unifying whole—procedurally emulates the synthetic design strategies that organic architects deployed nearly two generations earlier in the United States. Despite the perceived architectural genius accorded to individual members of the UN design committee—including the famed Le Corbusier, who wished to advance his own design for the project after failing to complete the Palace of the League of Nations—Harrison prevailed by synthetically integrating small gestures from multiple designers into a single aesthetic vision. I interpret this use of organic language as Hitchcock's attempts to identify the native genius of American designers that placed them ahead of other competitors from other national regions. While architectural historians have already examined Harrison's design approach for prefiguring the "democratic" function of the United Nations, I examine the racial discourses that emerged from his manifestation of American pragmatism as the native genius of the American businessman-architect. In the wake of the sociological consolidations of whiteness I describe in chapter 4, the racial politics of this moment continue to distinguish American native genius within an international political context.

Identifying the racialization of architectural character in the nineteenth-century paradigm of architectural organicism makes it possible to demonstrate the lateral influence of organic discourses on the International Style debates in the first half of the twentieth century. Once the scientific rationalization of modern architectural theory made race and style two empirical and interconnected entities in cultural history, it was hard to break the expectation that racial characters and architectural characters would continue to parallel one another in a progressive modernist history. Even when architects no longer looked directly to nature to provide them with explicit metaphors for design, the modern architect was forced to reintroduce this idea through other means in order to substantiate the individuality of American cultural production within the international avant-garde.

Part I

THE ARYAN CHARACTER OF ALPINE ARCHITECTURE

Figure 1.1. View of the first-floor studio in La Vedette, ca. 1880. Médiathèque the l'Architecture.

1

CAMPFIRES IN THE SALON

Viollet-le-Duc and the Modernization of the Aryan Hut

And it is to this natural method that is owing the "style" with which all of nature's works are imbued. From the largest mountain down to the finest crystal, from the lichen to the oaks of our forests, from the polyp to human beings, everything in terrestrial creation does indeed possess style—that is to say, a perfect harmony between the results obtained and the means employed to achieve them.

—**Eugène Emmanuel Viollet-le-Duc,**
Dictionnaire raisonné de l'architecture française

THE FRENCH ARCHITECT EUGÈNE EMMANUEL Viollet-le-Duc spent a great deal of his career interpreting the cultural origins and importance of medieval architecture. In his most celebrated work, the *Dictionnaire raisonné de l'architecture française du XIe au XVIe siècle* (1856–1864), he uses alphabetical entries of architectural terms to record the progression of French culture. This writing took place alongside an active career of repairing and restoring the medieval fabric that made up the physical patrimony of the state. By all accounts he was very influential in Paris as the codirector of the Commission of Historical Monuments during the 1850s and 1860s, even as he was forced, on occasion, to defend his theoretical interpretations of the past. By the 1870s, however, he seemed to be in retreat. After a failed attempt to reform the design culture of the École des Beaux-Arts, the most prominent center of design culture in France, and after witnessing the despoiling of Alsace and Lorraine during the Franco-Prussian War, he sought a reprieve to reconsider the origins of French culture once again. This time he did so from the resort town of Lausanne, Switzerland, a small city in the countryside adjacent to the picturesque expanse of the French-Swiss Alps (see plate 1). This mountain scenery became an important visual motif in Viollet-le-Duc's later work. During the last two decades of his life he built a modest home for himself in Lausanne that served as a resting place while he continued his work of writing and repairing medieval churches in the region.

If one stands on the Rue de Bourg and walk up to the elevation where this home was located it is possible to catch a glimpse of the Alps that sits just across Lake Geneva (see plate 2). Some version of this dramatic view—of the distant housing settlements spotted along the bottom of an incline that rises up to form numerous peaks amid the clouds—would have been visible from the paired double hung windows in the front room of his home. It was within this front room, or salon, that Viollet-le-Duc wrote some of his most popular books on architecture, completed a volume analyzing the prehistoric and contemporary conditions of Mont Blanc (the highest peak in the Alps), entertained guests, and spent many of his private moments near the warmth of his fireplace (fig. 1.1). Given his direct participation in the science of geology during the 1870s, it is not entirely surprising that he painted a reconstructed scene of the prehistoric Alps in this room nearly a year after it was constructed; all evidence suggests he wished to understand these mountains in every possible way.

Viollet-le-Duc's fascination with the French-Swiss Alps resonated with the scientific advancements of his time. As mountaineering continued to be a popular pastime in France, geology emerged as a discipline in its own right. The Alps constituted a major leitmotiv of Romantic literature, with picturesque depictions of Mont Blanc appearing in memoirs, novels, and poems, from the poem "Mont Blanc" by the British Romantic poet Percy Shelley in 1816 to the letters written by Victor Hugo during his trek to the mountains, published in *En voyage, Alpes et Pyrénées* (1890).[1] Shelley's work praises the creative capacity of nature revealed by the vastness of the mountains by comparing it with the power of the human imagination, the latter a consistent theme of Romantic poetry.

By the 1830s mountain ranges were also providing linguists with a natural backdrop for interpreting the migration of human language. French, German, and British philologists examined the common "organic" behavior of European language groups that they believed pointed toward a common Indo-European language that predated most contemporary tongues. As the label itself suggests, this primitive language was most likely spoken by a group of races that originated in Southeast Asia and migrated across the Caucasus Mountains into various areas of Western Europe. These archetypal migrants, or Aryans, as they were called, formed the centerpiece of a geographical theory of European development that placed great emphasis on the study of Sanskrit and the religious customs of Hindu worship. In time, ethnographers began to speculate on the physical traits that characterized these Eurasian peoples. As an architectural historian, Viollet-le-Duc was in a unique position to contribute to these debates.

He extended this period's romantic fascination with the mountainous origins of Aryan man by illustrating the architectural elements associated with his primitive world.

This chapter examines the dialectical relationship that emerged between race and style in Viollet-le-Duc's ethnographic history of vernacular construction during the last two decades of his career. During this time the French architect articulated an explicitly organic conception of architectural style, or design, which he elaborated within a racialist model of history. This theory was most comprehensively summarized in the publication *Histoire de l'habitation humaine* (1876), although it was implicit in his earlier writings. In contrast to art historical notions of architectural styles that cataloged the external features of ornamentation, Viollet-le-Duc outlined the underlying rational principles of construction that guided the artist's imagination in manipulating raw materials and the decoration of structure. To better demonstrate these design principles, he developed a scientific method for interpreting historical designs that was inspired by the collective findings of ethnography, philology, and geology:

> Our era, and our era alone, since the beginning of recorded history, has assumed toward the past a quite exceptional attitude as far as history is concerned. Our age has wished to analyze the past, classify it, compare it, and write its complete history, following step-by-step the procession, the progress, and the various transformations of humanity. A fact as novel as this new analytic attitude of our era cannot be dismissed, as some superficial observers have imagined, as merely some kind of temporary fashion, or whim, or weakness on our part. The entire phenomenon is exceedingly complex. Cuvier, by means of his studies of comparative anatomy, as well as of his geological research, unveiled to the public almost literally from one day to the next a very long history of the world that had preceded the reign of mankind. People were captivated by Cuvier's revelations and eager to travel down the new path he charted for them. Then philologists discovered the origins of European languages, all of them coming ultimately from the same source. Ethnographers, for their part, oriented their work in the direction of the study of races and of their various aptitudes. Finally, the archaeologists came on the scene, and, studying artistic productions from India through Egypt and on through Europe itself, they compared, discussed, and distinguished among these various productions, uncovered their origins and charted their interrelationships, and, following the same analytic method, eventually succeeded in classifying them according to certain general laws.[2]

What linked all of these fields for Viollet-le-Duc were the inner principles that guided the organic generation of all forms in history, whether they were created by nature or by human cultures. Just as geological principles could be used to account for the earth's physical formation, and ethnographic principles to clarify the hybridization of primitive race groups into contemporary ethnicities, an organic principle of history should offer the designer a principled means of explaining the variations of vernacular architectural forms. Viollet-le-Duc employed an ethnographic framework of analysis in *L'habitation humaine* to outline the organic principles of architectural style that regulated the evolution of construction from primitive times to the Middle Ages. At least one architectural historian has labeled this unique model of history as a "domestic ethnography" of primitive times.[3]

Viollet-le-Duc's enduring interest in reconstituting the past extended the principles of racial anthropology into a rational conception of primitive life. His examination of French medieval culture was most carefully delineated in the *Dictionnaire raisonné*, which was followed up by a comparative study of primitive vernacular culture in *L'habitation humaine* and a series of contemporary designs in *Habitations modernes* (1877). These three studies reveal the extent to which he developed a general methodology for interpreting the shifting relationships between race and style in cultural history, in both the past and the present. During the same decade that he began his two works on human habitation, he began to explore the Alps, which resulted in the publication of *Le massif du Mont Blanc* (1876) (see plates 3 and 4). These journeys back in time enabled him to metaphorically walk the path of his ancestors, whom he believed were the Aryan men who migrated from the East. He even attempted to update the primitive forms of vernacular Aryan culture into modern structures that were suited to his life in Lausanne. The most explicit revival of the past was manifest in his theoretical interest in the chalet house type that influenced a series of designs completed for mountainous territories, from a rustic cottage in the Chamonix mountain range (1872–1873) to a gardener's house for the Duke of Orléans family estate at the Château d'Eu (1874) and La Vedette (1876), a house studio he completed for himself in Lausanne. Viollet-le-Duc's rational analysis of Aryan life brought the past into the present in various forms, from literary interpretations of vernacular culture to cartography and modern building construction. In effect, he used his studies to modernize the portrait of Aryan man as a rational and technologically advanced conqueror of the world, a legacy he was happy to claim membership to as a leading French Romantic thinker.

To account for Viollet-le-Duc's racialist conception of style, this chapter examines the influence of the Aryan migration model of history as it was visualized through the chalet and its picturesque surroundings between 1856 and 1876. One primary source in which the French architect cites the remote origins of Aryan man is the inaugural lecture he delivered at the École des Beaux-Arts (1864), which outlines the beginning of art in human history. The Hindu myths and religious practices Viollet-le-Duc cites here rehearse the major aspects of the Aryan migration model circulated by figures in the fields of philology and ethnography.

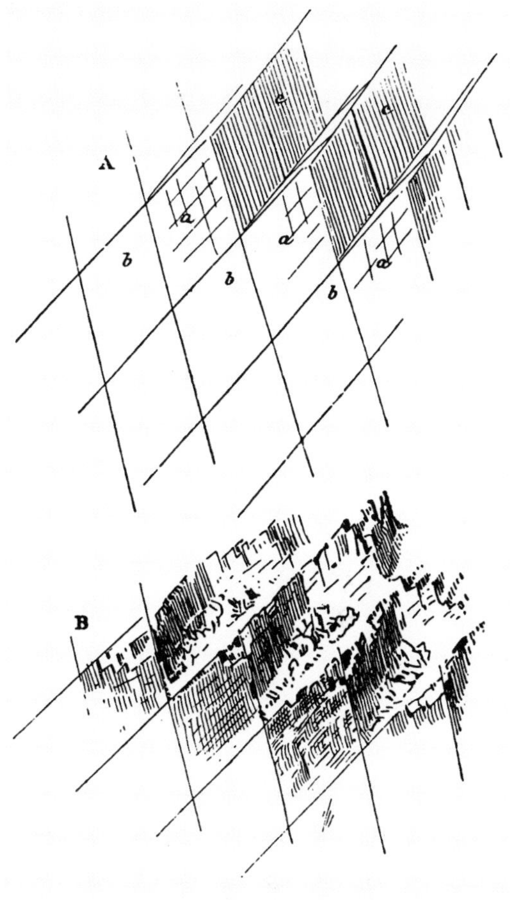

Figure 1.2. Viollet-le-Duc, geometrical analysis of tectonic plates, 1876. *Le massif de Mont Blanc,* plate 47.

This line of argumentation was anticipated by the Eastern themes of the "Style" entry of volume 8 of the *Dictionnaire raisonné.*[4] The architect engages in a curious discussion of the rhomboid geometry of granite and the geometric formation of the earth, which he later illustrates in his study on Mont Blanc (fig. 1.2).

After 1856, mountain imagery becomes a recurring image in the architect's discussion of primitive Aryan culture. This was especially clear in the narrative of the first three chapters of *L'habitation humaine.* The persistent dialectical relationship maintained between the racial characters of primitive man and the architectural character of vernacular construction establishes what Lauren O'Connell has called the "racial signature" of Viollet-le-Duc's architectural conception of primitive material culture.[5] These visual illustrations of race and style enliven the Aryan migration model of history that underwrites the narrative, which result in a discursive illustration of the broader principles of style. As this text synthesizes the findings of philology, ethnography, and geology with architectural history, it must be seen as a unique contribution to the racial discourses of the late nineteenth century.

The Aryan Migration Model of History

Philologists of the nineteenth century spent considerable time tracing the historical roots of an Indo-European language that was first spoken in the remote regions of the Himalayan mountain range. This historical development was traced back with the use of a comparative analysis of grammar between extant Sanskrit texts and modern European languages. Theorists such as Wilhelm von Humboldt, Jacob Grimm, Friedrich August Pott, Max Müller, and Franz Bopp believed that modern European languages were branches of an antique language that had been spoken by an extinct primitive people. Despite the fact that philologists used the term *race* to identify distinct strains of this Indo-European language, these labels were not intended to designate literal biological type forms. Instead, the term was used because language seemed to emulate the internal behavior of living organisms. However, the confusion between linguistic types and physiological entities does not seem very surprising in retrospect. According to a review of Adolphe Pictet's "Les origines indo-européennes, ou les Aryas primitifs," published in the British journal *Anthropological Review* in 1863, the Aryan migration theory had a profound effect on the critical assumptions of ethnographers: "When the great philological discovery of modern times was made, that all the languages of Europe, with a few exceptions, were sprung from one common tongue, most nearly represented by the ancient sacred language of India, the study of the branches sprung from this now extinct parent language became a matter of the highest moment to Ethnologists."[6] This discovery was of such great interest to ethnologists in part because of the eighteenth-century biological debates on the racial origins of man. The conception of a common biological root for the different races of mankind was still theory in the 1750s until the publication of Johann Friedrich Blumenbach's anthropological treatise *De Generis Humani Varietate Nativa.*[7] This scientific debate motivated natural philosophers like Immanuel Kant and Voltaire to elaborate the concepts of race and species, with the former endorsing a common root theory of species (monogenesis) and the latter endorsing the notion of separate species (epigenesis) that paralleled each racial variety in nature.[8] Adding the element of language simply made the scientific discourse on racial origins more heated and complex.

The fact that a primitive Aryan language group might possibly connect all of European culture made research in philology an international affair. Connecting European history to a single root or stock was clearly an assumption of this research, as the *Anthropological Review* article continues, "The evidence of language does prove beyond controversy, that the early race, which we call the Aryan, did once exist, and that, pouring itself out East and West in many waves of migration, it settled itself over almost all Europe."[9] This story of migration and conquest influenced Viollet-le-Duc's lecture of 1864 and the overall structure of *L'habitation humaine.* By the twentieth century Friedrich Schlegel was credited with inventing the *Indo-European* label while figures such as Pott helped to popularize it in Germany.[10] Pott's 1833 text *Etymologische Forschungen auf dem Gebiete der Indogermanischen Sprachen* was also seen to be the product of a new German national consciousness, which was manifest by his use of the term *Indo-Germanic languages.* Indo-European studies subsequently spread to England with the study of Indo-Celtic language groups in the personalities of James Cowles Prichard, the noted physician, and Pictet in the late 1830s and early 1840s. Pictet's work first appeared in 1837 as an essay titled "De l'affinité des langues celtiques avec le sanscrit" and, after several other essays and revisions in book form, in 1859 under the title *Origines indo-européennes.* Both works were published in French. Müller, another German Sanskrit scholar, is credited with circulating the Aryan designation for a British audience as late as 1861. Another source for British readers was Thomas Leslie Papillon's *Manual of Comparative Philology,* which corroborates Müller's claims, although by the time of its first publication in 1866 it was more of a summary of almost thirty years of work in philology across Europe.

Viollet-le-Duc's 1864 lecture at the École des Beaux-Arts makes only one explicit reference to a scientist of the nineteenth century: the philologist Louis Ferdinand Alfred Maury.[11] Viollet-le-Duc cites his work on "indigenous peoples" to reveal the collective efforts being undertaken by comparative grammarians and "German archeologists" to trace the ethnographic roots of Greek primitive art.[12] During the 1850s Maury contributed to an anthology that combined the findings of philologists, natural historians, anatomists, and ethnographers to produce a comprehensive natural history of man. This anthology, titled *Indigenous Races of the Earth* (1857), linked the spread of languages with the geographic distribution of races. Maury's essay specifically relates race, language, and geography in ways that anticipate Viollet-le-Duc's synthetic framework for cultural history. For example, Maury claims, "Languages are organisms that are all conceived on the same plan—one might almost say, upon the same skeleton, which in their development and their composition, follow fixed laws."[13] Both "languages and organisms" were considered to be organic in the same sense that Viollet-le-Duc interpreted structure in architecture. In addition, Maury states: "All these considerations show us, therefore, that the families of tongues are assemblages (*des ensembles*) very distinct, and the results of a diversified order of the creative faculty of speech. . . . [W]e must necessarily admit that it corresponds, under its different forms, to races of mankind possessing different faculties, as well for speech as for ideas. This is what the study of the principal classes or families of tongues will make still more evident; seeing that we shall find them in a relation sufficiently striking to the different human races."[14] Maury's analysis considers the historical evolution of language to be regulated by the same organic principles that made human races legibly distinct, which transformed language into an emblematic marker of racial differences. Viollet-le-Duc emulates the structure of this argument to connect variations in vernacular architecture with racial groups in cultural history.

Indigenous Races of the Earth produced several other seminal essays on American racial thought, including a contribution by George Gliddon on the debate between "the monogenists and the polygenists," an essay by Franz Pulszky that grouped "human races and their art," and two essays that related taxonomic characters and skulls to race types.[15] Pulszky's essay comes especially

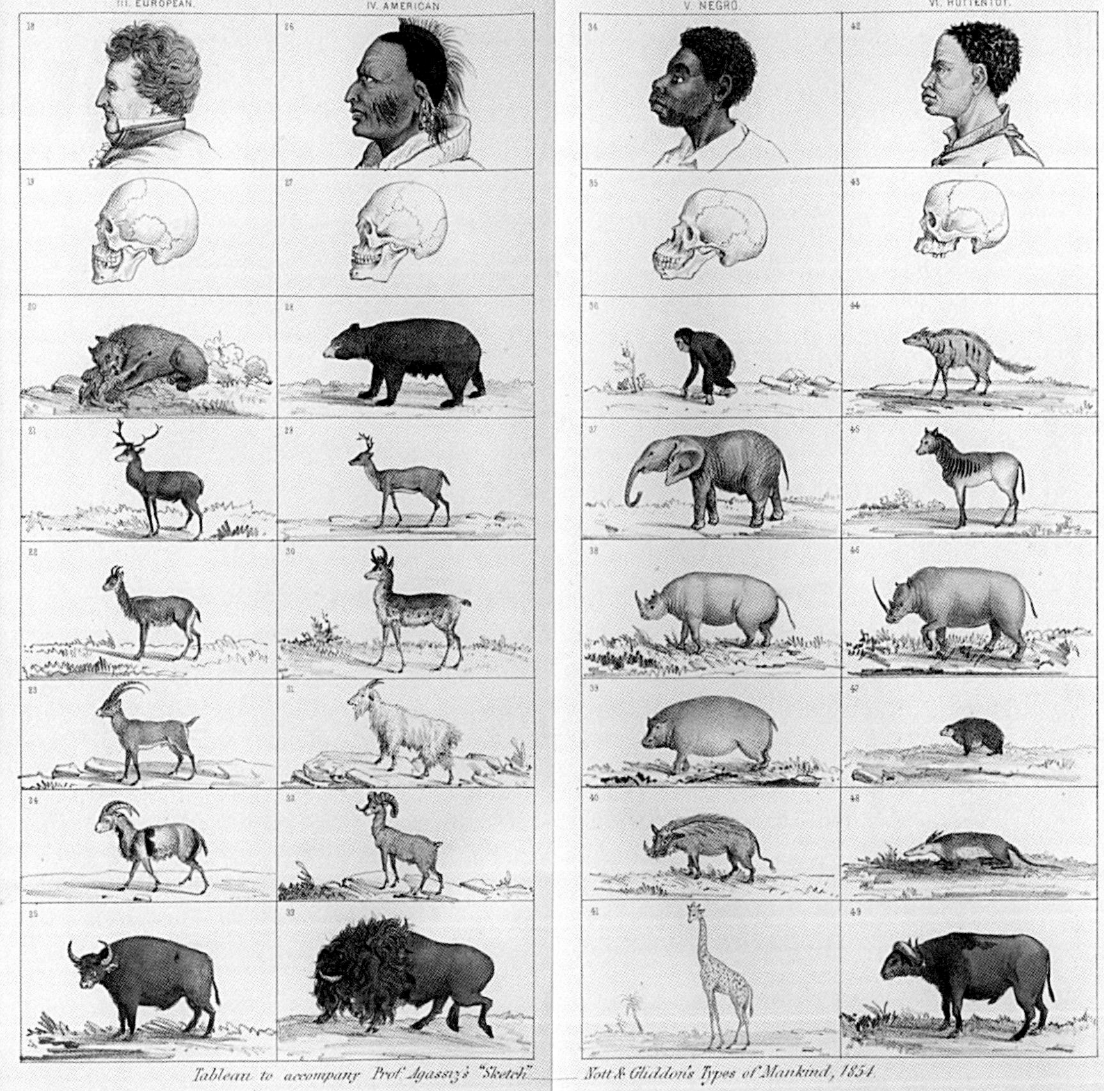

Figure 1.3. Chart of the indigenous organic species of various regions of the earth. *Types of Mankind.*

close to the Greek and Semitic themes outlined in Viollet-le-Duc's 1864 lecture, as it provided a detailed visual and narrative examination of Greek, Egyptian, and "Shemite" art forms.

The contributors to *Indigenous Races of the Earth* produced several diagrams that demonstrated an ecological understanding of the race idea, including one that clearly matched various race types to specific geographical regions of the earth (fig. 1.3). This chart, published in the text *Types of Mankind* (1854),

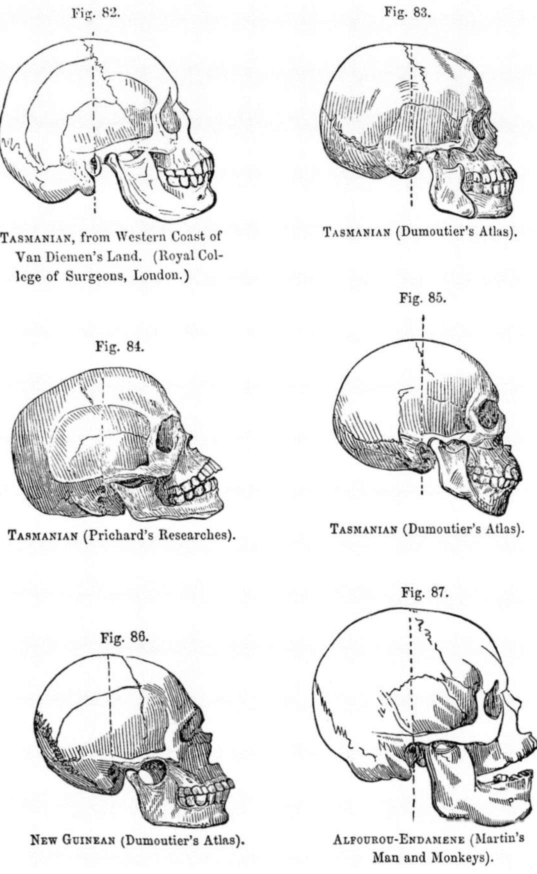

Figure 1.4. Comparison of human skulls from Tasmania and New Guinea in scientific literatures, 1857. From Josiah Nott, and L.-F.-Alfred Maury, eds.. *Indigenous Races of the Earth* (Philadelphia: J. B. Lippincott, 1857), 346.

catalogs the range of organic species found in regional geographies of the earth by coupling human race types with other species in zoology. This comprehensive catalog of life was based on a polygenic theory of the human species that speculated that each race constituted a distinct and separate species of mankind. Viollet-le-Duc was also familiar with the biological theory of monogenic reproduction. Such a gradualist conception of racial formation was evident in the work of the architect's friend Arthur de Gobineau's *Essai sur l'inégalité des races humaines.* This text credited the historical emergence of national characters to the biological degeneration of human race types from intermarriage, or miscegenation, as he called race mixing.

Both Gobineau's theory of national character and Maury's graphic representation of polygenic racial typologies depicted the transformation of the human body at the end of a teleological cycle of physical change. Even the skulls beneath each physiognomic profile in Maury's image attempt to explain race by means of an interior structure within the body. His image peers beneath the visual characteristics of racial taxonomy to detect the underlying structures that support these appearances. The use of craniometry in *Indigenous Races* and *Types of Mankind* became a consistent feature in nineteenth-century North American anthropology (fig. 1.4). The visual innovation of Maury's chart is its contextual placement of discrete specimens of the animal kingdom in relation to one another by their region of origin and habitation—a line of thinking that *L'habitation humaine* easily supplemented with its addition of architectural typologies in 1876.

Race and Nature in the *Dictionnaire raisonné*

Before Viollet-le-Duc defines style as the "manifestation of an ideal based on a principle," he opens his essay with a provisional distinction that characterizes what he considers to be the abuse of the term in the French architectural style debates. He qualifies the term by stating that "there is style" and "then there are styles," and he cites the latter to refer to the taxonomic practice of cataloguing common architectural features by period or epoch. In this sense, Viollet-le-Duc distinguishes his task from a mere identification of formal similarity. He was after the internal principles of architectural production. To create a distance in his reader's mind between the external and internal characteristics of style, he went so far as to identify what fueled the production of style in the fine arts. Painting, sculpture, and poetry were the foremost branches of the imitative arts, whereas architecture and music were nonimitative arts:

> For the architect, as for the musician, however, the psychology is different. These two types of artist do not take from an object or phenomenon of nature a feeling or sensation of their own that is then transformed by them into a work of art. Rather, the work of art must issue from out of their own intelligence; the work of art must arise in embryonic state in keeping with their possession of the faculty of reasoning. It is then their task to develop it by nourishing it with the observations that they have borrowed from nature, science, or earlier artistic creations.[16]

For Viollet-le-Duc, the relationship between style and nature in architecture was the inverse of its relationship in painting, sculpture, and poetry. What begins as an impression of form in the latter must start as "a conception of the human mind" for the architect, as an idea or a concept.[17] He uses a biological metaphor to distinguish the initial "embryonic" idea that issues from the architect's imagination that is only subsequently trained by the faculty of reasoning to produce style. In this way, the architect uses "nature, science, and earlier artistic creations" as a tutor for concretely manifesting their idea into form.[18] Once a viewer could detect the idea or concept in the distribution of parts, then the product of architecture could be said to possess style. Style, then, was the marking or imprinting of a central idea onto form.

Viollet-le-Duc went one step further in his definition of style when he claimed that science and nature served as such great tutors for the architect because they each possessed a sense of style in and of themselves. He considered it the limitation of the human mind to have to use something as a tutor in order to produce style in architecture: "Architecture as an art is a human creation. Such is our inferiority that, in order to achieve this type of creation, we are obliged to proceed as nature proceeds in the things she creates. We are obliged to employ the same elements and the same logical method as nature; we are obliged to observe the same submission to certain natural laws and to observe the same transitions. . . . Architecture, this most human of creations, is but an application of principles that are born outside of us—principles that we appropriate by observation."[19] Put this way, one can understand the architect and the fine artist to be observers of nature, but the architect was supposed to emulate nature's means of creating form and not the literal form of an object. By emulating the principles of style that were observed in the creation of natural objects, an architect could learn to lawfully apply a rational principle to their own work.

According to Viollet-le-Duc, the range of natural phenomena open to the architect's observation was vast. He cites mountains, crystals, lichens, polyps, oaks and human beings as possessing style, which he defined as "a perfect harmony between the results obtained and the means employed to achieve them."[20] His attempts to reconstruct the primitive state of landmasses from glacier movements proved that this statement was both literal and metaphorical in nature. Several aspects of his statement resonate with the findings of nineteenth-century race science. For one, the reference to the common life principles that link "the polyp to human beings" is a clear reference to the experiments that Blumenbach conducted on polyps in the late eighteenth century. Speculating on an inborn intelligence in organisms that directed their internal processes of generation, he took to deforming the "eyes" of sea polyps to note whether or not they would grow back.[21] Since each polyp attempted to grow back its missing "eyes," Blumenbach speculated that there was an internal imprint or idea of their final form embedded in each polyp that he called its *Bildungstrieb* (formative force). He later used this theory to explain the process of degeneration that was inherent to primitive man. According to Blumenbach, there was initially only one type of primitive man that migrated across the earth. As this type settled and adapted to their local geographies it developed into the five race types that he identified in his treaties. Over time these changes or degenerations became a permanent idea within mankind's internal makeup, which resisted any further ecological changes in response to external environments.[22] Like the polyp, race types were an internally conditioned idea that persisted in the form of successive generations. In Viollet-le-Duc's words, they were "a perfect harmony between the results obtained" (i.e., race types) "and the means employed" (i.e., geographic forces) "to achieve them."[23]

Viollet-le-Duc's citation of race science anticipates several aspects of his ethnographic framework for architectural construction. For example, as an aside to his discussion of the constructive principle that the Gallic Frenchmen of medieval times had invented with Gothic architecture, he stated how naturally primitive ethnographic artifacts embodied mankind's instinct for creating style:

> In proceeding thus, art acts in the same fashion as nature does, style in nature being the corollary of principle. All this is very simple in the case of primitive civilizations, where everything human has its own style: religion, customs, manners and morals, arts, and dress are all imbued with a distinct flavor deriving from direct and unsophisticated observations. The mythology of the Vedas, like that of the ancient Egyptians, arose out of this kind of direct observation; and these mythologies are accordingly penetrated with a style *par excellence*. Those arts that were an expression of these mythologies similarly possess style.[24]

It is important to note that the references to the Indian Vedic scriptures and Egyptian mythology are both expanded in Viollet-le-Duc's later writings: the former at the Beaux-Arts lecture of 1864 and the second in several chapters of *L'habitation humaine*. At the time of his writing the *Dictionnaire raisonné*, however, there already seems to be an implicit continuum between the naturalism that was expressed in interpreting race as style and the immediate sense of style that was produced by primitive man. According to Viollet-le-Duc, "all this is very simple in the case of primitive civilizations" because everything that was produced in the antique world seemed to automatically have style.[25] This provided a heuristic role for what we might call the racialized aspect of the principle of style in the primitive world.

Although the sense of style created by Gallic traders was not as immediate as what was created by the primitive Indian or Egyptian peoples, Viollet-le-Duc held their constructive principles of equilibrium up as an exemplary case for contemporary study. This position was partially in support of the correlation he made between the contemporary republican politics of France and the nascent liberal politics of the artisans who collaborated on Gothic architecture. In a nod to the state of nineteenth-century French politics, Viollet-le-Duc situates the political awakening that precipitated the rise of Gothic architecture within a nascent republican spirit:

> In the communes the old Gallic spirit was being revived. These communes were almost constantly in turmoil, constantly struggling with the feudal nobility. Though they were both industrious and rich, the bourgeois were divided into different bodies in accordance with the art or craft that they practiced. . . . These groups became foyers of municipal liberties, and schools of lay artists were formed within them. When the day came that they were able to work independently, without reference to the monastic establishments, the bishops recognized in them a potential for helping the bishops carry out their projects in the face of the power of the abbeys and of the lay nobility; the bishops thus turned to these schools of lay artists in order to secure their help in building a worthy and proper monument to the city itself, namely, the cathedral.[26]

His consideration of the class, religious, and political elements of Gothic architecture anticipates his 1864 discussion of Indian religious architecture in two ways. First, he states that the innovations of Gothic architecture "was confined to a single class in society," which mirrors his claim that the Hindu faith that fueled monumental Indian architecture was restricted to the highest caste of society.[27] This makes sense, given that Viollet-le-Duc considered the Gothic innovation to have "involved a return to a more primitive state" of being, a second nod to the themes isolated by his 1864 lecture at the École des Beaux-Arts.

The Racial Anthropology of the Beaux-Arts Lecture, 1864

In November of 1863, Viollet-le-Duc was appointed professor of art and aesthetics at the École des Beaux-Arts in an apparent effort to reform its educational program.[28] The proof of a migration from the mountains to the plains below was an important element for Viollet-le-Duc's inaugural lecture at the Beaux-Arts in 1864. According to this lecture, the outgrowth of human culture from the plains was implicit in the parallels between the gods of Hindu myth and those of the Greeks; the Hindu Indra is paralleled by the Greek Argus, Sivitri is also Poseidon, and Ogha is Oceanus.[29] The Brahmas of India represent for Viollet-le-Duc the people of the mountains, the oldest origins of artistic imagination in the East. The connections established between Sanskrit texts and the introduction of art in the upper Indus is, for Viollet-le-Duc, the result of deliberate efforts on the part of the purified cultural elite to preserve their faith. These two aims worked in tandem, although the use of the plastic arts had an undeniable religious purpose at its origin.

According to the lecture there is no initial separation between the utility of an object and a consciousness of its symbolic power: "From pure abstraction, man is thus drawn to expression through the medium of myths and symbols: from that moment the artist had to intervene, to interpret these concepts by finite forms, engraving them on men's minds. . . . Thus the ordinary worshipper is initiated by an image representing phenomena caused by the divine power, and deciphers in a concrete way the enigma whose mystical sense is only understood by the Brahmans."[30] Thus, there is a separation between the appreciation of myth in the Brahmans, the keepers and interpreters of tradition, and the ordinary worshipper who requires mediation for understanding.

For Viollet-le-Duc it was no coincidence that the groups in charge of developing the religious myths are the vanguard of early culture. They even preserve the integrity of their bloodlines to keep any admixture of faith that is inevitable in social mixing from contaminating their tradition. In a line of thinking similar to Gobineau's, this cultural elite is the group most devout in maintaining their original bloodlines. Though Viollet-le-Duc disagrees with Gobineau's elite vision for the nineteenth century, the two men see eye to eye on the role of the elite in the origins of art. Toward this end Viollet-le-Duc reads the law of caste separation in India as a legal principle that grows from the evolution of Indian art.

Scientific explanation for degeneration appears to be influential in the Beaux-Arts lecture in several ways, although its reference to permanent race characters initially seems to corroborate a purely taxonomic reading of the subject. The polemical tone of Viollet-le-Duc's language on race does not make this subtlety easy to distinguish. He makes several essentialist distinctions between the black and white race groups regarding their artistic output:

> Let us first establish certain overriding facts. The various human races are not equal, and to take the two extremes, it is clear that the white races, which have occupied Europe for some three thousand years, are infinitely superior to the black races that have inhabited a large part of Africa since time immemorial. The former have had an orderly history, a series of more or less advancing civilisations, with moments of astonishing splendour; the latter are still where they were twenty centuries ago . . . without putting them on the path to progress. . . . The further back we go into the distant past, the more marked become these differences, observable in the finite results that they produced.[31]

This statement explains why Viollet-le-Duc consistently paired white and black in oppositional terms historically. It also explains why he never mentioned the primitive architectural forms of black Africans, since he considered their artistic accomplishments to be stuck at a primitive stage of development that did not yield artistic results.

If this weren't enough, Viollet-le-Duc comments on the seemingly inherent instinct that Aryans possess that distinguish their talent for painting when he says: "Aryan peoples had a supremely high level of skill, or if you wish, instinct, in producing color contributions that were agreeable to the eye. Some may say that this was no more than the influence of the beauty of the climate, and of the natural world that surrounded them. I cannot accept this argument; if it were true all peoples living at the same latitude under similar climatic conditions would have developed the same skill, which is far from being the case."[32] In this context Viollet-le-Duc's essentialist reading of the inherent characters of racial groups in the development of art seems to subdue any environmentalist consideration for the race idea. However, if one remembers that Maury and Gobineau trace the environmental factors that shape the original formation of each race group then one can recover what is masked by the determinism inherent in Viollet-le-Duc's description of permanent race characteristics.

Given Viollet-le-Duc's interest in exploring the origins of culture and his knowledge of Gobineau's essay it is reasonable to assume that he is aware and interested in this aspect of nineteenth-century racial discourse. But why does he not simply say so directly in his texts? One reason may be in the very purpose of the Beaux-Arts lectures. He states at the opening of his talk that the purpose of his explorations in history is not "to turn out archeologists or art historians; we must above all train and seek to produce artists, practising artists, who will give a splendour to [French] art which is worthy both of the present and the past. . . . It is by going back to past origins, by concentrating on the study of what caused the periods when great art blossomed, that we can bring identity of purpose to all the energy which is today dispersed and, it must be admitted, largely wasted."[33] In this context the inherent characters of each race group are the decisive precondition for the active social dynamics that will cause the periods of great art; Viollet-le-Duc will turn to investigating the active factors of the migration of peoples and the synthesis this causes with the fusion of cultural groups to address the issue of art's evolution. The original formation or degeneration of man into races can be taken as a given in this case, since its explanation does not directly inform our knowledge of migration and exchange. But the process of degeneration is fundamental to Viollet-le-Duc's understanding of style and cannot be tossed aside. Though only a precondition in his 1864 lecture, it is still clearly one of the fundamental natural processes that aids in the architect's understanding of style in the *Dictionnaire raisonné*; it was simply not germane to the discussion at hand.

He continues by noting a preference for the active dynamics of ethnography when he states a preference for specific race mixtures for the production of art. He claims, "It seems that this mixture of Aryan blood with that of the Semites produces the most favourable ethnological conditions for developments in the arts."[34] We will see a similar dynamic described in the narration of *L'habitation humaine*, outlined below. In this way the dialectic between an essentialist understanding of racial characters and the evolution of these characters in different hybrid cultures begins to emerge that repeats itself in the illustration and narration of *L'habitation humaine*.

The Representations of Race and Style in *Histoire de l'habitation humaine*

As one looks back at Viollet-le-Duc's work on vernacular architecture in the 1860s and 1870s we see that he was developing an explicit interest in the origins of architecture among the different races of man. Benjamin Bucknall notes this interest in his introduction to the English translation of *Histoire de l'habitation humaine*, published under the title *Habitations of Man in All Ages*, when he says that this "instructive and interesting book, a translation of which I now present to the English reader, describes the origin and development of Domestic Architecture among the several races of mankind, the modes in which human dwellings have been constructed, and the appearance and manners of their inhabitants from prehistoric down to modern times."[35] Bucknall makes it clear that this text provides the reader with a historical narrative of constructive systems proper to each race group and a comprehensive syntax of constructive systems that parallels the ethnography of each race group outlined in Viollet-le-Duc's history of construction.

We are to understand Viollet-le-Duc's narrative history as a progressive story. This does not mean that contemporary technological means have eclipsed previous ones but that contemporary techniques have been progressively integrated into the social milieu. This is illustrated by the allegorical role of Epergos and Doxius as fictional characters in the narration. These two semidivine narrators introduce a temporal dialectic between progress and tradition in their prose and in their literal traveling through time. Key features for visualizing the progressive narrative outlined in the text are the book's illustrations. As promised, the text provides a parallel description of construction details alongside the ethnographic details of habitation with illustrations that supplement these textual descriptions. For example, at several points in *L'habitation humaine* we are privy to the interaction between the inhabitants, their means of labor, and the construction details of their dwellings; in figure 25 of the text we sense the rhythm of the Egyptian workers as they tie together reed guides for rammed earth exterior walls, and in figure 22 we watch slaves infill the wood frame of an Aryan house with the baked bricks Epergos mentions in chapter 2. Vast interior shots reveal the private lives of those in recline or welcoming guests; in figure 12 the fat Fau welcomes Epergos and Doxius, while figure 66 depicts a toast in the triclinium of a Greek house, and in figure 71 we espy a private conversation between two women seated in a courtyard of a Roman villa (fig. 1.5). Bucknall states of these illustrations that "the pencil of the artist has aided our imagination vividly to realise all the chief features of this progress."[36]

If we take the role of the images in the text to be to assist in the presentation of a progressive narrative of history, then what role does the introduction of taxonomic descriptions play? Well, just as the dwellings of each phase of human development are shown, so are the stages of development of the various races. Alongside scenes of everyday life that depict inhabitants using their domestic space, Viollet-le-Duc provides the taxonomic profile of each group. Akin to the rational depiction of building details, the author offers up taxonomies of the human condition as being as rational as the plan or section of a house. Looking ahead in the text, thirteen of its twenty-eight chapters close with a taxonomic portrayal of the race groups described therein; they are the Dasyu of the Upper Indus (also known as the Naïrriti), the Aryan of the Upper Indus, the "Chinaman," the Mongolian of Central Asia, the Egyptian of the upper Nile Delta, the Semite, the Assyrian, the Asiatic Ionian, the Greek Hellene, the Roman, the Indian Buddhist, the Cashmere of the Far East, and the Peruvian (figs. 1.6, 1.7). At least one architectural historian notes that this breakdown follows Arthur

Figure 1.5. Viollet-le-Duc, "Interior of the Chinese house." From *Histoire de l'habitation humaine* (1876), 32.

de Gobineau's tripartite division of man of white, yellow, and black in contradistinction to the quadripartite division of man in white, black, brown (or red), and yellow of the late eighteenth century.[37]

Upon closer inspection we see that a taxonomic profile closes every chapter that has a new racial formation. For example, we see an artistic depiction

Figure 1.6 (*top left*). Viollet-le-Duc, physiognomic profile of Dasyus. *Histoire de l'habitation humaine* (1876), 7.

Figure 1.7 (*bottom left*). Viollet-le-Duc, physiognomic profile of Aryan man. *Histoire de l'habitation humaine* (1876), 14.

of the Aryans first in chapter 2, when they meet Epergos and Doxius hiding under a rock in the mountains from the storm. After this an Aryan profile is not redrawn until chapter 6, when a racial mixture produces the Egyptians of the Upper Nile Delta. In parallel with the reappearance of the Aryans is the reappearance of their conflict with the Dasyus. Thus, the patterns of race mixture and race conflict provide principal elements of Viollet-le-Duc's history of primitive man. Chapter 9 mentions a conflict between the Asiatic Egyptians of the northern Delta and the dark-skinned Nubians to the south. This opposition repeats itself in chapter 12 between the Aryans of the Upper Media and their neighboring black inhabitants. On two occasions Viollet-le-Duc uses antique terms for the non-European other to identify nonwhite Aryans; in chapter 11 he identifies blacks with the term Dasyus from the Rig-Veda and in chapter 15 he identifies all non-Greeks as Tyrrhenians.

A curious feature about the taxonomies in the text is the sex and profile of its images; every image is male and is done in side or three-quarter profile. This pattern of representation places *L'habitation humaine* squarely in the physiognomic tradition of art, although the text falls closer to Petrus Camper's use of facial angles, which are a prelude to nineteenth-century phrenology, than to the ideal geometric precision of Jean-Jacques Lequeu's treatise (fig. 1.8). As is always the case with Viollet-le-Duc's innovative incorporation of drawing, his text replaces the reduced aesthetics of Camper and Lequeu's geometric constructions with a finished profile, hatched and shaded in to reinforce the

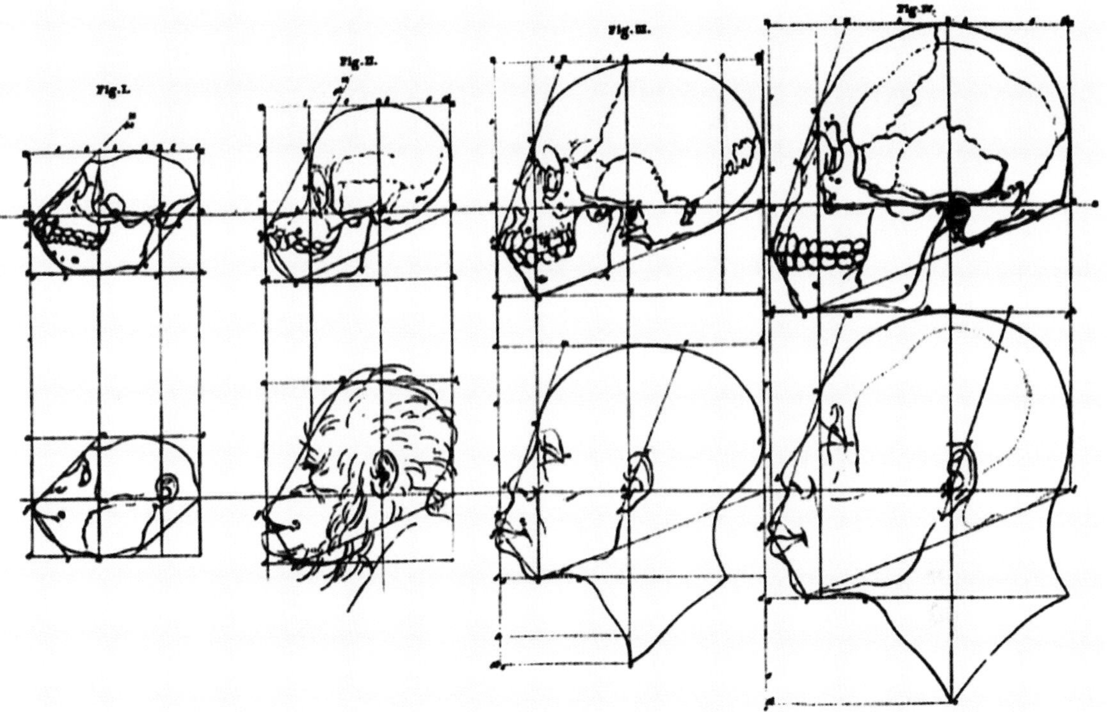

Figure 1.8. Facial angles of an ape, orangutan, a Kalmuck, and an African. Petrus Camper, 1791.

characteristics of their faces. Alongside the narration the reader is given a vivid summary of the character of each race type, which in the absence of any comparative profiling is nothing less than a visual stereotype. We are given a visual impression of the characteristics of the story's races. This is how, as Bucknall notes, the illustrations make Viollet-le-Duc's text come to life for the young reader. Although this technique of representation perpetuates racist stereotypes of nonwhite subjects, it must also be seen for its racial logic: it functions as a tutor for visualizing an Aryan historical narrative while allowing the reader to appropriate an aesthetic sensibility for the beauty of whiteness referenced in the artistic traditions of physiognomy, with its discussions of beauty and character. In this context the side profiles of the Asiatic Ionian, the Greek Hellene, and the Roman cannot be seen as accidental or neutral offerings. This reference might explain the absence of any black figures, which presents these subjects—through omission—as having no history. The exotic nature of the depiction of the Dasyu, the Chinaman, the Mongolian, and the Peruvian, by comparison, are all physical types that diverge from the beauty of whiteness.

Figure 1.9. Viollet-le-Duc, "The Primitive House of the Arya." *Histoire de l'habitation humaine* (1876), 11.

Viollet-le-Duc's progressive narrative complements the illustrative logic of racial taxonomies with a narrative and pictorial description of the organic principles of style in architecture. These principles were most clearly expressed in the transformation of constructive systems and materiality of vernacular architectures. Viollet-le-Duc provides a clear example of this in the physical transformation of the traditional Aryan hut as its people migrated from the mountain plateaus to the river valleys below. In chapter 2 of *L'habitation humaine* he introduces the reader to the most primitive state of the Aryan hut, which consisted of a pile of overlapping logs abutting a rock face (fig. 1.9).

As climate was an important element of Viollet-le-Duc's constructive theory, he uses it to introduce the reader to the mountain ranges that were a prominent part of the Aryan migration theory: "It is a vast plateau, commanded on the north by a chain of mountains whose summits, lost in the mists, are seldom visible. Wide and deep valleys furrow the plateau, and torrents rush down the slopes and along their beds, which are covered with rocky fragments and forests. Eternal snows clothe the heights. Accumulating, they spread out in long glaciers as far as the bottom of the valleys, hollowing out gleaming furrows, and pushing before them rocks and sand."[38] What is interesting about this description is that it couples the Aryan with the mountain peaks of the Aryan migration theory, while simultaneously introducing the reader to the generative powers of nature in the acclimate weather that accompanied this setting. This weather prepared the plains below by "hollowing out gleaming furrows, and pushing before them rocks and sand," which ironically helped prepare the land for the Aryan migration in subsequent chapters of the text. Due to the lack of water runoff on the roof, the chimney and roof of the Aryan dwelling gave way. In response to this disaster, the narration takes the reader step by step through the design decisions that were employed to resolve the issue of water damage; the top of the crag was prepared so that water could be directed away from the roof, and a stone base and stone walls were created to add durability to the shelter that was fitting to its climate (fig. 1.10). In physical appearance the outline of the Aryan dwelling remained the same, but in the second version the skin had changed. It was now more suited to its climate, which paralleled the ecological relationship biologists suggested guided the formation of race types. The only difference in this parallel was that the inherent capability of the Aryans was related to the use of timber; they learned to use stone out of necessity.

If the transition from a timber dwelling to a masonry structure demonstrates an internal organic principle of style that was akin to a race type in biology, then the next transformation of the Aryan dwelling exemplifies an ethnographic principle in the "mixed system of construction" that was produced.[39] Viollet-le-Duc uses the dynamic cultural exchanges that were the result of trade, conquest, and intermarriage to explain the hybrid forms that were manifest in the next stage of the Aryan dwelling. The narrative description of physical migrations establishes the setting for explaining the constructive changes to the initial type form.

In chapter 6 of *L'habitation humaine*, the Aryans migrate from the mountain peaks to the valleys below, as they had "been vanquished by the great families from the North," only to make slaves of the native "men of yellow complexion."[40] Ironically, the Aryans were aware of the Dasyus of the valleys because they had traded wool with them before. Although the Dasyus were easily subjugated in battle, Viollet-le-Duc credited them with a more complex knowledge of

Figure 1.10. Viollet-le-Duc, "Rebuilt House of the Aryas." *Histoire de l'habitation humaine* (1876), 23.

"industrial occupations"; they worked metals and stone, fashioned woods, made bricks, and even employed a polychrome decoration to insulate materials from wear. Due to the fair weather in the valley, the native homes were of lighter

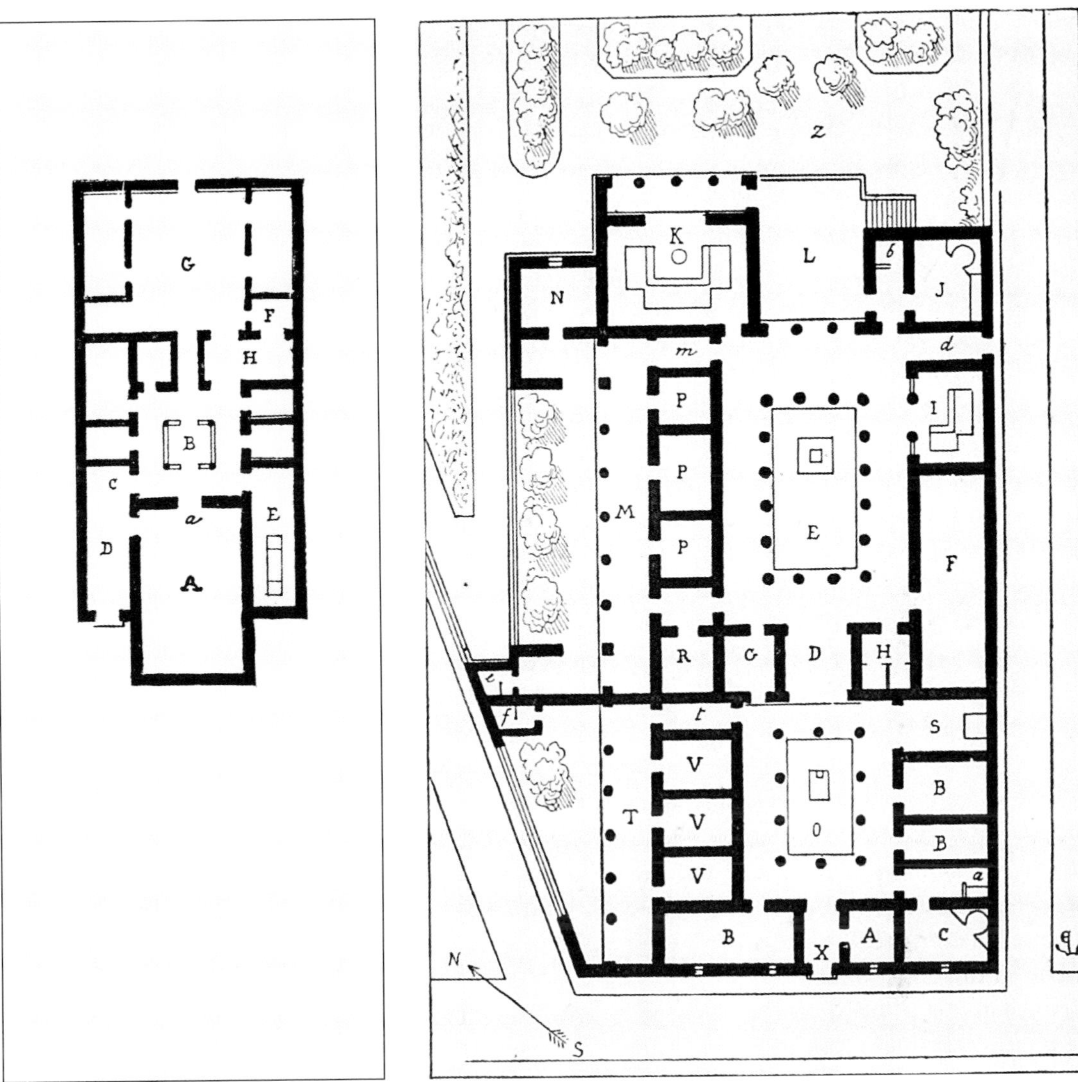

Figure 1.11 (*above left*). Viollet-le-Duc, "Plan of House of Aryas settled in the Upper Indus." *Histoire de l'habitation humaine* (1876), 49.

Figure 1.12 (*above right*). Viollet-le-Duc, "Plan of Athenian House." *Histoire de l'habitation humaine* (1876), 198.

materials, consisting of reeds stacked with a pisé pebble aggregate. The Aryans directed the natives to produce an architecture that was reminiscent of their traditional forms, but "gave only general orders . . . leaving their execution to the natives."[41] In this way, the plan and broad outline of the new dwellings were of an Aryan tradition, but the execution was of Dasyus origin.

Figure 1.13. Composite image of the illustrations in *L'habitation humaine* (1876) that illustrate the parallel vernacular types generated by the Dasyus (*top*) and the Aryans (*below*).

Viollet-le-Duc has already prepared the reader in chapter 6 by providing a general plan of the Aryan dwelling (fig. 1.11), to relate this layout to subsequent Hellenic innovations in chapters 16 and 17 that correlate with literal archaeological fragments (fig. 1.12). Thus, in the first few chapters the reader has been prepared to dialectically relate the narration and illustration of style to interpret an organic principle operating within the development of the Aryan dwelling, to identify the Aryan roots of Hellenic developments, and to relate both processes back to a primitive system of trabeated construction (fig. 1.13).

The principles of style Viollet-le-Duc introduces in the visual story of the Aryan dwelling had application to nineteenth-century constructive systems as well. Bucknall's introduction speaks of the complex relations that existed between contemporary constructive systems and their primitive precedents. In one section he identifies the dynamics that give primitive forms their beauty:

> Methods of construction adopted in times of primitive simplicity leave traces in the architecture of later periods, when that simplicity has been exchanged for luxury and refinement. On the other hand, we observe how, in the domestic architecture of the past, the main features of construction are determined by a consideration of habits, exigencies of climate and situation, the nature of the materials and the means of execution at the command of the builders; while we find them succeeding in giving even to the most primitive conceptions and modest structures that charm which arises from the free expression of a rational application of means to an end, and which, in human works, constitutes Art.[42]

According to Bucknall, not only do primitive constructive systems leave their trace in contemporary forms but the ethnographic customs informing the creation of primitive domestic details constitute some of the ends for which man creates art in architecture. The role that Bucknall sees for Viollet-le-Duc's history of primitive construction in the contemporary moment is the provision of a tool for reconstituting the art of the present; with a growing knowledge of the logic of primitive construction one can more easily match contemporary technologies (or means) with their present-day problems (or ends). By studying the traces that primitive forms leave for the architect one learns to identify the generative principles still relevant to the contemporary period. This was the power of primitive patterns as Bucknall interprets it in his introduction to Viollet-le-Duc's text.

Bucknall's explicit reference to the idea of "national genius" helps us answer the question of the anthropological basis of his earlier reference to race.[43] This nationalized conception of ethnography originates with Johann Gottfried Herder and is a part of his efforts to expand the discourse surrounding the race concept. His most famous work on human anthropology is *Outlines of a Philosophy of the History of Man*, an ambitious and unfinished work that he compiled between 1784 and 1791. Implicit in the phrase "national genius" is an inherent tension between deterministic biological factors that affect human form and the environmentalism of socially minded anthropologists of the nineteenth century. Herder's interpretation of the several races of mankind supplements a focus on biological criteria with environmentally formed characters one adopts while in their nation of origin. According to Herder, only some of the factors that the environment contributes to the constitution of the human body come from nature, like one's climate and diet. However, on the manmade side, forces like culture and politics also play a role in human development. The temperament of a culture expressed in one's national traditions may artificially "deform" one's physical traits in ways that are not genetic, but nonetheless recurring features of human form. National groups in Herder's text are described as having certain postures, facial expressions, and hand gestures that are ubiquitous learned behaviors.

This expansive definition fits well with Viollet-le-Duc's focus on ethnographic exchanges in the history of mankind. Yet even though this definition shifts the focus from the racial determinism described in biology to the notion of national genius, national genius did not obliterate the reference to human biology, as Herder's own text suggests. Such a reliance on primitive origins had been manifest in the discussion of abstractions of taxonomic traits in *L'habitation humaine*, as well as the obvious fact that every ethnographic development had to have a starting point. In this text the pairing of the Aryans with the Dasyus begins our march toward progress. At best Herder complicates the reductive consideration of race at a time when nationhood has become the more important factor to consider in the development of historical patrimony.

And we know of Viollet-le-Duc's interest in preserving the patrimony of the French state.

To complicate this discussion of the difference between ethnography and race theory, one can turn to the vitalism of nineteenth-century biologists to uncover yet another generative principle for human form. The progressive interest of race theorists in the early nineteenth century lies in their pursuit of the ultimate causes for the finite characters that appear on the outside. For them, race is only an external endpoint, an abstract designation for the internal relationships at stake in the body. Blood humors, phlogiston, germs, and vitalist processes are the principal aspects of this discourse in the life sciences. Race theory in this context develops the environmental aspects of the relation between the details of the visible and formative nature of the invisible. Buffon's introduction to the contingencies of hereditary traits in animal sexuality in the treatise *L'histoire naturelle*, of 1747, is the first step in exploring this direction. Kant read this treatise and expands the assumptions of its argument to account for the varieties we see in mankind in the essay "On the Different Races of Man," which first appeared in 1775. In it, Kant uses a deductive approach to posit the necessity of a teleological ecology within the body that fixes the external appearance of man over time. This fixing of physical character, or the degeneration from an ideal form, as Kant puts it, happens in response to environmental factors like climate and diet. These factors included what types of nutrients were present in the foods available, which, when combined with diet and climate, produced a racial taxonomy indicative of these inputs. Blumenbach takes Kant's speculative essay and verifies it with a comparative anatomical study of human skulls taken from the various race groups. This comparative approach to human form greatly influences the development of physical anthropology and phrenology in the late nineteenth century. Paul Erickson notes how proponents of anthropology and phrenology in England, Germany, France, and areas of the Netherlands simultaneously practice this comparative method.[44] This contextualizes the discourse of the race within scientific efforts to calve these fields from the previous rubrics of natural history in the nineteenth century. It also demonstrates the continued relevance of the race idea for anthropology from at least the end of the eighteenth century in the revisions to Buffon's model by Kant, to the establishment of cultural anthropology as a distinct field of study in the early twentieth century.

From the preceding review of the importance the race concept has for nineteenth-century ethnographers, we see how it is possible to preserve the static categories of racial taxonomy while complicating this superficial system with the pursuit of internal causes. Bucknall's reference to race in the phrase "the several races of mankind" indexes this discourse in all of the aspects mentioned above; he notes Viollet-le-Duc's interest in constructing a parallel history between the origin and development of construction details alongside an ethnographic consideration of the contingencies that inform these details, as well as pointing out the possibility of structuring this progressive history under the stable taxonomic categories of the three race groups of Gobineau's text. The presence of taxonomic figures at the close of thirteen chapters in *L'habitation humaine* establishes a visual referent as stable as a racial taxonomy, while the progressive narrative of the text complicates a simplistic reading. In short, Viollet-le-Duc tries to have it both ways: he writes with the dynamics of ethnography in mind while freezing the process in the visual language of racial taxonomy to make each phase clearly understood. Herder's definition helps Viollet-le-Duc's historical narrative complicate the reductive focus on taxonomic race forms by positing a larger field of factors for consideration by the historian. Yet a tension remains between the text's descriptive narrative and its static profiling of male types, which is obviously racist. One is tempted to rely on Bucknall and Bressani's idea of a dialectical principle fundamental to Viollet-le-Duc's historical method in order to account for these extremes.

Viollet-le-Duc would use other scientific tutors as analogies for identifying generative principles of design in the nineteenth century; geology, linguistics, and comparative anatomy are only the most regular sources quoted by scholars. Since the narratives of construction and racial anthropology are so closely linked in *L'habitation humaine,* the race idea is yet another source of inspiration for Viollet-le-Duc. Insofar as the intellectual context of the nineteenth century suggests an emphasis in the field of anthropology on developing racial schemas that account for multiple environmental factors, Bucknall's use of "national genius" necessarily indexes that discourse. It is also interesting to note that Petit Jean, the antagonist of *Histoire d'un dessinateur* (another popular history written by Viollet-le-Duc in the late 1870s) finishes his training by going on an expedition of the mountains.[45] Apparently, recording the mountains in drawings helps young Jean to see more clearly, which is no surprise given the emphasis that Viollet-le-Duc puts on drawing for clarifying hidden relationships. The racial aspect of this novella appears most visibly in chapter fifteen, where the student begins to learn how to see by drawing the facial angles of famous pieces of art, a practice that Petrus Camper popularized in the eighteenth century with his treatise *On the Points of Similarity between the Human Species, Quadrupeds, Birds, and Fish; with Rules for Drawing, founded on this Similarity* of 1778. Thus, in this period we can already begin to see race and style meeting for Viollet-le-Duc in the image of the mountain.

Figure 1.14. Viollet-le-Duc, "Le Chalet des Aryas," 1875. *Histoire de l'habitation humaine* (1876), 383.

The Swiss architectural historian Jacques Gubler notes the influence of tourist culture on Viollet-le-Duc's romantic interpretation of rural architectures.[47] According to Gubler, the chalet at Chamonix served as an outpost for mountaineers and travelers looking for a resting post—a practice the architect would have been familiar with given his mapmaking expeditions through the Alps.[48] The second- and third-story spaces that housed visitors were decorated in a romantic style that recalled the primitive origins of the chalet type form, while the ground floor that housed the innkeepers or permanent residents was treated more austerely (with concrete) to keep out the cold weather. Gubler also notes Viollet-le-Duc's revival of the communal function of fireplaces for collecting people around the hearth, which transformed the direct simplicity of the single-loaded corridor in the primitive hut into a double-loaded corridor that contained the growing complexities of the modern program. What remains unclear, however, in Gubler's analysis is the symbolic purpose of the fireplace in these more recent designs. If one revisits the "primitive house of the [Aryans]" illustrated in *L'habitation humaine*, one notes the functional distinction that had already occurred between the fireplace contained within the main dwelling, which was used for warmth, and the stone hearth in the central courtyard that operated as an altar to the ancestors (see figs. 1.9, 1.10). The audiences for both spaces were strictly enforced: the internal hearth was used to collect members of the immediate family while the elders of the household used the exterior hearth to communicate with members of the family cult. This separation is now duplicated inside of the interior, with the dining room serving as a remnant of the interior hearth and the fireplace of the "salon," or study, serving as the area of communion with history. In this sense, Viollet-le-Duc's solution not only achieves a strict functional separation between the public and the private spaces of the chalet but also revives the symbolic importance of the religious family cult in the contemporary salon.

The Maison du Jardinier was completed for the Chateau d'Eu, a residence of the royal family since the sixteenth century.[49] This modest structure continues the double-loaded corridor that revives the spatial separation between the interior and exterior fireplaces of the Aryan primitive hut. (fig. 1.16) The Maison du Jardinier initially served as a family home for the estate's gardener, who provided support services for the larger chateau, until a member of the royal family was forced to live there during his exile from England. The flexibility of this program to serve both the royal family and its support staff communicates the suitability of this modern program for all members of the French nation-state.

A distinct physiognomic feature of this building is its use of brick, which was briefly introduced in the narrative of *L'habitation humaine* as a finishing material for the primitive Aryan hut.[50] This material was probably chosen to coordinate with the brick finish of the baroque façade of the main house, which

Figure 1.16. Maison du Jardinier. Note the brick façade with wood inlay. Viollet-le-Duc, ca. 1874–1875. Médiathèque de l'Architecture.

employs inlaid ashlar quoins, arches, and pilasters to ennoble the four-story structure. The inlaid wood details of the Maison du Jardinier recall the primitive origins of this building type in a subtler way than the romantic finishes of Chamonix. The crisscross patterning of the spandrel panels above the entryway rise along the central axis of the front façade, which meets at the apex of the roof adorned with large wooden brackets. As a composition, the brick finishing of this building presents an image of a rustic hut that echoes the country houses that Friedrich Weinbrenner designed in Karlsruhe. Both regions were associated with local construction techniques that combined wood inlay with stucco or brick infill, and these building traditions often served as a visual sign of the growing importance of farming in remote agricultural economies. The Maison du Jardinier also serves as an aesthetic midpoint between Viollet-le-Duc's romantic quotation of primitive wooden structures and his concrete translation of wooden architectural forms in La Vedette (fig. 1.17).[51]

Lausanne was the perfect site for Viollet-le-Duc's architectural practice in many ways, with its public culture intent on preserving the traditional rhythms of a market town in the face of efforts to modernize provincial France. It also had

Figure 1.17. Villa à Lausanne. Note the complete masonry façade. Viollet-le-Duc, 1875. From *Habitations modernes* (1877), plate 161.

a formative development, to which Viollet-le-Duc contributed directly with a construction of a new church and the restoration of another. He was working on a plan for the steeple of the town's church upon his death, when the project went to another architect. The dialectical struggle between tradition and technology that was so fundamental to the architect's preservation efforts in France and his publication of *Habitations modernes* and *L'habitation humaine* seemed to be alive in this provincial town.

La Vedette first appeared as a speculative adaptation of the chalet house type in Viollet-le-Duc's *Habitations modernes* the same year that construction was completed in Lausanne, Switzerland, and one year before the publication of *L'habitation humaine.* Viollet-le-Duc believed that the chalet type was indigenous to the hilly regions of Switzerland and selected it over the Gothic architecture he was used to working with. In fact, each house in *Habitations modernes* is accompanied by a description of the region that it was designed for and a short explanation of its vernacular roots. As a counterpoint to the primitive narration of *L'habitations humaine*, which depicts the ethnographic birthplace of the Aryan in the mountainous East, *Habitations modernes* revives a primitive vernacular model of the home for a mountainous region that survived into the nineteenth century. Viollet-le-Duc's conception of such primitive settings permitted him to endow contemporary forms with historical characteristics.

Shortly before his death and almost a year after the original construction, a mural of a mountain range was added to the salon drawing room of the first floor of La Vedette (see fig. 1.1). In producing a reading of the representational significance of this mural, there are several textual parallels with the Aryan migration model of history discussed earlier in this chapter. As the narrative goes, the visual descent from the mountains to the plains below mirrors the path philologists thought the primitive Aryan tribes had taken when they conquered other races on their way toward civilization. Akin to the shifting dimensions of the literal mountains that Viollet-le-Duc visited after 1870, human civilization preserved a record of its own stresses and conflicts in ethnographic and architectural terms. This parallel was implicit in the late inclusion of the mountain mural, especially given its appearance after the bulk of Viollet-le-Duc's exhibitions through the Alps (see plate 5). In painting this scene, Viollet-le-Duc mirrored the mythical behavior of the Aryan tribes he read about from Maury and the German archaeologists: they not only worshipped their gods up in the mountains but in turn memorialized this presence with the ornamentation of their vernacular architecture. According to the narrative of *L'habitation humaine*, these forms registered the hybrid aspects of the conqueror and the conquered, akin to the process of blood mixture that occurred between hybrid race groups. The correlation between the narrative and illustrations of this text created a step-by-step reconstruction of Aryan primitive development, resulting in a comprehensive historical narrative of primitive life that Gubler believes to be fundamental to the design of La Vedette. Viollet-le-Duc not only integrated three existing narratives of the philological, the anthropological, and the architectural but materialized the historical impulses of these narratives.

Since the existing documentation on this house is limited, one must speculate on the manner in which the specifics of the interior aligned with its surroundings. The painting of an outdoor scene in an interior space, specifically an interior space with direct views to the outside, expanded the normal dimensions of the interior. From the history of Lausanne's economic development, it is evident that the Swiss Alps could be seen as a backdrop for miles from the lower elevation of the town at least until the buildup after the 1890s. This no doubt would have created a resonance between the interior mural scene and the mountains in the distance. The cross-axes created by the openings in the perimeter walls

Figure 1.18. Elevation of northern wall inside of salon, La Vedette, ca. 1876. Médiathèque de l'Architecture.

of the salon are also suggestive since they permit the entering subject to extend their views beyond the walls of the space. For example, the double doors that opened from the foyer into the salon diagonally aligned with the view framed by the middle two sashes of the bay window. The single door that opened from the innermost corridor into the salon aligned with the two windows set into the exterior wall to the south, and the fireplace along the northeast interior wall mirrored this arrangement. Upon entering the room from either door, the subject is presented with both literal and speculative views of the mountains beyond. Casual views up from the centrally located table would provide a visual dialogue between the reconstructed views of the interior and views of the mountain range outside. It is tempting to think that the snowcapped mountains painted on the interior were a reconstructed view of what was visible through the two oversized windows set into the southern face of the house.

The isolation of the fireplace along the interior northern wall seems to recall the idea of a campfire situated within the eastern half of the salon (fig. 1.18). As the sun moved east to west, the eastern half of the room would run out of daylight first. The placement of this element would have given the occupant an immediate spatial orientation of the chalet's situation within the site; an internal compass, if you will. And would not the weary Aryan traveler have benefited from a compass? Following the conspicuous ornamental post that divided the room in two brings one's attention to the rusticated banding that lined the perimeter of the space. If this mural was supposed to evoke an outdoor scene, then perhaps the timber framing elicited the impression of an outdoor patio, with the rusticated stone base eliciting the memory of a masonry plinth. Sitting beneath this trellised patio and looking out into the mountain range beyond—in either direction, no less—would have given a viewer the semblance of looking beyond into the exterior.

Yet there were enough signals within the composition to give evidence that this constructed view was a ruse, a constructed order meant to emulate nature, but not completely replace it. For example, the post in the northwest corner of the room would have fulfilled this function as it was slightly pushed into the wall, putting it slightly out of alignment with the middle post. This element was aligned just enough to suggest that it was still a support, but displaced so that the construction of the panorama took precedence over the literal construction of space. The rusticated wainscot also provides something of a disjunction between the panorama and the painted rocks beyond. It is almost as if Viollet-le-Duc wanted to be sure that the mural, the polychrome coating that weatherized the wall, was not given too much of a reality of its own. Its function was only partially symbolic, partially representational. It must still be identified as a coating. As the architect sat himself by the warmth of the fire, at a temporal vantage point where he could look back upon the passage of time and reconstruct the primitive that opposing views of the mountain range provided him, it might be fair to call this drawing room a contemplative space, maybe even the perfect space for an architect to observe nature and perhaps even emulate her principles.

In the spirit of the ethnographic narrative of *L'habitation humaine*, this private vista permitted the architect to stand in the plains of yesteryear and witness the beginning of the plastic arts, never far removed from the rusticated wainscot that recalled the geometric principle inherent in the mountain itself. The top of the drafting table sat midway between the datum of the plains and the heights of the mountain peaks, showing how contemporary man was stuck somewhere between his primitive roots and the perfection of the Greeks. It was also clearly a reminder that Frenchman consisted of some of the last root of this noble line of Aryans. In a sense, Viollet-le-Duc painted himself as the prototypical Aryan man, enlightened from his forays into history, and finally being made victorious by his universal knowledge of nature. He literally climbed the mountain of Mont Blanc to unearth her secrets and invented one of the most elaborate historical narratives for architects of the nineteenth century, and without the race concept so dear to the time period, he might never have made it to the top.

Despite Viollet-le-Duc's clear rejection of neoclassical anthropomorphic metaphors for architectural style, he continued to reference the human body in his architectural writings. His turn toward organic metaphors for style implicitly introduced a biological image of human development, which was most explicitly expressed in the narration and illustration of *Histoire de l'habitation humaine.* The seeds of this intellectual development date back to the organic redefinition of "Style" outlined in the *Dictionnaire raisonné de l'architecture française* of 1864, and by 1875 Viollet-le-Duc had constructed a comprehensive and comparative ethnographic framework for interpreting the development of style in vernacular primitive architecture. The paradigm shift introduced by this definition of style parallels methodological innovations in the natural sciences that replaced the taxonomic categories of racial difference common in natural history texts of the late eighteenth century with the teleological principles of biological development outlined in the nineteenth century. The comparative historical framework Viollet-le-Duc introduced for racial typologies and vernacular construction typologies in *L'habitation humaine* ultimately encouraged him to interpret race as style in the context of his architecture theory. This innovation established a discursive interpretation of organic architecture that emulated the generative principles of scientific models of racial difference in the nineteenth century.

Traditional accounts of Viollet-le-Duc's style theory have taken his interest in race theory as an incidental reference of his late intellectual development, or have focused on the general "organic" character of his scientific metaphors for design. Isolating his explicit interest in the representation of the human body makes us reconsider the racial and ethnic content of his structural preoccupations, which in turn should help us to be more critical of what racial biases were likely to have been built into his contributions to French structural rationalism. Since part of Viollet-le-Duc's fascination with architectural history was guided by his need to identify appropriate historical precedents for contemporary design, the racial and ethnographic content of history was not an incidental part of his style theory. He constructed a synthetic relationship between the national aspirations, ethnographic origins, racial dispositions, and structural innovations of material culture as a rational basis for regulating the practical methodology of nineteenth-century design. Considering the fact that the legitimacy of race science was not discredited until the mid-1940s, the dissemination of Viollet-le-Duc's organicism perpetuated a methodological bias for emulating the findings and tacit assumptions of nineteenth- and twentieth-century racial anthropology (biology and ethnography). To put it another way, when we consider what this means with respect to the French racial discourses most common to the late nineteenth and early twentieth century, Viollet-le-Duc's style theory offered the architect no internal checks against the tacit racist assumptions of these scientific discourses, a fact that is aptly illustrated by his own architectural writings.

What was most innovative about his consideration of race, however, was the clear identification of a common organic principle in the teleological conceptions of racial and ethnographic development. With this developmental model, race was no longer restricted to the taxonomic characteristics most central to anthropomorphic considerations of the human body. Instead, surface characters became indicative of internal predispositions: as the rib vault and flying buttress clearly expressed the load-bearing capacity of Gothic architecture, so did the physical complexion and taxonomic features of a race type indicate an ecological resolution of internal teleological properties and external geographical factors. Race in Viollet-le-Duc's style theory became a natural illustration of the universal principles of form.

Figure 2.1. Samuel Wale, frontispiece to the English translation of Marc-Antoine Laugier's *Essay on Architecture* (1755).

2

BEYOND THE PRIMITIVE HUT

Gottfried Semper and the Material Embodiment of German Character

> In ancient and modern times the store of architectural forms has often been portrayed as mainly conditioned by and arising from the material, yet by regarding construction as the essence of architecture we, while believing to liberate it from false accessories, have thus placed it in fetters. Architecture, like its great teacher, nature, should choose and apply its material according to the laws conditioned by nature, yet should it not also make the form and character of its creations dependent on the ideas embodied in them, and not on the material?
>
> —**Gottfried Semper,**
> **"Four Elements of Architecture"**

IN THE FIRST FIVE YEARS of the 1860s, the expatriated Dresden architect Gottfried Semper published a treatise titled *Der Stil in der technischen und tektonischen Kunsten, oder, Praktische Ästhetik* (*Style in the Technical and Tectonic Arts, or, a Practical Aesthetics*) from his academic post at the Eidgenössische Technische Hochschule (ETH) in Zurich.[1] This text outlines an anthropological interpretation of architectural style that traces the origins of representational ornament back to the symbolic meanings of premodern motifs used to decorate the practical arts. The anthropological framework of *Der Stil* advances several of the themes discussed in Semper's earlier writings, including an 1851 essay titled "The Four Elements of Architecture," which proposed a new origin theory for domestic architecture. This latter essay was radical for its time because it challenged the canonical role of the primitive hut in modern architectural theory. As Joseph Rykwert notes in *On Adam's House in Paradise,* the primitive hut operated from antiquity to the Renaissance and beyond as a conceptual model of design that stripped down architecture to its most basic components.[2] In the Vitruvian tradition, this origin myth visualized the perfect harmony that could be achieved between man and nature in the built environment, a social and aesthetic ideal that was embodied by the geometrical proportions of the human body. By the eighteenth century, the critical meaning of the primitive hut had been progressively transformed by the rational ideals of the European Enlightenments to represent a different portrait of man in nature. Instead of referencing the divine clockwork that regulated the universal laws of nature, anthropological models of cultural development were molding the architect's understanding of the past (fig. 2.1). Semper directly contributed to this scientific transformation of modern architectural theory by deriving a set of design principles from the ethnographical histories of premodern cultural groups published in the nineteenth century.

From his lectures of the 1840s to his treatise of the early 1860s, Semper consistently examined the material cultures of premodern peoples for clues to deduce the essential elements of architecture.[3] His textual references to the facial tattoos of New Zealand natives or the constructive motifs of the Caribbean hut participate in the scholarly tradition of reimagining architecture's origins, but from the perspective of ethnographical history. They also anticipate the ethnographical documentation of Germany's colonies in the islands of the South Seas nearly a decade after the architect's passing. Semper's methodological departure in architectural theory initially appears to subvert the necessity for the human-body metaphors of Vitruvian theory. Of what further use was a metaphorical representation of natural order when the empirical methodologies of natural science were providing direct answers to how natural phenomena worked? This epistemological shift has led some scholars to argue that the scientific rationalization of European architectural theory rendered the necessity of a human-body metaphor in modern architecture effectively obsolete.[4] Yet at least one paradigm continued to maintain a metaphorical relationship between man and nature as a critical foundation for architectural invention, although on entirely new grounds.

For proponents of architectural organicism, the human body remained one of several case studies capable of illustrating the generative principles of nature. However, these principles were no longer communicated through a mimetic image of the human body but in the scientific accounting of the invisible processes that constituted its final form. As Caroline van Eck notes in her study of architectural organicism, proponents of this approach began to emulate the processes of nature instead of its visual appearances.[5] Within this disciplinary context, the typological and medicalized interpretation of the human body would have provided the modern architect with an empirical illustration of nature's capacity to stylize organic life, one that would have seemed immediately relevant to the design and construction of new national building traditions. Given the procedural focus of nineteenth-century architecture theory, perhaps the best way of framing the shifting importance of the human body is to account for the productivities that emerged from this new procedural interpretation of nature. In the anthropological discourses that inspired Semper's radical challenge to canonical interpretations of the primitive hut, the image of the human body had splintered from one universal image of man into a series of discrete race types that categorize the variations of cultural differences found in history. Answering the question of what further purpose the human body served in architectural organicism requires us to take a closer look at a seminal idea of the biological and anthropological sciences: the race concept.

The scientific rubrics that fostered the core ideas of racial anthropology were taken from a wide range of fields, including biology, linguistics, ethnography, and art history. Ethnography and art history especially functioned as umbrella fields that synthetically related the constellation of data on human culture into a holistic frame of analysis. During the nineteenth century philosophers and scientists debated what value the race concept had for resolving the fundamental nature of the human species. Was human diversity caused by variations within a single species, or did different race groups represent entirely distinct species? Proponents of polygenetic species origins for mankind believed that the intellectual aptitudes and temperaments of different groups seemed to point toward a physiological cause, but there was no consensus on why, from the time Linnaeus invented the species-genera typological system of categorization until the late eighteenth century.

Robert Bernasconi has reconstructed the historical correspondence that arose between the German philosopher Immanuel Kant and the German anatomist and anthropologist Johann Friedrich Blumenbach that supported a monogenetic conception of the human species.[6] This innovative breakthrough sprang from an epistemological debate over the analytical value of the race concept.[7] According to Bernasconi, Kant should be credited with inventing the modern notion of the race concept, as he uses it to rationalize the systematic relationships that must exist in order for species, genera, and variations to have scientific meaning. In Blumenbach's subsequent illustrations of five racial types, represented by lithographs of five human skulls, he attempts to demonstrate the physiological principles that imperceptibly transformed the archetypal races of man into the cultural variations then seen around the globe. Even before Charles Darwin's theory of natural selection, the immanence and mutability of racial characters made the morphological notions of hybridity and miscegenation a heuristic lens for conceptualizing the social and political effects of cross-cultural exchanges.[8]

Contemporary studies of the European architectural style debates have only recently begun to account for the potential influence of race science on nineteenth-century debates.[9] These innovations have been slow to reach studies of Semper's architectural style theory, although some pioneering studies do exist.[10] Despite a steady stream of academic studies documenting Semper's interest in natural science and anthropology, very few are dedicated to the critical function of the race concept in his style theory or the racial discourses generated by his writings have been forthcoming. One reason for this omission is likely the narrow focus of disciplinary histories that tend to privilege the architectural value of Semper's work in lieu of a cross-disciplinary analysis of the broader implications of his ideas. A prime example of this can be seen in the intellectual frameworks of academic studies that account for Semper's anthropological interpretation of architecture. Rykwert, Wolfgang Herrmann, and Harry Francis Mallgrave have done the most work in recovering the anthropological themes and hermeneutical strategies that distinguished Semper's notion of design from the academicism, materialism, and structuralism of his time. This research has reversed a negative conception of Semper's writings that was popularized by many after his death, from the art historian Alois Riegl, who famously critiqued *Der Stil* as a reductive materialist theory of design, to the biological interpretation of this treatise published by Semper's son and biographer.[11] These postwar revisionist histories note Semper's 1869 rejection of Darwinian evolutionary theory as evidence that his theory is not Darwinian in nature. Such corrections have shielded Semper's architectural legacy from being associated with the Social Darwinist paradigms of the early twentieth century or the Aryan nationalisms of the mid-twentieth century.[12] Yet to defend Semper against undue claims of ethnonational racism should not prevent us from making a careful examination of the formal principles he would have gleaned from his exposure to the race concept. Such a reactive viewpoint prevents us from interpreting the racialist structure of Semper's arguments and the broader political implications of his work.

An important step in interpreting the inevitable consequences of Semper's anthropological interpretation of architectural style is to clearly distinguish between the generative principles that were typically associated with evolutionary models of development and the race idea. Evolutionary models of development such as Darwin's theory of natural selection were not the only means of interpreting cultural differences or substantiating cultural hierarchies in the nineteenth century. The French naturalist and zoologist Georges Cuvier, a historical figure commonly cited as a primary influence in Semper's career in academic studies, found it possible to reject the theory of biological evolution while supporting the existence of biological race types.[13] Cuvier even expounded upon the essential qualities of racial character when it suited his needs to explain the differences between white and nonwhite characters (fig. 2.2). His fascination with the Hottentot Venus is now well documented, as is his scientific interpretation of race types as an inherent factor of biology and anthropological research.[14]

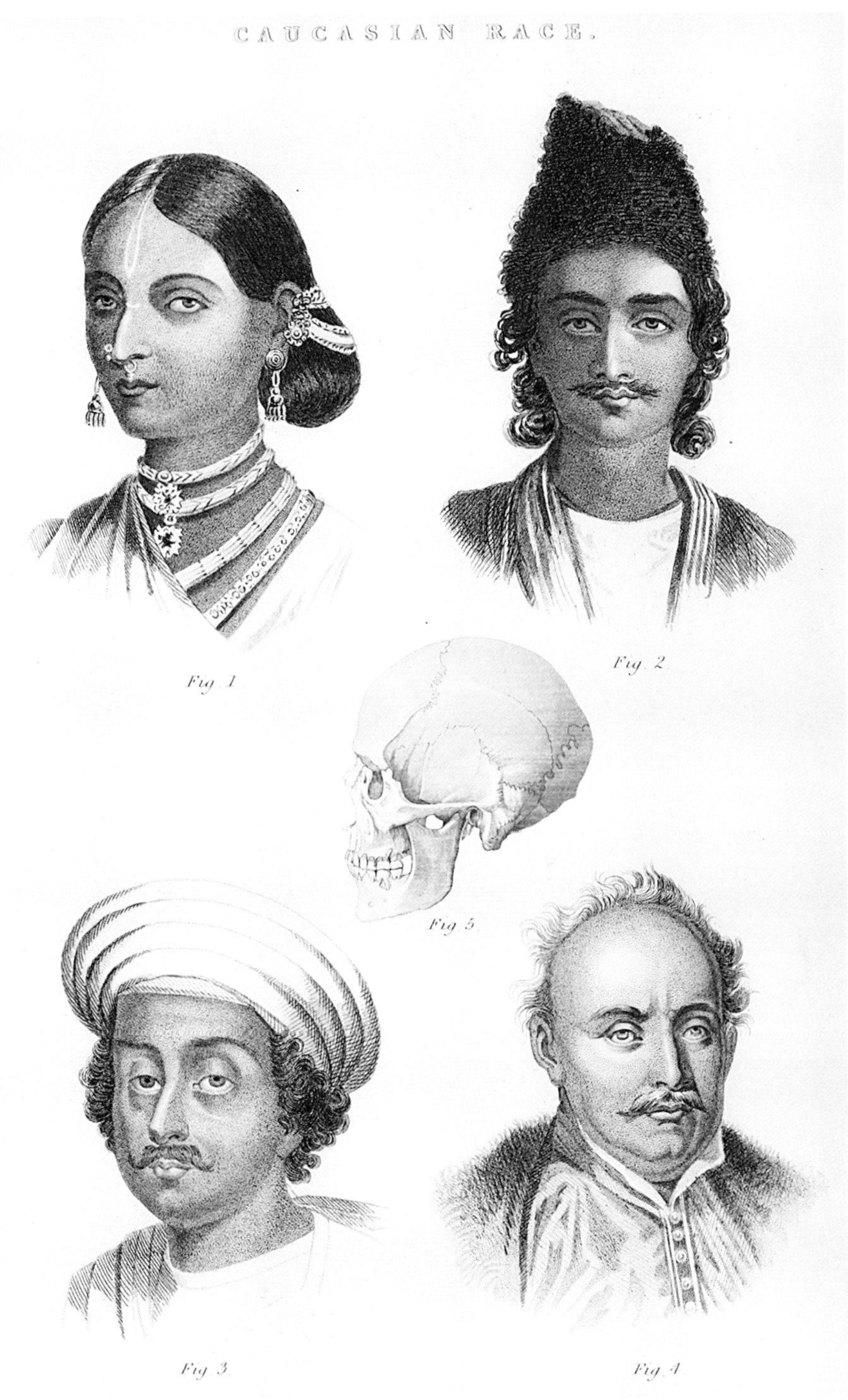

Figure 2.2. Georges Cuvier, illustration of the Caucasian race. From *The Animal Kingdom: Arranged According to its Organization, Forming a Natural History of Animals and an Introduction to Comparative Anatomy* (1851).

In addition to nonevolutionary conceptions of human difference, architectural theorists did not require an evolutionary model of history to imagine the steady transformation of architecture culture, as ideological theories of morphological development had already been introduced through Johann Wolfgang von Goethe's concept of the *Urpflanze* or Friedrich Schlegel's conception of the plasticity of the German language.[15] As Semper's case so clearly demonstrates, one can be interested in the particularities of race, language, and formal morphology without having to endorse Darwinian theories of natural selection or evolutionary models of historical change. It was also possible to value the positive traits of so-called primitive tribes, as Semper does in his discussion of the aesthetic impulse behind tattooing, and still find oneself implicated in the negative implications of colonial politics. Even as Semper struggled to present a narrative of historical change that considered each tradition of material culture as a product of a particular time and place, his outsized love of Greek culture and his desire to promote a liberally based German state directly contribute to nineteenth-century ethnonationalism—a tendency that was expressed by liberal approaches to German unification and the progressive instrumentalization of ethnographical history in the colonial projects of the 1870s and 1880s.[16]

This chapter uses the lens of scientific type theory to identify the epistemic racialism of Semper's anthropological interpretation of architectural style, which introduced embodied notions of racial character into the German paradigm of architectural tectonics. It argues that the typological structure of Semper's synthesis of the four elements of architecture metaphorically transfers the immanence and mutability of biological race types onto the transformation of material culture. This operation resulted in an embodied representation of racial characters that was associated with visual representations of the human body in the natural sciences, but no longer required the literal representation of the human body in the context of architectural theory.

Semper first advanced a typological interpretation of the primordial origins of architectural style in "Four Elements of Architecture," which he later refined with the anthropological framework of his architectural treatise *Der Stil*. The parallel status that he maintains between race and style in these two publications emulates the visual economy of nineteenth-century racial anthropology, which treated these two phenomena as physical evidence for the underlying characters of national groups. The interchangeability of race and style categories in Semper's writings effectively personifies his interpretation of material culture with the racial characteristics of its creators. An embodied notion of racial character is most clearly manifested in Semper's interpretation of the formal properties of Greek temple architecture in "Four Elements of Architecture" and the Greek hydria and the Egyptian situla in *Der Stil*, although each work contains other examples of embodied racial characters as well.

A remarkable resonance between the realism of Semper's style theory and the political debates of his time can be found in his use of the physiological concept of *Stoffwechsel* (metabolism), which introduced a new notion of morphology to *Der Stil* but was also influential in nutritionist debates of the nineteenth century. The nutritionist and social reformer Jacob Moleschott, a peer of Semper's at the ETH in Zurich, employed the principles of metabolism to shape key segments of the population to modify the moral and intellectual characters of the nation-state. Semper's textual references to Stoffwechsel places his work within a political context where scientific expertise was valorized for directing the future character of the German people. These conceptual themes were no doubt relevant to his own attempts to translate German national characters into representative architectural forms.

Further examples of the broader social and political implications of Semper's style theory were exemplified in both positive and negative ways. For example, Semper's search for historical origins was partially manifested by his search for an architectural style that might potentially give rise to a modern German nation-state. This impulse was present in his textual parallels of Greek and German culture in "Four Elements of Architecture" and his historical outline of the autochthonous roots of German culture in the rural housing traditions of the Bavarian Alps in *Der Stil*. Like Viollet-le-Duc's speculation of the Alpine roots of French Aryan culture, Semper's style theory similarly locates a native origin for German culture in the Rhaetian Alps.[17]

These references collectively legitimized the perceived Greco-Italic origins of Germanic culture that ultimately contributed to Semper's preference for a proto-Roman architectural style of building. This stylistic choice for a contemporary modern architecture constituted an architectural revivalism that was theoretically capable of synthetically integrating the ethnic, religious, and political pluralism manifested throughout the federation of states associated with the Prussian-controlled northern and Austro-Hungarian-controlled southern regions of modern Germany. On the one hand, the cultural allusions of Semper's architectural style enabled the cultural assimilation of certain ethnic minorities such as the wealthy Jewish elites who adopted the secular ideals of the nation-state. On the other hand, Semper's earnest fascination with the aesthetic practices of nonwhite "primitives" such as the Māori was indicative of a subsequent instrumentalization of scientific knowledge through political support for German colonialism in Africa, northern China, and the islands of the South Seas.[18] As Susanne Zantop notes, the ethnographic categorizations of the nineteenth century created an implicit visual cartography of the expanding geographical extents of the German empire, from the native white populations at home to the potential nonwhite subjects of colonialism living abroad.[19] By the time of his death, the social and political contexts of Semper's career transformed many of his architectural designs of the 1850 and 1860s into a visual allegory of Germany's search for a homogenous national identity, from its internal struggles to define the common roots of the body politic to its colonial aspirations as a leading nation of Western Europe.

The Narrative Structure of "The Four Elements of Architecture"

"The Four Elements of Architecture" outlines the fundamental principles of Semper's anthropological interpretation of architectural style. The essay is organized into six main sections, the first four of which detail his shifting position on polychrome decoration in classical Greek temple architecture. The final two turn their attention back toward the course of architectural style throughout cultural history, with section V outlining the four elements of architecture that were passed on from one generation to the next and section VI providing a few practical applications of this fourfold theory for contemporary design.

Semper's essay incorporates the race concept in both thematic content and the typological structure of his argument. The former modality was an explicit attempt to align the latest findings of racial anthropology into his critical assessment of the central importance of polychrome decoration in antiquity. The latter modality was an inherent consequence of Semper's emulation of the structural principles of scientific type theory, which was an organizational paradigm of the sciences that classified both the biological traits of individuals and the common trends of national groups into racial categories.

In terms of thematic content, "Four Elements of Architecture" constitutes an apologia for the superiority of Greek culture. This tradition was hailed in the nineteenth century for establishing many of the tenets of Western civilization, including the birth of democratic culture in the ancient world. Several passages from Semper's essay intimate the parallel traits he perceived between the democratic culture that bound the Greek city-states into a functioning political unit and the historic potential for Germany to become a unified liberal state in Western Europe. One of the most suggestive passages can be found near the end of the essay, where he cites the obstacles that Greek citizens had to overcome to achieve a common "national feeling" among the citizenry: "Composed of a mixture of tribes, the Greeks were not ready for a free development toward national unity until war, piracy, and trade had deprived them of their traditional, moral, and tellurian bonds. The democratic element emerging from these unruly conditions would have consumed itself early had not the flame of democracy occasionally been fueled with long-lasting logs of wood."[20] He later credits "the free Ionic spirit" that dominated national ideas for synthesizing the artistic trends of foreign cultures into the political philosophy that gave birth to a new plateau in architecture.[21]

Semper's narrative presents the Greeks as the first "historians" of art who learned to base "their art on the traditions of other people."[22] The rhetorical parallels between a democratic Greece and a liberal Germany would have been tacit in the minds of his German-speaking readers as they could discern the ways that the political structure of their Zollverein, or the economic confederation of distinct principalities in the region, approximated the political structure of Greek governance. After all, Germany had also suffered the trials of "war, piracy, and trade" along the Rhine from routine French military incursions, a sentiment that was poetically expressed by Goethe's homage to the Strasbourg Cathedral in his epic poem "Von Deutsche Baukunst" as early as 1772.

"Four Elements of Architecture" establishes several important principles that guided Semper's consideration of the race concept during the 1850s and 1860s. One parameter that conditioned his thinking was an organic conception of architectural design. His brand of architectural organicism provided a holistic intellectual framework for updating the metaphorical relationships that connected man and nature in the classical tradition. Section V of his essay opens with the claim that "architecture, like its great teacher, nature, should choose and apply its material according to the laws conditioned by nature."[23] Semper's critique of reductive materialism is countered by an important caveat that identifies the new source of meaning in his architecture theory: "the ideas embodied within them."[24] This addendum is instructive because it credits the "form and character" of architectural styles to the ideas embodied by their material details but not immanent in these details themselves. These underlying ideas consisted of the essential cultural beliefs that regulated the production of material culture, and later of monumental architectures.

Semper explicitly cites race as a correlational factor in the morphological transformation of architectural styles: "According to how different human societies developed under the varied influences of climate, natural surroundings, social relations, and different racial dispositions, the combinations in which the four elements of architecture were arranged also had to change, with some elements becoming more developed while others receded into the background. At the same time the different technical skills of man became organized according to these elements: *ceramics* and afterwards metal works around the *hearth*, *water* and *masonry works* around the *mound*, *carpentry* around the *roof* and its accessories."[25] The organic relationships that linked the essential traits of a people's "racial dispositions" and the morphological transformation of their material culture, while suggestive, is still a very schematic metric for tracing the historical lineage of cultural ideas. At first glance, the influence of racial characters appears to operate on material culture from the outside as the essential characters of material culture, which Semper would identify as the four elements of architecture, seem to have a life of their own. However, this perspective must yield to two very important limitations. First, Semper makes it clear that style cannot progress in a vacuum; it needs the stuff of culture to transform itself. And second, since the arts and architecture emulate natural principles of generation, then the organic principles of development found in the progression of material culture constitute a second-level order that emulates the natural principles that established the racial characters of historical groups. As we will see, these characters were considered from the perspective of individuals and the common cultures that emerged within national groups.

Another parameter of Semper's essay that conditions the critical function of the race concept in his theory is the typological structure of his argument, which employs the four elements of architecture as historical origin points for tracing parallel developments in architectural history. In a structural sense, the four elements of architecture constitute a primary set of archetypal categories that operate as discrete origin points for subsequent artistic developments in cultural history. This establishes a structural parallel between race and style categories that is recapitulated at the level of material culture. In analytical terms, Semper's approach enables him to use the organic behavior of race types as a metaphor for describing the behavior of the four elements of architecture; namely, in the stability of the latter's aesthetic motifs over several generations of change. He states this explicitly in this essay when he says that "the original constituent parts [of the four elements] can still be distinguished, and it is essential to trace them in order to understand certain manifestations of Greek art that seem, unfortunately, inexplicable and contradictory when viewed out of context."[26]

The narration of "The Four Elements of Architecture" establishes an implicit hierarchy of the social and political traits associated with each cultural group in the ancient world. These textual comparisons take place against the backdrop of the transnational exchanges of economic trade and colonial conquest. A few broad categories emerge that provide an organizational matrix for his understanding the past. As an example, Semper divides the spatial, structural, and ornamental features of premodern architectures into two broad architectural types: the "hut" and "the court building."[27] He associates the former with the social and political customs of nomadic cultures, including "the Saxon settlements of North Germany."[28] The two dominant architectural elements of this type are "the terrace and the roof," which he explores as shifting over time in response to the base temperaments of different groups in history.

A rhetorical parallel between the racial and architectural characters of these cultures can be found in his descriptions of the formal independence of the autonomous structures of these tent architectures, which were capped with a series of sloping roofs to demarcate the aggregation of individuals inside. For Semper, these architectural features constitute an external sign of the freedom and independence that also organized daily practices. Such a liberal way of life is directly contrasted with the underlying characteristics of court architectures, which were supposedly hampered by a centralized autocratic or monarchical rulership that subordinated all individual expression beneath an aggrandizement of the ruler himself.

Figure 2.3. Imperial audience hall in Peking. From M. G. Pauthier and M. Bazin, *Chine Moderne, ou, description historique geographique et littéraire* (1853).

The racial imprint of architectural styles was also manifest in the polarities Semper perceived between the so-called primitive and advanced cultures on his scale of civilizational status. Certain forms of Asiatic architecture, despite being a historical antecedent of Hellenic culture, are depicted as stuck in the past: "In China, where architecture has stood still since primitive times and where the four architectural elements most clearly have remained separate from one another, the partition wall, which is for the most part movable, retains its original meaning independent of the roof and the masonry wall. The interior of the house is divided up by such partition walls, which relate as little to the actual structure as do the outside walls, built of bricks yet hollow and dressed with braided reeds and carpets."[29] In a relative sense, these cultures exist outside of time, a phenomenon that freezes our understanding of the racial characters underlying these architectural forms. Period illustrations of the royal and religious Chinese architectures visually codified this interpretation of regional culture (fig. 2.3). A similar status of backwardness was perceived to exist in the ritual architectures of India, Native Americans, and of course "the huts of the savages."[30] Such comparisons lay the groundwork for Semper's use of the Caribbean hut as a similarly frozen exemplar of the four elements of architecture in *Der Stil*.

Semper continues to develop the idea of racial dispositions in his essay by proposing their relative stability over time, a trait that makes them an ideal category for tracing historical changes. His description of human culture proceeds from premodern nomadic tribes to late civilizational empires, with the artistic development of each cultural group progressing along an independent trajectory of teleological changes that inflects the essential characteristics of a people. In his discussion of the Jewish lineage on Phoenician culture, Semper claims that their racial dispositions were manifested by both the biological lineage of "these two racially related nations" and the spiritual content of "the sacred and profane" writings of both cultural groups.[31] This is an important passage to consider, as it elucidates the dual nature in which the term *race* is expressed in the 1851 essay. Throughout the narrative, race is expressed as both a biological marker of human differences and an analytical category for identifying the fixed (spiritual) characteristics of entire national or civilizational groups. The cases most explicitly linked to biologically determined racial characters occur in the farthest reaches of the past, where mankind is forced to respond to his needs in the most immediate and pragmatic ways. The aesthetic motifs that are created during this phase of cultural development are preserved in the decoration of various implements of the practical arts, although these ideas can be passed on to others. Conversely, at the moment when monumental architectures have finally emerged, a new breed of characters—national characters—emerges that seems to develop a relative sense of stability that now expresses the dominant traits of a larger and more complex body of citizens.

In this sense, it is possible to read Semper's interpretation of the Greeks as "a free people sustained by a national feeling" as an emulation of the anthropologists who used the term *race* to categorize the fixed traits of different national groups.[32] Thus, one could speak of the racial characters of Native Americans as conditioned by their inferior biology as well as those of the Greek race that were synthetically arrived at, through a detailed analysis of the past. What is important here is not the different causes that one might conceive of motivating the individual or the collective responses to art, but the categorical parallels that are maintained in these two extreme positions: while operating as a primary motivating factor in early stages of cultural development and outside of material culture at the more advanced stages, the organic properties of the race concept provided a heuristic tool for conceptualizing the historical development of architectural styles across time.

Debating the Role of Autochthonous Genius in Greek Architecture

If one looks closely, the theme of embodied racial character can also be seen in the academic debates between Semper and the archaeologists, anthropologists, and architectural critics writing about the role of autochthonous genius in architectural history. This was a persistent point of conflict in scholarly debates on the use of polychromy in Greek architecture, as many considered the use of color to be a sign of primitive cultural development. The most ardent Grecophones of the nineteenth century romanticized the base temperaments of the leading Greek ethnic groups. The influence of this ideal on political debates in the eighteenth and nineteenth century was considerable, as it provided a strong civic model for many contemporary Europeans. European nations competed with one another to become the seat of Continental power, a position that was partially expressed by a dominance in artistic culture. Such a political context gave rise to competing claims of continuing the legacy of Western civilization, especially through the lens of revising the grand ideals of Greek and Roman culture. In Semper's native Germany, this included a range of progressive artists and political theorists who believed that the loose political structure of modern-day Germany might one day emulate the civilizational height of Greek culture by becoming a unified liberal nation in Europe.

Given the political stakes of this artistic question, historical accounts of the causes of Greek superiority could have serious consequences. Herrmann notes the historical dispute that arose between Semper and the archaeologist Karl Bötticher over the cultural influences they believed were most responsible for the artistic refinements of Greek temple architecture.[33] While Herrmann does not explicitly account for the critical influence of racial anthropology on either man's thinking, one can infer from their respective writings an inverse relationship on the role of autochthonous genius in artistic development. These ideas can be mined both for their immediate disciplinary significance and for their grander political implications.

For Semper, the influence of racial characters was strongest at the dawn of time, for it was at this time in history that all other factors were relatively minor by comparison. As we have shown above, he claims racial determinism is arguably most evident in the cultural groups situated at the lowest stage of cultural development. It was during these early beginnings that the archetypal forms of the four elements of architecture supposedly first came into being. Semper theorized in 1851 that all people begin at this stage of cultural development, but in modern times only a few remained stuck there due to consistent periods of geographical isolation or by finding themselves subject to a hierarchical political culture that mandated the preservation of archetypal motifs associated with a ruler's culture. By contrast, advanced civilizations progressed beyond this stage by engaging in cross-cultural exchanges through historical patterns of trade, conquest, or treaty building, which resulted in a merging of the essential characteristics of their architectural motifs with others. In a structural recapitulation of primitive racial characters, the material culture of advanced civilizations established new standards of art that proved to be just as stable as the archetypal forms of the past. For this reason Semper believed he could identify the national characteristics of historical groups by interpreting the ways they handled material in physical objects of culture. Bötticher departed from Semper's position on autochthonous genius in several ways. His interpretation of Greek temple architecture suggested that racial character operated at both the dawn of time and in critical moments when the artistic achievements of a cultural groups were so profound that they radically broke with historical precedent to create a new artistic tradition. In this way, Bötticher applied a principle of racial determinism to account for the singularity of Greek art and architecture. While both Semper and Bötticher supported the position that Greek architecture was a singular achievement in cultural history, their dispute reveals the varying degrees to which both figures applied the race concept in their typological analysis of architectural style.

The critical function of the race concept in Bötticher's architecture theory was conditioned by the organicist rhetoric he used to interpret the creative process of architectural design. As a student of Karl Friedrich Schinkel, a Prussian architect and prominent theorist of German tectonics, Bötticher set out to summarize the main principles of his mentor's architectural theory. Schinkel began summarizing his approach to design in the 1840s with the unpublished "Architektonisches Lehrbuch," a text that purposefully imitates the title of the Karlsruhe architect Friedrich Weinbrenner's pedagogical manual of 1810. Two years after Schinkel's death, Bötticher delivered a speech that summarized his mentor's project of developing a fully articulated tectonic theory of architecture during a festschrift in his honor. This speech was published as the essay "Andeutungen über das Heilige und Profane in der Baukunst der Hellenen: Eine Gedachtnisschrift zur Geburtstagsfeier Schinkels" (The principles of Hellenic and German ways of building with regard to their applications to our present way of building) in 1846, and it is notable for its use of organic language to explain Schinkel's approach to design.[34]

Using bodily terms taken from comparative anatomy, Bötticher claims that Schinkel found a way of clothing the bones of medieval construction with the skin of Hellenic ornamental motifs.[35] This description indicates not a simple application of architectural ornament along aesthetic lines but an embodied approach to form that used the representational meaning of architectural ornaments to express the underlying spatial and structural constitution of a building.

Figure 2.4. Georges Buffon, "Races of Man." From Buffon's *Natural History of Man, the Globe, and of Quadrupeds* (1857).

Bötticher defends this approach as consistent with the laws of nature that created organic forms by coordinating all of the functional elements of a body through one underlying idea. Using Schinkel's design for the Freiderichswerder Church in Berlin as a case study, Bötticher claims that this structure organically synthesizes the primary elements of two historical languages of architecture into one overriding form: in this structure, the Gothic principles of construction are visually expressed by a Hellenic style of ornamentation.

Bötticher's warning to contemporary architects against forcing an ill-fated marriage between two incompatible systems of architecture that will produce inorganic or monstrous forms emulates the principles of sexual reproduction put forward by the French naturalist Georges Buffon.[36] This organicist rhetoric employs the language that biologists used to account for the marriage or mating of two organic specimens as test for revealing whether both organisms are members of the same species, with species being understood as an underlying idea that would determine the form of each category of organic life. Buffon famously used the example of the sterile mule or hinny to illustrate the natural principle of sexual selection that mandates that only animals within the same species can produce offspring that can go on to reproduce more of their kind.[37] This theory was offered as proof that the notion of character was universal in all human creation and that human beings of different race types were indeed members of the same species (fig. 2.4). In addition to sterile progeny, Buffon speculated on the types of monstrous forms that could emerge in nature if biological inbreeding occurred within a single family line or was purposefully hybridized through the cross-breeding of species shaped by incongruous physiological criterion. Bötticher's tectonics poetically employs this organicist language to naturalize Schinkel's theory of architectural style in comparison to what he considered the inorganic character of most stylistic forms of eclecticism in the nineteenth century. Bötticher encourages the designer to familiarize himself with the complex history of individual examples of architectural styles so as not to apply them against their essential nature. Only a purposeful revival of their cultural uses would guarantee their lawful use in a contemporary setting.

At the same time that Bötticher uses zoological and anatomical language to illustrate the perils of architectural eclecticism, he distinguishes the primary elements of Schinkel's monumental architecture with two new architectural concepts: the *Kern-form* (work form) and the *Kunst-form* (art form). The structural members of the work form are largely situated within the body of the building, although they precondition the formal profile and scale of architectural physiognomy. The art form, on the other hand, consists of the architectural ornaments used to dress or cover these structural elements and operate as a visual sign of what lies inside. For Bötticher, Gothic construction is the most efficient type of work form, while Hellenic ornamentation is privileged as the art form with the greatest legibility in the nineteenth century. He uses the terms *Körpern* (body), *tektonischen Körpers* (tectonic bodies), and *Körperbildung* (bodily formation) to outline the organic principles for integrating these two components in the introduction of *Die Tektonik der Hellenen* (The architectonics of the Greeks). In his narrative of architectural history, architectural ornament initially evolves as an aesthetic practice invented to protect raw materials, which in time serves as a visible mask that calls attention to the work performed by each structural member. These primitive utilizations of ornament finally synthesize into one integrated art form in the treatment of Syrian columns and monumental Greek stone architecture. In the Syrian case, Bötticher proposes that the metal skins surrounding the wood columns eventually thicken to the point where the structural task initially performed by the interior wood structure is taken over by the aesthetic mask itself. In the case of Greek stone architecture, the structural tasks of previously used wooden structural members is embodied within the details of the stone ornament, which again effectively integrates the elements of aesthetic expression and structural performance into one synthetic artistic form.

Bötticher's proposal that modern architects use the elements of construction to regulate the placement of visual ornamentation renews the critical emphasis on architectural embodiment that was central to German tectonic discourse. The proponents of this paradigm of architectural organicism thought of design as the rational articulation of a constructive body that was conditioned by a range of historical factors, from the materials used to the social and political systems regulating the functional spaces of its interior. Like a living organism that slowly grows from an embryological state into a complex form, Bötticher's account of Schinkel's design process began with the cultural requirements of a space that came into gradual appearance with the placement of a structural frame around that space and the layering of structural members and architectural ornamentation. By the end of this organic design process, the resulting building operated like a fully integrated corporeal body that used ornament to refer back to the original spatial requirements of its making. This ornamental program made the social and political conditions that regulated its final form plainly visible on its outside form.

According to the architectural historian Mitchell Schwarzer, Bötticher's organic interpretation of architectural style was disseminated in Germany by at least two disciples in the nineteenth century, the architect Heinzerling and Sigismund Wolff.[38] Heinzerling rearticulated Bötticher's style theory in the form of a methodological primer that reveals the creative implications of this approach for designers. He divides the design process into four principal steps, each of which is associated with a formal concept. *Nutzform* (functional form) is the term used to identify the spatial components of an architectural program. *Werkform* (structural form) corresponds with Bötticher's concept of Kern-form, which details the articulation of spatial needs with the placement of structure. *Begriffsform* (conceptual form) is the term used to identify the ideal of the whole that regulates the aesthetic dressing of construction in the form of connections or joinery.[39] And finally, *Sinnform* (perceptual form) corresponds with Bötticher's concept of Kunst-form. All of these features considered the social and cultural demands of a project to be the conceptual origins or main idea of architecture.

Despite these parallels, however, there were some key departures from Bötticher's scientific model of design. For example, Heinzerling chose to invent ahistorical artistic ornaments that directly imitated natural organisms in order to provide architecture with a sense of character, a mimetic gesture that revives the anthropomorphic foundations of Vitruvian theory.[40] This ornament explicitly uses botanical and zoological specimens to integrate architecture into its regional contexts, which Heinzerling believed was necessary to represent the naturalistic basis of art. He expanded the procedural rules for architectural design with a detailed explanation of the organic principles behind his theory in an 1869 essay, "Die Bildungsgesetze der Formen in der Architektur" (The generative laws of architectural form). The term *Bildung* was an important leitmotiv of eighteenth-century German political debates—Alexander von Humboldt often used it to describe the process of individual enlightenment or education that was the result of self-improvement in modern civic culture.

This avenue of improvement was now available to a wider public as a result of the political reforms taking place in Germany's short experiments with democratic institutions. *Bildung* also appears in scientific debates that describe the internal idea or motivation behind the self-formation or physical development of natural organisms. At each level, a sense of teleological development lay beneath external manifestations of character.

By the 1850s Bötticher was convinced that Greek stone architecture was entirely unique in antiquity, and was only made possible because of the republican ideals and racial character of its citizens. His environmental interpretation of autochthonous genius attributes the superiority and inferiority of racial character to biological traits.[41] The debate between Bötticher and Semper mirrors the debates that occurred between scientists who credited racial characters with directly shaping cultural history and those who considered race to be one of several factors that groups used to disseminate social norms in cultural history. Bötticher's theory was influenced by several figures, including the work of the Berlin scholar and fellow Grecophile Karl Otfried Müller. Müller praises Hellenic culture in his text *The History and Antiquities of the Doric Race* (1839) by claiming that the republican ideals of Greek politics precipitated the racial integration of the multiple tribes of the empire, a gesture that cemented the overall character of the nation-state. While he admits that each tribe was made up of many racial and ethnic groups, he proposes that the characteristic of the Aryan type dominated early Greek culture. Bötticher follows up on Müller's ethnographic thesis by supporting his findings with a range of art historical evidence for the influence of Greece's natural climate on the promotion of philosophical reflection and physical perfection in life and art. Bötticher reasoned that if Greek autochthonous genius could lead to the creation of a perfect stone architecture, perhaps modern Germany might be able to produce a uniquely modern style of architecture that used the new material of iron—a historical parallel between Greece and Germany found in Semper's 1851 essay.

While Semper borrows heavily from Bötticher's organic theory, even supporting his elevated view of Greek artistic genius, he rejects a deterministic relationship between racial genius and architectural style that elides the influence of historical precedent. This position did not constitute a rejection of the existence of race types or a disavowal of essential racial characters in cultural history. As already outlined, there is much to suggest that Semper not only believed in the scientific validity of biological race types but was consciously aware of the typological principles that scientists used to account for racial variations in history. His focus on the gradual transformation of artistic culture, however, required him to apply the principles of scientific type theory in an entirely different way than did his peer Bötticher.

For Semper, the creation and development of an organically integrated architectural style was not always guaranteed in cultural history, nor was it becoming easier to do so as time progressed: the most influential national building traditions were the result of profound artistic contemplation and the purposeful interpretation of the historical conditions of art that permitted an architect to intervene without disrupting or distorting dominant cultural trends. Instances of decadent periods in world civilizations where the imitation of historical art forms drowned out all other principled innovations were plentiful in ethnographical accounts. In order to separate these unprincipled (i.e., inorganic) applications of style in history, Semper privileges the ethnographer's incremental and empirical analysis of cultural history by rhetorically constructing a stable origin point for the transformation of material culture that resisted substantive changes to its essential characteristics; a principle of order that enabled him to empirically trace the morphological transformation of premodern artistic motifs. Such a typological interpretation of architectural history permits Semper to track the parallel status of race and style through time.

If we restate Semper's and Bötticher's academic debates on Greek temple architecture in the terms that were outlined by scientific type theory, then there are some key parallels between each figure's intellectual position on racial character in the content and structure of their theoretical arguments. While they agreed that architectural styles should emulate the organic processes of natural generation and each held Greek autochthone culture in high esteem, they disagreed over the specific role of racial characters in shaping architectural styles. Bötticher proposed that the essential traits of Greek ethnic character could directly account for the synchronic breaks with tradition that were represented by the innovations of Greek temple architecture. Semper, however, preferred to contextualize the role of racial character with the influences of climate, geography, and political doctrine in a diachronic analysis of Greek temple architecture's assimilation of historical precedents. Yet at the level of epistemology Semper moved beyond Bötticher in his emulation of the typological properties of the race concept. By the 1860s the structural parallels that existed between the race and style categories of anthropological discourses enabled Semper to treat material culture as a physical proxy for the racial and national characters of historical groups.

The Embodiment of Racial Character in *Der Stil*

Semper made his most enduring contributions to modern architectural theory with the publication of the two-volume treatise *Der Stil*. Despite the critical reception of this work in the 1870s and 1880s as a materialist history of art, he opens his text with a critique of a rigid materialist or academic approach to architecture.[42] He takes aim at "the false premise that the world of architectural forms arises solely from structural and material considerations."[43] Instead, he prefers

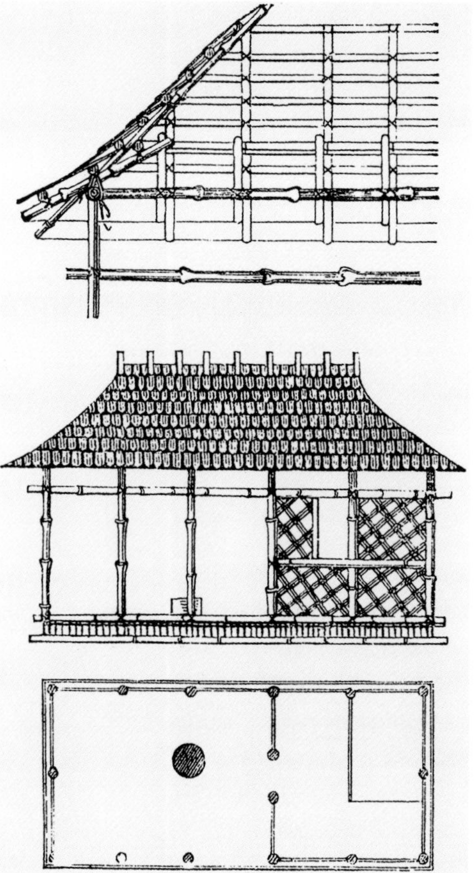

Figure 2.5. Gottfried Semper, Caribbean hut. From *Style in the Technical and Tectonic Arts, or, a Practical Aesthetic*, vol. 2, 666 (1863).

to think of materials as being "subservient to the idea," by which he means the social and political values associated with particular architectural forms.[44] With respects to the antiquarians and historicists that strictly imitate archaeological styles, he criticizes this group's tendency to "depreciate the present tradition" by trying to "make the demands of the present" fit into past forms.[45] Throughout *Der Stil*, Semper strives to maintain a balance between the self-awareness of the architectural historian and the contemporary designer's pragmatic response to newly engineered materials and spatial programs.

In the introduction to his treatise, Semper considers historicism to be a mixed blessing insofar as it becomes a crutch that prevents the designer from developing a natural instinct for problem solving. In contrast to the innate capacity that he believes primitive man held for harmonizing art with the principles of nature, he portrays modern man as incapable of making advances without scientifically recovering and reviving the organic relationship between form and culture in previous historical styles. Semper chooses to illustrate the Caribbean hut to represent the purest expression of the four elements of architecture, a reference that replaces the Chinese pagoda forms of 1851 (fig. 2.5). Again, he identifies these four elements as: the hearth as the place where clay was first hardened into solid finishing materials; the roof as the first place where the wood frame became the technology of enclosure; the woven mats that made "the knot" the principle motif of enclosure; and the mound or earthwork that provided a solid base for collecting all of these elements. Of course, these material techniques were important not in and of themselves but as material emblems of the cultural practices they represented. Semper considered the hearth to be the moral core of the home as it originally served as the location for the birth of language, dance, and other communal activities. In addition, the knotted patterns of literal textiles were associated with both physical binding elements and two-dimensional binding

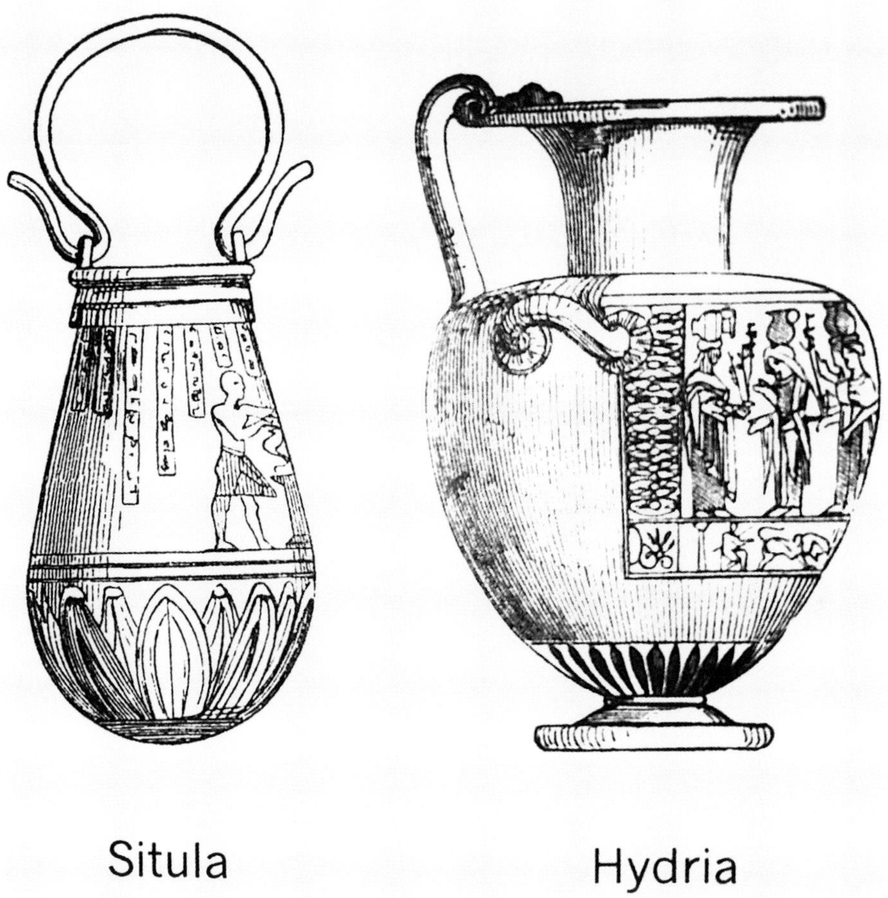

Figure 2.6. Gottfried Semper, "Situla und Hydria." From *Style in the Technical and Tectonic Arts, or, a Practical Aesthetic*, vol. 2 (1863), 4.

patterns in clothing, carpets, furniture, and architectural ornaments. Semper's ethnographic interpretation of material culture provided him with a rational means of reconstructing the organic principles that he believed were necessary to compensate for the lost aesthetic instincts of modern man.

Under the ethnographical framework of *Der Stil*, the textual description of national characters and the illustration of objects of material culture established a discursive framework for interpreting character that made race and style two mutually reinforcing elements of civilizational change. Perhaps the most famous example of the visual representation of national character in Semper's treatise is his comparison of the symbolic meaning of Greek and Egyptian ceramic forms (fig. 2.6). According to Semper, the Greek hydria and the Egyptian situla were used as ceremonial religious forms for carrying water in each culture. He interprets the formal qualities of these objects as a visual and material index of the cultural traits that predominated in each group. The single directional axis of the Egyptian situla is read as a visual manifestation of the top-down, hierarchical character of their political system that permeated their thoughts and actions. By contrast, the Greek hydria seems to be developed in all three axes at once. Its liberated form is taken as a material sign of the liberal character of their republican politics. While never literally representing the racial profiles of Greek or Egyptian peoples, Semper's embodied representation of national character advances the visual economy of ethnography, which tethers illustrations of race types with that of material cultures to codify cultural differences.

During the nineteenth century, the term *race* is used in scientific type theory to represent categories of like objects from the perspective of both the taxonomic and the cultural traits of groups of people. This tendency accounts for the coexistence of biological descriptions of race that were predicated on the physical characteristics of the white, black, yellow, and red races proposed by scientists and the anthropological description of the national groups such as the German race, which categorized peoples by the acculturation of similar political myths. This categorical tendency can be seen in the many ways that race was associated with various forms of phenomena in the fields of philology, biology, and anthropology. Philologists such as Max Müller used the term *race* to identify linguistic type forms that had developed from earlier language systems, but were unique enough to be declared autonomous grammatical systems. The claim that these languages exhibited organic behaviors such as the potential to breed supports the notion that *race* was an appropriate label for these entities, even though it was metaphorical; the organic behavior of these systems was limited to their structures, not their appearance. In biology, however, race types were associated with physical characters that were emblematic of the physiological causes of human variation. Biologists initially used the term *race* to continue the taxonomic categorization of the natural world that Linnaeus began in the eighteenth century. However, their search for the invisible causes of natural variation attempted to peer beneath apparent physical differences. The visual display of difference was understood to be an emblematic sign of the ecological causes that were responsible for racial variations. It wasn't until the second half of the nineteenth century, when anthropology became an umbrella field for consolidating all of natural history, that scientists attempted to resolve the analytical functions of the term *race*. Over time, the critical function of the race concept was to categorize elements that were deemed similar as a result of an underlying organic process of generation into type categories.

Examining the typological structure of Semper's argument enables us to identify the tacit parallels that exist between the organic principles of development outlined in *Der Stil* and other scientific texts of the period, including those explicitly associated with scientific race theory. For example, although no direct reference to Blumenbach's theories of comparative anatomy has ever been found in the architect's writings, the typological properties of Blumenbach's biological concept of *Bildungstrieb* (formative force) structurally mirrors a reference that has been explicitly connected to Semper's style theory—the ethnologist Gustav Klemm's notion of *Kunsttrieb* (artistic force).[46] Klemm invented his developmental model of culture to explain the anthropological drive of primitive peoples to express themselves through artistic concepts, which was manifest by innovations in religious customs, dance, and other spiritual pursuits.[47] The developmental principles of Klemm's artistic force parallels those of Blumenbach's formative force, which posits the existence of an unseen teleological process of development that internally drove the physical transformation of all living organisms. The structural dynamics of Klemm's theory translates the teleological principles of developmental models found in biological and ethnographical theory into an underlying force of cultural history.

Klemm went on to visualize the material consequences of his synthetic concept of Kunsttrieb with a strategic pairing of racial and stylistic type forms. In the first few volumes of *Allgemeine Kultur-geschichte der Menschheit*, he illustrates the historical struggle between what he called the "passive" and "active" race types of mankind (fig. 2.7). Anticipating Semper's complete substitution of the human body with material culture, Klemm organizes the different races of man above the physical specimens of material culture most closely associated with them in cultural history. This visual alignment of race and style type forms portrays the historical conflict between Aryan and non-Aryan peoples in the plains below primitive mountain ranges around the world as a conflict between the spiritual essence or psychological mindsets of different groups. However, Klemm's material index for national characters operates well within the structural logic established by racial anthropology in the nineteenth century. The conflict between race groups in Klemm's theory and those between national groups in Semper's theory parallels the pattern established in Viollet-le-Duc's architecture theory between the Aryan and Dasyus races. While in Klemm's theory the sedentary patterns of the passive races generally permitted them to develop more sophisticated agricultural and material finishing practices, the active races were more natural rulers as conquering peoples and thus served as the elite in most hybrid cultures. The epistemological structure of type theory provided a discursive framework for relating race in style in both explicit and implicit ways.

In order to construct a metanarrative for the transformation of style in cultural history, Semper engaged in a comparative study of the archetypal motifs found in the practical arts of the ancient world and subsequent movements in architectural history. Combining the findings of ethnographers, archaeologists,

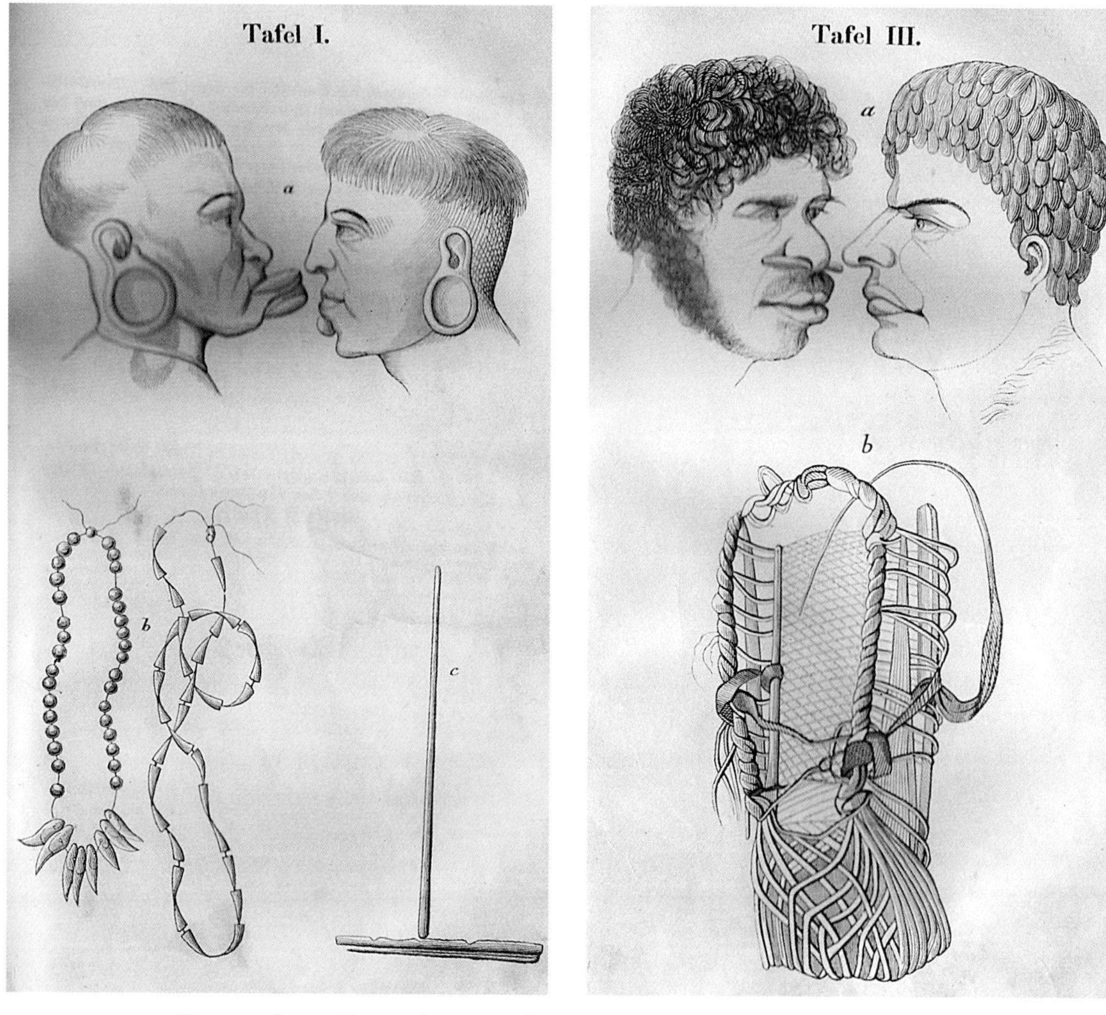

Figure 2.7. Gustav Klemm, illustration of primitive man and his material culture. From *Allgemeine Cultur-Geschichte der Menschheit* (1843).

and art historians, he deduced a historical mechanism responsible for propelling the transformation of these elements in the ancient world—a principle that he labeled *Stoffwechsel*. While Semper was careful to distance himself from a materialistic interpretation of formal change, he employed a term that was burdened by many political associations in nineteenth-century Germany. The concept of Stoffwechsel was first employed in the field of biology as a means of explaining the transformation of food into nutrients that the body could use to sustain its physical growth and development. In Semper's hands, this model of nourishment and growth became a metaphorical lens for illustrating the organic principles of conversion that directed the transformation of material culture. According to his theory, the symbolic meanings of the artistic motifs created from finishing raw materials in the ancient world continued to be transformed in the history of art as the realm of art expanded to include more and more objects of everyday use. The original connection between social meanings and material practices was not invented anew in each historical age but instead was transformed to reflect key changes to a practical object's material composition, functional use, and symbolic meaning. Once fine art had reached the stage of monumental architecture, the most efficient means of preserving this history was architectural ornament. As a practical basis for contemporary design, the principle of Stoffwechsel would have guaranteed the authenticity of modern architectural designs by empirically reviving the meaning of stylistic motifs with crucial trends from the past. Only a lawful transmission of cultural ideals would preserve the historical continuity of national character in the form of architectural ornament, an element that Semper claimed gave artistic motifs a distinctive formal "physiognomy."[48] Even if the contemporary aesthetic of German architecture was extremely diverse, as it was during the nineteenth century, the primitive roots of national artistic traditions and the common mentality that artists used to transform these art forms provided a hidden basis for interpreting the oneness of national identity.

German nutritionists used the principle of Stoffwechsel during the second half of the nineteenth century to theorize the physiological processes that contributed to the formation of individual character. During the 1840s and 1850s, Jacob Moleschott popularized this term in tracts and publications circulated in Germany to reform public taste.[49] Moleschott repackaged the scientific findings of Dutch biologists to educate general audiences about the manner in which the human body transforms raw materials into the nutrition required to sustain itself. As the historian Frederick Gregory explains, Moleschott depicted food "as the raw building blocks of the body" that affected one's mental abilities and physical constitution.[50] He suggested changing one's diet as a direct means of socially engineering a healthy and vigorous citizenry, literally stylizing living organisms for integration into modern society. In this sense, Moleschott's rhetoric was a physiological version of Humboldt's concept of Bildung in the educational sphere at the beginning of the nineteenth century. Moleschott collaborated in the publication of two books on nutrition and physiological development: *Die Physiologie der Nahrungsmittel: Ein Handbuch der Diätetik* in 1850 and *Der Krieslauf des Lebens* in 1875. Anticipating the contemporary maxim "you are what you eat," *Die Physiologie* outlines specific dietary regimes for reforming the minds of artists, philosophers, politicians, and even the social habits of the poor. His fascination with the integration of *Kraft* (force) and *Stoff* (matter) anticipates Semper's explanations of stylistic change in *Der Stil*, even attributing historical transformations to an underlying organic principle that regulated the visual expression of national characters over time.

While Semper was likely aware of Moleschott's explanation for human character, having served with him at the ETH in Zurich, his application of Stoffwechsel did not fully attribute the visual expression of artistic character to strict materialist causes.[51] Instead, Semper sublimates the material origins of Stoffwechsel by using it as a metaphor for the morphological principles that regulate the material transformation of ornament in cultural history. In this sense, Stoffwechsel "signified the [historical] process by which artistic forms undergo changes of material by carrying forward vestiges or residues of" earlier stages of development, "symbolically alluding . . . to the materials used in the past" without literally being constituted by these material elements.[52] In *Der Stil*, the ultimate cause for stylistic change is attributed to the underlying ideas of artistic motifs that reflect mankind's inborn drive to order the built environment. This universal *Motiv* (drive) underwrote the visual expression of style over time via the artistic motifs of the practical arts. Despite Semper's sublimation of Moleschott's materialism, however, both figures attributed great importance to the critical function of Stoffwechsel for interpreting (and potentially even shaping) human character. The fact that its use covers both the physical and spiritual elements of character building suggests its critical function in establishing a common rhetoric for character judgments in modern Germany. The formation of one's self in the present time is always bound by the activities of the past, be they in the form of one's diet or the patrimonial legacy of the nation-state. Semper expands the conceptual territory of character judgments when he borrows the dynamics of physiology to make his ethnographic analysis of material culture. The nature of this extension—from biological to national races—contributes to the confusing reception of Semper's ideas.

An embodied representation of racial and national characters can be found at several critical junctures in *Der Stil*. In addition to the representation of the Greek hydria and the Egyptian situla, a parallel organicist interpretation of race (via the human body) and style (via material culture) is expressed in Semper's analysis of ceramic art forms. In a general introduction to clay form, Semper describes the most primitive use of ceramics to establish the essential nature of ceramic forms in all its guises:

> *Ceramics* alludes in the first instance only to the material to be treated—namely, clay (κεροµοζ)—which was the first material to be used for this technique and which in its many guises has continually asserted its claim to being the plastic material par excellence throughout all stages of this art's development. Because clay has been of general importance for all branches of the technique in question (forming, so to speak, its material basis), and because clay, as the first plastic material, to some extent established the style to be followed for other materials later, we are perhaps justified here in assigning to the word a more general meaning than it had for the Greeks.[53]

While the firing of clay was originally reserved for the making of pots and vessels for containing liquids, this material process is extended to include any plastic material fired to maintain a solid form, such as roof tiles and terra cotta wall panels. The conceptual relationship established here between blood and soil, or men of clay and vessels of clay, emerges in the religious function of ceramics, which appears "long before the appearance of monumental architecture, which they influenced significantly."[54] Treating ceramic forms as fossils that mirror the function of bones in natural history, Semper proceeds to read the spiritual or psychological state of world cultures from two of their most representative objects. He is not ambiguous about his intentions, for he states, "If one examines the pots produced by a given group of people, it is usually possible to say what they were like and what stage of development they had reached!" Each form preserves a memory of its earlier function: the teardrop shape of the Egyptian situla recalls the leather pouches previously used to collect water from a rushing river, while the Greeks collected liquids from fountains and other sources of falling water. In addition to this functional reading, Semper ascertains the spiritual state of their cultures by comparing and contrasting the aesthetic states of each vessel: "How significantly the soaring, spiritual, and lucid essence of the spring-worshiping Hellenes emerges symbolically from this subordinated artistic form, in contrast to the situla, which expresses the physical law of gravity and balance in a way quite opposite but no less appropriate to the spirit of the Egyptian people."[55] Though he does not provide more specific instructions of how to go about interpreting the spiritual essence of ceramic forms in this instance, he provides at least two other images that suggest that one can personify the objects of material culture.

At least one diagram illustrates the organic principles of Stoffwechsel in ceramics that emulates the hereditary principles for phylogenetic growth in the animal kingdom. This diagram, taken from Jules Claude Ziegler's Études céramiques (1850) describes the family of ceramic bowl types that contributed to the generation of formal hybrids in the past (fig. 2.8). Beginning with the ideal geometries of the square and the circle, Ziegler's diagram illustrates the possible range of hybridized type forms that could be generated by these ideal starting points. Such an image visually materializes the natural historical principle of how to detect unity within a diversity of external forms. Semper follows this ideal diagram with a sectional analysis of seven ceramic pots taken from antiquity, including the Greek hydria mentioned above. Semper's analysis is interesting in part because of his geometrical attempts to illustrate the different characters of national peoples. Each sectional diagram isolates the spatial relationship that existed between the gripping angle of the handle and the horizon line that dictated the pouring moment of each vessel. This line also provides the constant datum of the earth, the literal horizon against which one can understand the situational specificity of each object.

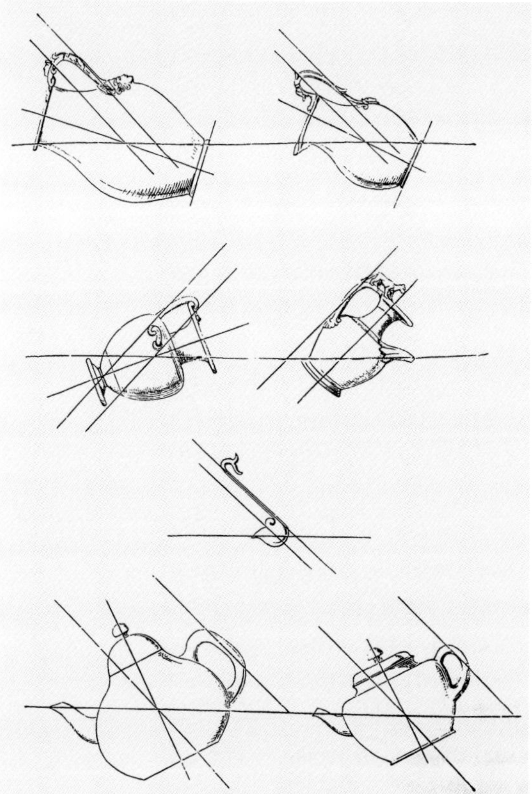

Figure 2.8. Pouring moment of pitchers from around the world. From *Style in the Technical and Tectonic Arts, or, a Practical Aesthetic*, vol. 2 (1863), 112.

Visual parallels between race and place can also be found in Semper's description of the carpentry traditions, or tectonics, of historical peoples. He attempts to trace the "Greco-Italic" roots of contemporary German timber architectures in the "technical-historical" section of the chapter dedicated to tectonics. Semper proposes that the architectural form of the Tuscan-Roman temple consisted of a mixture of wooden elements dressed in stone ornaments. According to him, this sacred arrangement was an outgrowth of simpler housing forms, perhaps even the "rural construction style of southern Germany," which was brought to the region by Etruscan migrants traveling through Italy via the Rhaetian Alps. He cites Karl Otfried Müller directly in this passage as support for his reconstruction of "late Italic colonization."[56] Using this historical lineage, Semper identifies the vernacular roots of German architecture in late Roman, or what he called Greco-Italic, forms. He follows up his historical narrative for Roman antiquity with a discussion of the tectonics of European's barbarian tribes during the medieval period, including the works of Scandinavian and German architects.

Though it may not be common sense today, many art historians of the time believed that several European cultures initially met in the far north of Europe during the Roman Empire.[57] The writings of art historians such as Johan Christian Dahl, who was known to Semper, provided evidence of a mixture of German and Scandinavian cultures during the medieval periods. The essence of Scandinavian civil society was expressed in illustration of ceremonial stave churches, which were believed to have evolved from wooden barn structures and earlier utilitarian prototypes. Dahl's illustrations of Borgund Stave Church furniture appears in volume 2 of *Der Stil*, where Semper explores the tectonic principles of wooden furniture that, again, preserves in miniature the principles of monumental architectural forms (fig. 2.9). Nordic myths of Aryan race purity

Figure 2.9. Burstol, "Pew from Bo (rear view)." From *Style in the Technical and Tectonic Arts, or, a Practical Aesthetic*, vol. 2 (1863), 672.

have been traced back to nineteenth-century speculations, although Semper's analysis of these building traditions do not reflect the racial superiority that has charged late Nazi thinking. This turn would not happen for several decades. Contemporary politics is evident, however, in Semper's rhetorical nod to Germany's resistance to French conquests in the past: "The conquests of German tribes in the territories of the Roman empire were accompanied in the provinces by a revolution in social forms and in building methods, which can be explained only by assuming that there was a conscious and active resistance to extant political and architectural principles in the aging Roman civilization."[58] As was characteristic of Semper's discussion of ceramic forms, he examines Scandinavian manors and churches for their reflection of national characters.

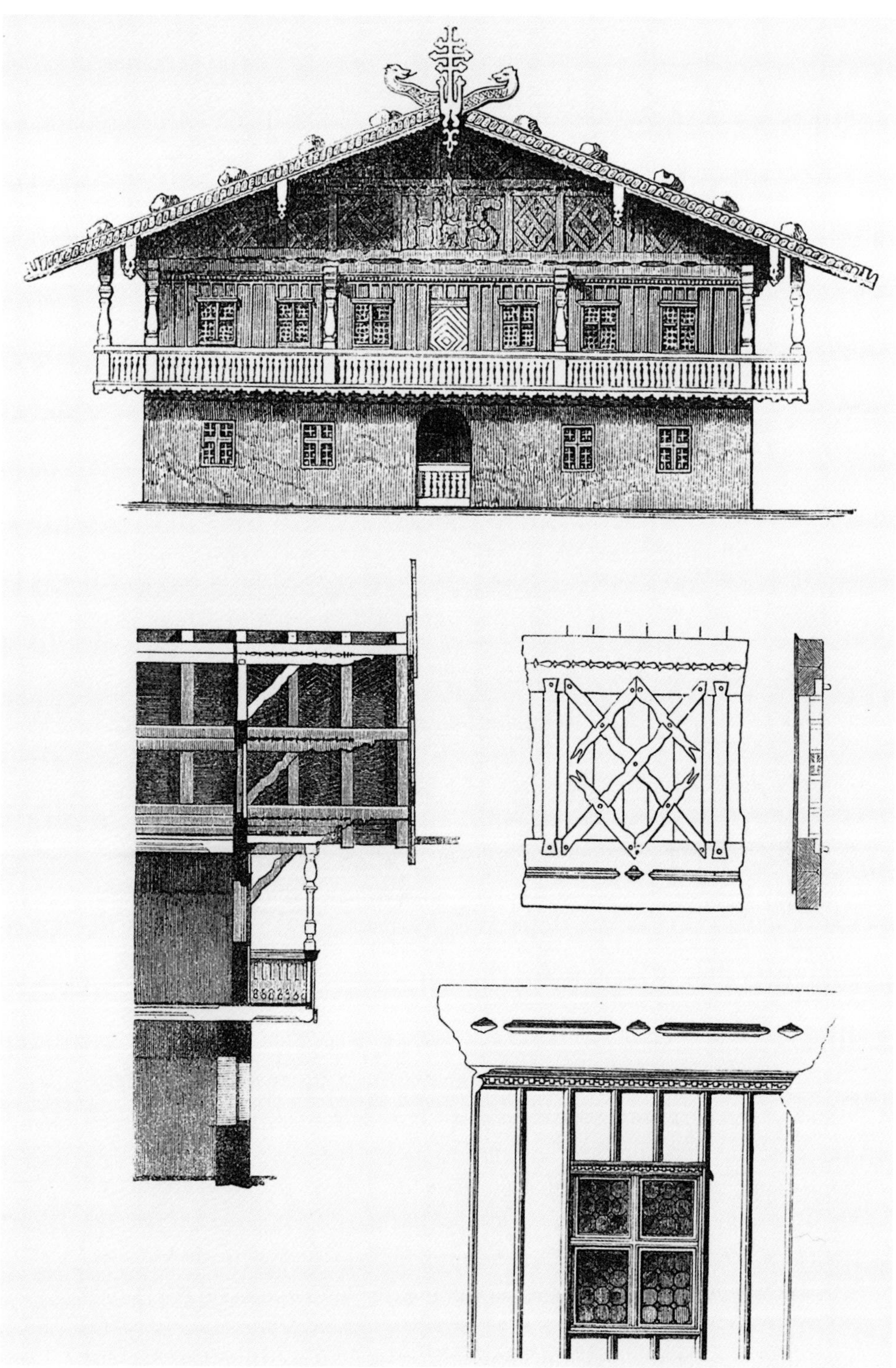

Figure 2.10. "Bavarian Tyrolean house," from *Style in the Technical and Tectonic Arts, or, a Practical Aesthetic*, vol. 2 (1863), 686.

Figure 2.11. "Details of the Mill," from *Style in the Technical and Tectonic Arts, or, a Practical Aesthetic*, vol. 2 (1863), 689.

After his discussion of Scandinavian medieval forms, Semper turns his attention toward the medieval architectures of western and southeastern Germany, including the Bavarian-Tyrolean hut he cites as a contemporary example of an extant primitive type form (figs. 2.10 and 2.11). Despite the dissemination of Gothic structural types in surrounding areas, Semper claims that the social isolation caused by the mountain ranges of southern Germany protected this culture's original way of life:

> The southern German timber house represents a Greco-Italic type in its *whole appearance*: a shallow gable roof that cantilevers considerably, with a purlin structure, a *tabulatum* that runs round the house or at least around several sides (reminiscent of the *mesodme* and *pergula* of the Hellenic and Roman house). The mixture of stone construction with timber structure, especially the principle of dressing that occurs here, of boarding and beading wall surfaces and door and window frames, as well as the antepagments on the facings of purlins and beams, the adornment of which is more painterly-polychrome than sculptural—all of this combines to make plausible the suggestion already made by Leo von Klenze that in these buildings an ancient building tradition has been retained in a relatively pure form.[59]

His discussion of carpentry forms is again predicated on detecting the implicit origins of style that were usually lost to the past. With the comparative methodologies of ethnography, it was possible to look to contemporary case studies of the primitive to reconstruct their conditions in the past. Like the Caribbean hut, the Bavarian-Tyrolean hut represents a modern-day ethnographical proof of the validity of his style theory. But of course, the social and political status of these primitives in contemporary Europe would have also affected the German's reception of such cultures. Rural primitives in German territories legitimized the urban lifestyles of the metropolis while those in colonial territories primarily provided material support through raw materials and labor. Semper's reference to von Klenze is also not incidental. Von Klenze speculated that his Greek revivalist architectural style was entirely appropriate for modernizing Germany, as it visually expressed the antique customs that were passed down from the Greeks. While Semper would turn to "Italian architecture of the early sixteenth century" to commemorate the cultural origins of modern Germany, both architects represent serious attempts to fashion a unified cultural narrative out of the past that was visualized by a synthetic architectural formalism.[60]

In addition, the geographical circuit that Semper uses to explore tectonics—from Greco-Italic structures to medieval Scandinavian and German structures—traces the geographical route of the Alps mountain range. Semper uses this microhistory within *Der Stil* to clarify the tectonic roots of German character. It is not surprising that he closes the section on tectonics with a discussion of Renaissance architecture. He considers this style of architecture to be a refinement of the simpler principles established during the Greco-Italian migrations of the primitive world. Most of Semper's monumental buildings were constructed in a Renaissance revivalist style, including the architectural programs that most squarely defined modern society: the opera house and the museum are only two of the most distinctive program types Semper built in Germany and Switzerland. The role of the Alps in sustaining primitive German habitus also provides a geographical framework for relating Semper's constructions in Switzerland to his study of German culture. Such constructions in the modern period would not completely obey nation-state boundaries if they self-consciously revived aspects of the primitive world that existed before these boundaries existed.

Semper's Materialization of German National Character

Contemporary scholars in European history, cultural studies, and postcolonial theory have expounded upon the racial and national discourses that emerged from instrumentalizing the findings of racial anthropology, from legitimizing (or eliminating) the assimilation of minority groups within the nation-state to the colonization of nonwhite peoples living abroad.[61] Germany was no exception to these trends, as professional scientists pioneered new research in the race sciences and politicians experimented with colonialism in various areas of Africa, Asia, and the South Seas. The critical importance of the race concept in nineteenth-century anthropology and the racial politics it spawned in nineteenth-century Germany prompts the question of what critical role it might have played in Semper's anthropological interpretation of architectural style. Since Semper uses racial anthropology to establish the historical origins of architecture, we might begin to answer these questions by interrogating the visual economies that were invoked with his textual references to such empirical case studies.

Semper's invocation of the material cultures of Chinese and Caribbean natives was not meant to settle the matter of historical origins for all time but instead served as a prompt for locating an infinite number of discrete origin points in cultural history. This included by implication the historical origins of even the modern nation-states of Western Europe. His discussion of tectonic, or wood-structured, vernacular architectures explicitly speculates on the rural building traditions of German architectures of the Bavarian Alps. In a manner that parallels Viollet-le-Duc's nineteenth-century studies of Aryan migrations in the French Alps, *Der Stil* considers the similarities between Germanic and Scandinavian housing types as possible evidence of premodern nomadic Saxons who previously migrated through the Bavarian Alps.[62]

Semper and von Klenze's ethnographical speculations on the cultural origins of the German body politic are just two instances in a long line of origin thinking within German romanticism.[63] Folk historians such as Jacob and Wilhelm Grimm, ethnographers such as Johann Gottfried Herder, and linguists such as Franz Bopp, Max Müller, and the Schlegel brothers collected a broad range of material and expressive cultural artifacts from premodern Germany to illuminate the historical origins of medieval *volk* (folk) life.[64] Semper's architectural speculations parallel their publications of medieval fairy tales, folk songs, ethnographical histories, and national origin myths in both academic circles and various realms of popular culture. The literal reconstruction of premodern dwellings in nineteenth-century ski resort towns provided mass entertainment for tourists visiting the Bavarian Alps and the historical study of folk myths provided a new set of political tools for shoring up a unified conception of German nationhood that was proving to be historically elusive. Continually pitted against the French as cultural stewards of the Rhine valley, German military units in the Prussian north and the Austro-Hungarian south struggled to maintain the Zollverein, the economic confederation that emerged between the surviving remnants of the Habsburg empire. The political fragmentation of this political regime into hundreds of independent kingdoms and principalities elicited fierce intellectual debates on the potential future of a unified modern Germany. If such an arrangement was indeed possible, what language or religious traditions would dominate the official institutions of this new nation-state? Romantic images of the German past were both a symptom of these political debates and a visual emblem of a deep psychological desire to develop an organic social basis for growing and maintaining a contemporary German nationalism. Semper's theoretical invocation of the Caribbean hut as a remote origin for architectural invention made it possible to search for the ethnographical roots of a new common culture in modern Germany that could shape national character for many years to come. It is important to account for the latent conceptual parallels that connected racial character and architectural character in such cases.

Stylistic revivals were often motivated by an implicit ethnographical interpretation of one's national origins. Architectural historians have documented the fashion for Renaissance revivalist forms that arose among social elites in Dresden and Vienna from the late 1830s to the mid-1870s.[65] This fashion affected the monumental building programs that defined the liberal state as well as the private villas that housed its most privileged citizens. This craze was also fueled by historical investigations into Roman history such as Jacob Burckhardt's *Cultur der Renaissance in Italien* (1860), which had an incredible influence on reviving Roman aesthetic motifs at this time. Semper was an early proponent of Renaissance revivalism in Germany, as evidenced by several designs for Martin Wilhelm Oppenheim, a Jewish banker living in Dresden. He constructed at least three structures for the local Jewish community, including a villa and palazzo for the Oppenheim family (both in the Renaissance style) and a synagogue in Dresden (in a Romanesque style).[66] It is interesting to note that the same structure that inaugurated the fashion for Renaissance villas in Dresden was also a very important material index of the successful "Germanization" of Jewish minorities living there.[67] (This acceptance was also aided, in part, by Oppenheim's conversion to Protestantism, as was the case for many Jews seeking acceptance in modern Germany.) The social acceptance of this Jewish minority was made possible by the Emancipation Edict of 1812 that officially protected the rights of German Jews in the city, which was later expanded in 1837 with laws making the practice of Judaism legal within the boundaries of the city.

The Dresden Synagogue (1838–1840) is an eclectic design that combines a restrained Romanesque exterior with an opulently decorated Moorish interior (see plate 6 and fig. 2.12).[68] Its floor plan consists of two square volumes centered on a Greek cross plan with a wooden dome directly overhead. A series of heavily ornamented columns provides support for two gallery levels above for women congregants and standing room space. The ground floor is reserved for male congregants situated directly across from the rabbi presenting the daily scripture. An elevated platform at the northern wall supports a small interior canopy that opened to the congregation through a Palladian arched opening that held the bimah (the platform for reading the Torah). An ornamented Moorish dome that rose to the full three-story height of the interior caps this entire ensemble. Semper's solution for the Dresden Synagogue emulates the exterior buttressing and masonry finish of San Vitale at Ravenna, which gave the entire project the feeling of being a Byzantine historical fragment. This fragmentary character was heightened by the fact that the synagogue was part of a complex of buildings contained by a half-story perimeter wall. Given that Jewish specialists had served the Saxon court since the fifteenth century and the Romanesque style of Semper's design was associated with a revival of the Saxon roots of the German nation-state, it is tempting to interpret the exterior features of this synagogue as physical evidence of the Germanness of its Jewish minority. (Coincidentally, the Asiatic origins of the exoticized Moorish interior might have inversely recalled the common geographical roots of Indo-European peoples and historical Jews.) The Germanic face of the Dresden Synagogue, however, was not able to save it from demolition during Kristallnacht in November 1938 as the Nazi regime swung back toward arguments for racial purity. The only remnant of the building was an ornament, a Jewish star, designed by Semper, that was restored to the reconstructed synagogue in the 1940s.

The physical designs for Villa Rosa and the Palais Oppenheim, both completed for the banker Oppenheim, express some of the lessons Semper learned from his ethnographic study of tectonic structures. For example, as monumental architectural forms it was the job of the building's ornamentation to refer to the artistic motifs that were revived in its construction, whether these details were taken from the immediate building itself or the historical situations that gave rise to the initial use of each artistic motive. This interpretation departs from Gothic enthusiasts such as Viollet-le-Duc who endorse a strict alignment between the underlying construction of a building and the final placement of architectural ornament. Semper was more interested in reviving the antique spirit of his ancestors than being archaeologically bound to the features of their

Figure 2.12. Interior of the Dresden Synagogue, Hugo Licht, *Die Architektur des XX. Jahrhunderts, Zeitschrift für moderne Baukunst* (1901).

physical constructions. This liberal interpretation of the past could easily be achieved with the appropriate use of stucco: "It was only by dressing ceilings and walls with stucco that the Renaissance reached perfection, for this technique, as has been shown in other places, is eminently antique."[69] In his design for Villa Rosa, we see Semper reviving the foursquare alignment of Andrea Palladio's Villa Rotunda, but he substitutes the circular geometry of its atrium for an octagon (figs. 2.13–2.15). This geometrical substitution occurs yet again in Palais Oppenheim. Such a gesture brings the exterior features of the dome that tops the Dresden Synagogue to the interior of the home. This central space not only ties together the sequence of the plan but recalls the antique tablinum of Roman homes, where the head of the household would meet with visitors.[70] In Villa Rosa, this space would have synthesized a dramatic two-story view of family portraits with the patrimony of the estate. Given that the villa is named after Martin's wife, Rosa Oppenheim, it would be most appropriate to say that this space connected members of the matrilineal line to the setting, especially since matrilineal descent is an important feature for conferring Jewish status onto children.

Semper was still constructing Roman villas in the 1860s, although he demonstrated his ability to moderate the ornamental aspects of this type when it required a more modest or rustic feel. This is evident in his design for Villa Garbald, in Castasegna, near the border of Italy and Switzerland. This design emulates the features of a Tuscan country villa, the same historical form that inspired Schinkel's design of a Roman bath that is near the Charlottenhof Palace in Potsdam. Despite the fact that a country villa comes closest to the half-timber construction systems of contemporary buildings found in western and southwestern Germany, Semper's use of stucco and applied ornament attempts to rise above the lack of feeling for the antique manifest by these cases: "This was partly due to its excessively dry approach to the structural elements of decoration—handled not in an antique or symbolic way, but according to a literal technical spirit—and partly, though to a greater degree, a result of transferring motives that originated in the vaulting system of stone church naves to secular buildings in lighter timber frameworks."[71] In this way, Semper can simultaneously praise the contemporary Bavarian-Tyrolean hut as a pure manifestation of primitive Greco-Italic architecture, and thus support its revival in contemporary design, while still seeking to innovate its formal expression in modern building forms.

Two prominent features of the Tuscan villa that Semper revives are the Egyptian malkaf, or "windscreen that helped to block the sun" and "admitted a cool breeze into the interior courtyard," and the pergola that springs forth from the central volume of the building and leads back toward a nearby garden or relieving landscape.[72] The former is prominent in Semper's earliest designs for Villa Garbald, which alternate between the hip and gabled roof forms he

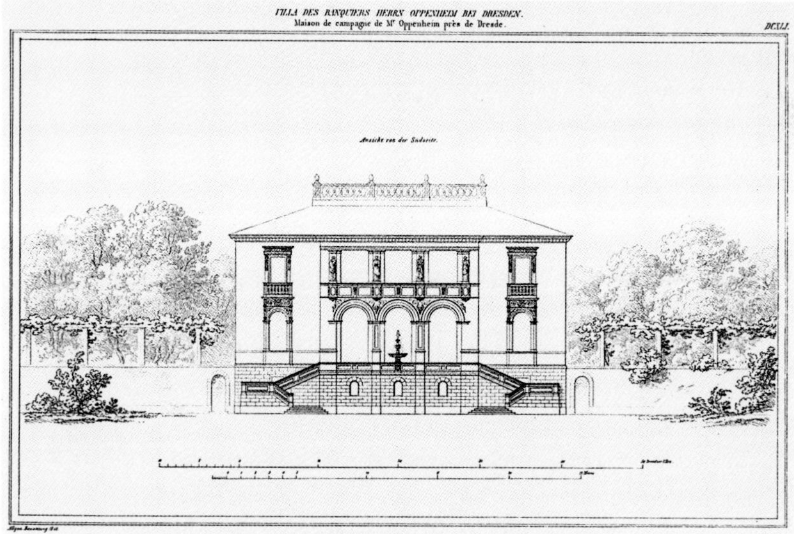

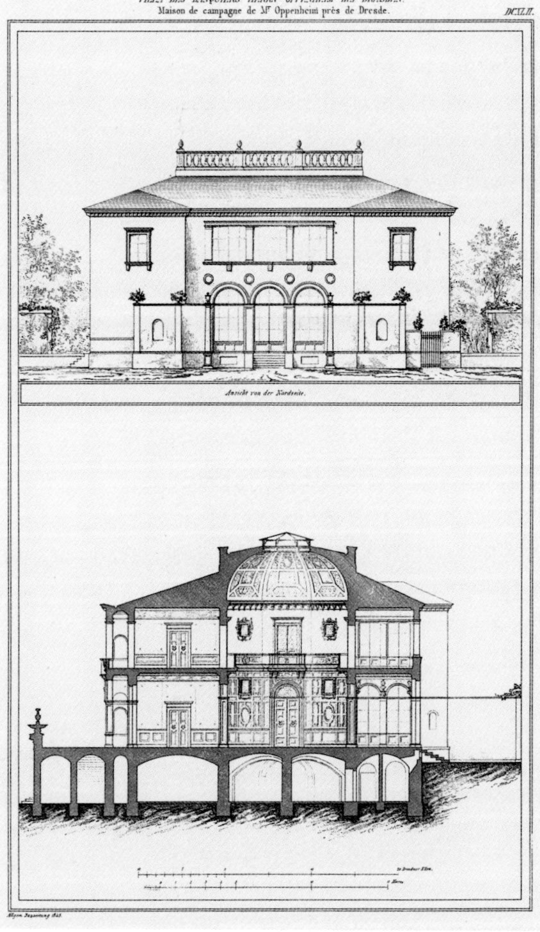

Figure 2.13 (*above*). Front elevation of Villa Rosa, near Dresden. From *Allgemeine Bauzeitung* (1845).

Figure 2.14 (*left*). Back elevation and section of Villa Rosa, near Dresden. From *Allgemeine Bauzeitung* (1845).

Figure 2.15 (*opposite*). Photo of two-story interior atrium, Villa Rosa, near Dresden, 1900.

Figure 2.16. Villa Garbald with variation, Castasegna, Switzerland, 1865. Courtesy of gta Archives / ETH Zurich (holding Gottfried Semper).

Figure 2.17. Photo of perimeter wall with pergola above, 1880. Schweizerische Bauzeitung, vol. 67 (1916), plate 40.

believed were most often employed in Tuscan villas (figs. 2.16 and 2.17). It is both a nod to the demands of climate and a romantic gesture that returns its user to the position of the agrarian landowner overlooking his territory. In an interesting parallel, Agostino Garbald, the owner of Villa Garbald, was a director of customs, which made his job one of managing the political boundaries that cropped up in this region. Semper's architecture returned Garbald and his wife to a time when the lines of division between Switzerland, Italy, and Germany were unified by a common Indo-European culture. In this way, the Alps play a role in reviving the past, even if not only for those of Germanic descent.

This chapter argues that the racial content of Semper's "practical aesthetic" was a direct result of his ethnographic interpretation of architectural style. The structural logic of nineteenth-century racial anthropology (i.e., type theory) conditioned Semper's aesthetic schema for style to exemplify the parallel status of race and style categories in ethnography.

In addition to the racial essentialisms that burdened nineteenth-century ethnography, the physical objects of material culture stand in as visual proxies for the ephemeral characteristics of racial and ethnic groups, which made the display of historical art forms operate as a mirror of racial development in cultural history. The conceptual parallels between racial character and architectural character that are overtly displayed in the illustrations of Viollet-le-Duc's *L'histoire de l'habitations* are more covertly manifest in Semper's *Der Stil*, which treats material culture as a physical proxy for the racial and national characters of historic peoples. The dialectic between race and style categories in *Der Stil* is especially clear in Semper's comparison of the Greek hydria and the Egyptian situla, as well as in the mythical origins of the Bavarian-Tyrolean hut as a culturally pure German-type form. His style theory reinforces a racialized interpretation of cultural history without needing to make an explicit reference to the biological race concept to relay the productivities of representing the human body as an empirical model for architectural invention.

From a political perspective, Semper's written descriptions of the Bavarian-Tyrolean hut recall the lost glories of the Habsburg empire. His claim that this structure represents a pure historical type form that has been passed down from medieval times to the present insulates these vernacular architectures from the contaminations of historical change that might have resulted from contemporary traditions. The Roman lineage of the Bavarian-Tyrolean hut also colors his preference for Renaissance precedents in contemporary architectural design. This specific interpretation of southern German culture was only made possible by Semper's dream of collecting a full record of the cultural past.

One aspect of Semper's style theory that needs to be studied further is the colonial gaze that is implicit in his ethnographic approach to cultural history.

While not a literal colonialist, his desire to possess the entire catalog of cultural history is a representational project that parallels the colonial activities that would occur under Otto von Bismarck in the 1880s. The central importance of tattooing in *Der Stil* anticipates the national interest in Papua New Guinea as a colonial territory nearly two decades before it officially became a German protectorate. In a manner that parallels actual colonialism, his desire to possess the world's cultural heritage, or to define the other, in postcolonial parlance, was a necessary step for legitimizing a synthetic interpretation of the German present. As Susanne Zantop suggests in her book *Colonial Fantasies,* German elites did not have to actually possess foreign territories to be influenced by the cataloging practices of colonialism—these impulses were an integral element of colonial politics and the enlightenment rubrics that conditioned Semper's appreciation of cultural differences.

COLOR PLATES

Plate 1. Eugène Emmanuel Viollet-le-Duc, *View of Chamonix Mountain Range*, 1876. Médiathèque de l'Architecture et du Patrimoine.

Plate 2. View of the French-Swiss Alps taken near the site of La Vedette, 2016. Photo by author.

Plate 3. Eugène Emmanuel Viollet-le-Duc, drawing of existing state of Chamonix Mountain valley, 1874. Médiathèque de l'Architecture et du Patrimoine.

Plate 5. Eugène Emmanuel Viollet-le-Duc, interior mural of La Vedette with reconstructed state of the Alps, 1874–1875. Médiathèque de l'Architecture et du Patrimoine.

Plate 4. Eugène Emmanuel Viollet-le-Duc, drawing of reconstructed state of Chamonix Mountain with glacier, 1874. Médiathèque de l'Architecture et du Patrimoine.

Plate 6. "Die Sinagoge zu Dresden." Illustration by Gustav Täubert, lithograph by Johann Riedel, printed by J. G. Braunsdorf, Dresden, published by v. G. Täubert, Dresden, ca. 1840. Courtesy of Rosenthal Judaica Collection, College of Charleston.

Plate 7. Pilgrim Baptist Church, Chicago, updated view of the enlarged stage area, 1960s. Richard Nickel Archive, Art Institute of Chicago.

Plate 8. Johnson & Lee, Ltd., proposed restoration of Pilgrim Baptist Church, Chicago, 2011. From Vikki Ortiz Healy, "Pilgrim Baptist to Be Born Again," *Chicago Tribune*, April 2, 2011.

Plate 9. Poster created by the New York City Housing Authority, October 20, 1936. Catalog no. 98518316, Work Projects Administration Poster Collection, Library of Congress.

Plate 10. River Gardens Housing Development. Site plan visualizing the cruciform housing blocks (*within white circle above*) invented by William Lescaze, ca. 1930. WELA, Special Collections Research Center, Syracuse University.

Plate 11. Heinz Warneke, *Man, the Provider*, sculpture located at Harlem River Houses, ca. 1937. Photo taken May 1988. Photo no. 02.005.064, La Guardia Archives, LaGuardia Community College, New York.

Plate 12. Ilya Bolotowsky, *Untitled*, from the Williamsburg Housing Project Murals. Oil on canvas, 85 × 211 in. This was the first abstract mural commissioned for the New York City Housing Authority, completed for a recreation room in the basement of Williamsburg Houses, ca. 1936. On long-term loan from the New York Housing Authority to the American Art Collection, Brooklyn Museum, accession no. L1990.1.1.

Part II

THE WHITENESS OF AMERICAN ARCHITECTURE

Figure 3.1. Dankmar Adler and Louis Sullivan, Kehilath Anshe Ma'ariv Synagogue, Chicago, 1891. Postcard. Richard Nickel Archive, Art Institute of Chicago.

3

THE SEARCH FOR AN AMERICAN ARCHITECTURE

Louis Sullivan and the Physiognomic Translation of American Character

> From the character of a pier may we not discern the character of a race: and from the slowly changing character of a developed pier may we not discern the temperamental changes taking place in a race: its growth, its fulfillment, its decay! Has man at any time, can man at any time, can he now lay his hand upon anything, can he focus his mind upon anything, without leaving upon that thing the impress of his character?
>
> —**Louis Sullivan,**
> ***Kindergarten Chats***

LIKE MANY OF HIS PEERS, Louis Sullivan spent the majority of his career trying to establish an authentic American architecture. His interpretation of architectural style was symptomatic of nineteenth-century theories that presupposed that national characters were reflected in the material details of regional architecture, but he raised fundamental questions about how an indigenous American architecture might be produced. Unlike revivalists who relied on the cultural associations of historical ornament, Sullivan believed that he could directly communicate national character with nonhistoricist ornament. He conceptualized style as the result of a rational process of design that was as immanent as nature itself and used geometry to create a verisimilitude between nature and architecture. In political terms, his architecture promoted national identity in direct and indirect ways: its spatial program fostered the development of national character in American citizens, while a building's style provided a visual representation of these national characteristics. Sullivan believed that his botanically inspired ornaments constituted a vernacular sign of the sociological context of the nation: they simultaneously represented the significance of nature in frontier life and man's spiritual connections to his surroundings, even in urban settings.

Architectural historians have successfully challenged a functionalist interpretation of Sullivan's oeuvre since the 1970s by recovering the poetic and spiritualist themes of his architectural theory.[1] Yet this literature has not fully accounted for how Sullivan's thought was influenced by the racial discourses of his day. This chapter builds upon recent studies of Sullivan's writings and buildings to more fully account for the cultural biases he absorbed from his social and political contexts.[2] It seeks to place his design practice in conversation with nineteenth-century nationalist discourses in order to reconstruct the tacit racial assumptions underlying his work. To this end, in this chapter I use the concepts of character and physiognomy as critical lenses for locating the racial content implicit in Sullivan's architectural representations of American character.[3] Sullivan believed that the common man would produce an indigenous local culture that was reflective of democratic ideals. However, the applicability of this theory was heavily affected by an assimilationist conception of national character that limited the value of his ideas for new waves of white ethnic immigrants and nonwhite peoples then living in the United States.

In his efforts to interpret and represent the essential qualities of American character, Sullivan had to contend with the changing social and political factors of American society that contributed to the racial and ethnic divisions of his native Chicago.[4] Westward expansion, new waves of European immigration, the emergence of unionized labor, and the continued segregation of whites and nonwhites produced an ethnically and economically segregated city. The cultural assumptions of native myths such as manifest destiny raised serious doubts about which groups were best positioned to contribute to American culture and define its general character. In a period when Irish Americans fought for social acceptance, Sullivan's inclusion as a luminary of American arts and letters was no foregone conclusion. Anthropological theories on the inferior moral and intellectual status of nonwhites persisted beyond the Civil War, affecting the public's reception of Asian and Mexican immigrants and recently freed slaves. Religion also played a role, as Jews and Catholics challenged the religious monopoly of Protestants within the political elite.

Within this socially fractured context, Sullivan employed the aesthetic principles of physiognomic theory to concretize the ephemeral qualities of individual and national character that he believed anchored the future trajectory of the nation-state. During the nineteenth century, biologists introduced new scientific criteria to account for the base temperaments of race groups, which extended the visual principles artists used to represent national characters in the eighteenth century.[5] The empirical content of physiognomic theory provided a conceptual hinge between Sullivan's textual and visual depictions of racial characters and his architectural representations of American character. He employed physiognomic language in his writings to describe the inner character of people, as well as the essential qualities of inorganic entities such as the natural landscape and architectural buildings. He also sketched caricatures of human character throughout his career, to represent both individual traits and those of nationalities. These aesthetic practices prepared him to transform the interpretive strategies of artistic physiognomy into a projective technique for materializing the ephemeral traits of American character.

By the mid-1880s Sullivan rejected the practice of European revivalism because he believed these historical styles were not capable of expressing the particularities of American life. Instead, he replaced these conventions with an ahistorical brand of botanical ornament that he created from scratch. He also extensively revised the exterior massing and profiles of modern building types to push his architecture beyond a mere imitation of past styles.

Using the artistic concept of physiognomy as an interpretive lens for reading Sullivan's thought, in this chapter I argue that the racial content of his architectural designs can be located in a synthetic theory of architectural physiognomy. The theoretical application of physiognomic concepts in architectural theory is evident in the ethnographic content of Sullivan's architectural writings and drawings that established the groundwork for architectural representation of national character.

Sullivan's physiognomic translations of American character can be examined in the physical case study of Kehilath Anshe Ma'ariv (K.A.M.) Synagogue (see fig. 3.1). This building manifests the physical implications of Sullivan's theory of architectural physiognomy for two minority groups: the German-speaking Jewish immigrants who first commissioned this structure and the black Baptist congregants who later occupied it after migrating to the South Side neighborhood of Chicago. In 1889, Dankmar Adler and Sullivan designed K.A.M. Synagogue to accommodate the first Jewish Reform congregation to settle in the South Side. The first wave of immigrants to arrive from central Germany consisted of highly educated subjects who desired a physical emblem of distinction that would mark their native social status and cultural capital. Adler and Sullivan worked closely with Reform leaders to determine how best to present this religious movement to new audiences in America. In order to mitigate the discrimination of Jewish immigrants perpetuated by Chicago's white Protestant elites, Adler and Sullivan created a physical environment where Reform Jews could present themselves as the social equivalent of good white Protestants. Newcomers who wished to emulate this dominant conception of religiosity learned to suppress the most exotic aspects of their material culture, either by rejecting the use of so-called Oriental architectural styles or restricting its use to the interior of religious spaces, to adopt an architectural sign of their accommodation of mainstream religious culture.

Adler and Sullivan's contribution to this process was a spatial and aesthetic realignment of several key elements of traditional Jewish synagogues with the most representative aspects of the Protestant church. Adler emulated the spatial layout of Protestant church interiors in the synagogue by treating its worship space as a simple auditorium, which secularized its function. In turn, Sullivan created a lush alternative to the Moorish motifs that were traditionally used to represent the exoticism of the Jewish faith with his own botanical ornaments, which used the visualization of floral growth and development to represent both the philosophical principles of Reform Judaism and the dominant characteristics of the nation's elite. This aestheticization of growth contains enough referential ambiguities to cast Jewish American identity as a parallel modality of contemporary Protestant reform efforts.

In 1921 Kehilath Anshe Ma'ariv Synagogue was purchased and occupied by Pilgrim Baptist Church, an upwardly mobile black congregation that historically fostered the rise of gospel music in Chicago. The black occupation of Kehilath Anshe Ma'ariv resulted in a slow and nuanced alteration of spatial practices that revised and expanded Sullivan's vision for American architecture over nearly half a decade. Church leaders such as Junius C. Austin modified the organic synthesis Adler and Sullivan had established between the built-in choir booths and botanical ornamentation surrounding the central stage of the auditorium to accommodate an increasing retinue of characters during weekly religious services. Austin's decision to incorporate a gospel choir on stage during his service was a controversial concession to new members arriving from the agrarian South who challenged the notions of black respectability that had regulated earlier singing practices. This class-based transformation of religious musical traditions resulted in a spatial challenge to the physical boundaries of the stage: the simple platform of Kehilath Anshe Ma'ariv was no longer big enough to contain the rising scale and importance of the gospel tradition that was coming to define black spirituality in the early years of the postwar period. Another formal change was manifest in the elimination of the decorative features of the exterior clerestory that contained the most overt symbols of Judaism on the building. This area was dramatically simplified by the 1960s and 1970s to save costs to the overall upkeep of the building—a loss that did not seem to diminish the new Christian associations of this structure.

The black occupation and alteration of Kehilath Anshe Ma'ariv Synagogue raises interesting questions regarding the historical legacies of Sullivan's representation of American character. Was his secular interpretation of religious space generous enough to represent the posthumous contributions that the gospel tradition has made to redefining American character? While Sullivan was never directly commissioned by an African American congregation, he purposefully established a secular ideal for religious space in order to promote the assimilation of any group that wished to be incorporated within the American body politic. Yet the most hegemonic nineteenth-century definitions for American character presented certain rhetorical limits to the inclusion of non-white subjects such as African Americans. What civic status did blacks have in Sullivan's political writings, and what effects did their racial identity and religious spatial practices introduce to Sullivan's aesthetic schema for Kehilath Anshe Ma'ariv Synagogue? These questions can only be answered by placing a disciplinary history of Sullivan's architectural thought in conversation with the broader trends of cultural history.

The racial and ethnic content of Sullivan's architecture theory has only recently become a subject in its own right.[6] A social history to his architecture enables us to interpret the theoretical and material implications of his rhetorical depictions of racial physiognomy and national character. Sullivan hoped that his buildings might contribute to the birth of a common culture in the United States. While this vision was dramatically limited by the assimilationist language of his architectural theory, the black stewardship of Sullivan's building ultimately demonstrated the latent capacity of these physical forms to spatially accommodate the contingent status of marginalized social minorities—despite the rhetorical exclusions of Sullivan's conception of the body politic. The research that informs this chapter builds upon nearly two decades of whiteness studies in the United States that have examined the historical struggles associated with Irish American and Jewish American assimilation.[7] David Roediger, Noel Ignatiev, Matthew Frye Jacobson, and others have outlined the historical shifts in the public perception of white racial identity that were the result of incorporating successive waves of European immigration to the United States. It also avails itself of numerous findings in African American studies and the counterpublic definitions of the body politic that emerged to challenge antiblack laws and practices.[8] These literatures provide valuable information on the strategies that upwardly mobile African Americans used to combat the seemingly permanent abject status of blackness in the Jim Crow South and the increasingly segregated Midwest. The historical legacy of Sullivan's American architecture would have been greatly limited were it not for the historical stewardship and critical interventions of these minority communities.

The Anglo-American Character of American Democracy

James B. Salazar's study of character reveals that it was commonly "understood as a theory of self-formation" by nineteenth-century writers and social reformers intent on developing modern forms of social capital.[9] The ideological function of character building was "to inculcate those forms of economic agency and social discrimination essential to the formation and regulation of a liberal, democratic public sphere in the United States."[10] One of the most influential theories of national character to emerge in the mid-nineteenth century originated from the philosophy of American transcendentalism. As architectural historians Sherman Paul, Robert Twombly, Narciso Menocal, and Lauren Weingarden have documented, Sullivan's writings were indebted to this school of thought.[11] Transcendentalism began as a religious reform movement within the Unitarian church, but its practice quickly expanded to encompass the reformation of civic affairs. Ralph Waldo Emerson, a key spokesman of the movement, proposed that democratic culture would expand only if its citizens embraced the credo of self-reliance and individualism. His essay "The Poet" (1844) outlines a key role for the arts in this task by using man's observation of nature to train his intellectual capacities for direct action. Emerson popularized a pantheistic interpretation of nature that suggested that "God"—or nature as the material exponent of divine law—was embedded within the human soul. This spiritual connection enabled individuals to see the divine operating in their surroundings without the use of revelation or other external aids. This democratization of sacred knowledge enabled everyday people to produce artworks that expressed their oneness with nature.[12]

Sullivan's writings bear the influence of transcendentalist attitudes toward American character, race, and nature. According to Twombly, Emerson's influence on Sullivan dates to his brief tenure in Frank Furness's office in Philadelphia in 1873.[13] Furness, an ardent abolitionist and Unitarian, translated Emerson's poetic study of nature into a new form of architectural organicism.[14] During his internships and travels, Sullivan continued to read the works of American transcendentalists and poets, developing a personal interpretation of these theories in the 1870s and 1880s.[15] For Sullivan, the highest calling of the architect was to construct poetic essays in brick and mortar capable of expressing Emerson's principle of oneness with nature. In 1887 he even wrote a letter to Walt Whitman praising Whitman's epic poem *Leaves of Grass* for providing a rhetorical model for creating an authentic American architecture.[16] Given Sullivan's interest in Whitman's poetry, he may also have familiarized himself with other examples of the poet's work, including the poems that explicitly discussed American race relations.

In a frequently cited passage from *Leaves of Grass*, Whitman depicts himself as a slave to illustrate the injustices of the Fugitive Slave Act.[17] While in this poem Whitman gives a sympathetic embodiment of blackness and recognizes the humanity of enslaved Africans, in reality he was never convinced of black Americans' equality with whites. The literary critic Martin Klammer notes the ways that Whitman's writings are split between poetic ideals of an inclusive amalgamation of the American race and journalistic diatribes on the amoral and lowly subjectivity of nonwhites.[18] Whitman's expositions on black character leave little doubt of his views on the inclusive amalgamation of the American race: "Who believes that the Whites and Blacks can ever amalgamate in America? Or who wishes it to happen? Nature has set an impassable seal against it. Besides, is not America for the Whites? And is it not better so? As long as the Blacks remain here how can they become anything like an independent and heroic race? There is no chance for it."[19] This bifurcated portrait of black racial character—optimistic in principle but pessimistic in reality—was the product of white working-class anxieties over labor competition from blacks: Whitman was a member of the Free Soil political party, which advocated the containment of slavery to southern states, which constituted an effort to minimize competing sources of labor that would undercut American white working classes. Sullivan's writings suggest that he emulated Whitman's view of American character as an amalgam of different nationalities, and he explicitly relates the poor state of white labor to the political precedent of slavery in the southern states.[20]

Sullivan was also aware of the political themes of Emerson's writings, in which the interpretation of Anglo-American character reveals the tacit racial assumptions of this period.[21] During the 1840s and 1850s, Emerson wrote several works that associate American character with the global development of "Englishness," to dispel claims that the untamed environments of North America's wilderness directly caused physical degeneration in its citizens.[22] His most concise explorations appear in the book *English Traits* (1856), which records the findings of two research trips to the United Kingdom: the first in 1833 and the second in 1847–1848. Emerson traces the evolution of English culture from the primitive migrations of Anglo-Saxon nomads in the British Isles to the earliest British settlers in the United States. These broad constructions of English character present the New World as the transatlantic edge of a robust diaspora of British migrants.[23] Emerson claimed that the hard life of the western frontier revivified the "virility" and "masculinity" of the Anglo-Saxon spirit in a way that promised to give North Americans an advantage in twentieth-century affairs.[24]

Emerson continued to use the term *race* in his theory of Anglo-American character, but he departed from the strict physiological criteria used by biological race theorists of the period.[25] He spent considerable time familiarizing himself with the findings of race science, but he was never fully convinced that a consensus had emerged regarding the empirical basis of biological race types.[26] Instead, he found greater consistency in the stability of national cultures over time, which he used to describe Indian, Celtic, Saxon, Jewish, and Negro peoples.[27] This criterion transfers the analytical value of biological race types, and the hierarchies they produced, to a comparative analysis of national cultures, which attributes the final causes of character to a synthetic constellation of biological and sociological factors. The only time he buffers this analysis with biological assessments of racial genius is in the most negative cases, such as in his analysis of the American Negro or other nonwhite minorities. This explains how Emerson could claim that nonwhites were naturally burdened by fixed moral, spiritual, and intellectual characters, but predict a great future for the development of the American race: he believed the fate of the nation was in the hands of the very best of its racial stock.[28]

The political themes of Sullivan's writings parallel several aspects of Emerson's theories. He emulates Emerson's geographical construction of American character by considering Chicago the frontier of Western civilization. Emerson influenced his romantic depiction of the West as a decisive context for America's future, and the culture and institutions of Continental Europe as a remnant of its feudal past.[29] Sullivan also studied the findings of evolutionary science in the 1870s and 1880s, claiming that "in Darwin he found much food."[30] He ultimately rejected the notion that biological race types can solely account for the progress of cultural history. Instead, he found that Herbert Spencer and Robert Huxley's applications of biological theory to sociology "seemed to fit his own case."[31] Using their principles of social organization as a guide, Sullivan analyzes the modern social typologies that emerged from the amalgamation of US national peoples in *Democracy: A Man Search* (1908).[32]

In *Democracy,* Sullivan outlines the range of social typologies that he believed hampered and propelled the contemporary development of American democracy. This manuscript, which was posthumously published in 1962, explicitly rejects all forms of slavery as latent remnants of Old World feudalism. Such a progressive attitude was common in the post–Civil War years, although it was consistently paired with a belief in determined racial character, another common refrain of the time. Nor was the abolitionist position an automatic endorsement of political pluralism or the social or biological hybridization of white and nonwhite racial groups, as slavery was thought to be a sign of malignance on the soul of white America instead of an affirmation of black American humanity. *Democracy* adheres to the assimilationist boundaries Sullivan established in earlier essays by focusing almost exclusively on the establishment of a common culture constructed by white ethnic assimilation. Like Emerson's view in *English Traits,* Sullivan's view of American character reframes the racial hierarchies of biology in sociological terms. This is evident in his use of physiognomic language in *Autobiography of an Idea* (1924): people's taxonomic traits become a visible sign of their level of cultural assimilation, which is negatively determined by racial identity in the most extreme cases. As the son of an Irishman, a sociological interpretation of amalgamated genius would have been a saving grace for Sullivan, who could thereby escape the attitude that nonwhite minorities—including the "white negroes," as the Irish were called—were unfit for self-governance.[33]

Formulating a Theory of Architectural Physiognomy

By the early 1900s Sullivan became more explicit in his claims that architectural character mirrors the character of the artist and the national context. He considers physiognomic interpretations of building culture to be "organic" insofar as the relationship between personal character and architectural character is involuntary and naturally emerges in vernacular styles. The self-reflexive depiction of his intellectual growth in *Autobiography* foregrounds such beliefs by illustrating the relationship that Sullivan believed existed between his education in the American Midwest and his formulation of an artist's sensitivity. This archetypal model of development presents a representative image of the formation of a creative intellect, the figure Sullivan believed heralded the future of American democracy. These views are confirmed in a 1922 letter he wrote to C. H. Whitaker, the editor of his serialized memoir in the American Institute of Architects' journal:

> In a talk I had with Andy a few evenings since, I brought up the subject of articles desired by you for the "Journal," and stated that my mind was a curious blank in regards to subjects for miscellaneous articles, as said mind was accustomed only to the idea of a developed thesis. After some miscellaneous discussion he said, "Why don't you write your Autobiography?" . . . After a while I got a 'flash' to the effect that such an Autobiography might prove to be made an effective medium in which to carry the vague beginnings, the gradual development, and the eventual form of my philosophy of architecture.[34]

The central theme of *Autobiography* is not the formation of a person per se but the formation of the creative faculty a person can express through their appreciation of nature. Using the literary form of the bildungsroman, Sullivan uses the structure and form of his memoir to analogically communicate this organic ideal of evolutionary development.

Sullivan offers a close recounting of his childhood in *Autobiography* as a conceptual model for outlining the process for assimilating into the American body politic. He describes himself as a "mongrel" citizen of French, Swiss, German, and Irish heritage.[35] This hybridized lineage exemplified what he believed was a common feature of the American experience. Instead of preserving the purity of one's national or cultural origins, each individual contributes to a transformation of these origins into a new hybridized reality. Sullivan uses physiognomic language to provide the reader with a vivid account of working- and middle-class relatives who conditioned his individual character. To contrast American character with European national genius, he repeats stereotypical depictions of Old World ethnic tropes that indicted the social mores of native Irishmen and unscrupulous Jewish speculators.

In the first chapter, titled "The Child," he tells the story of his grandparents' forced migration to the United States, which involved an unnamed Jewish speculator then living in Germany: "According also to family gossip, there seems to be no doubt that Henri List was tainted with cupidity. He speculated and finally lent ear to the wiles of a Jew. He ventured his all. The enterprise strangely and suddenly lost its credit, and the house of List tottered and collapsed in irretrievable ruin. Anna List borrowed money of her relatives to take the family to America, to forget the past and start anew in a strange land."[36] The reversal of Henri List's fortunes is portrayed as an inevitable consequence of associating with a citizen of such low moral character, as Jewish businessmen were routinely depicted in nineteenth-century French and German literature.[37] This episode could be seen as incidental if it did not dramatize the role of character in the victimization of his grandparents; if not for these misfortunes Sullivan might have been born a European, doomed to repeat the social limitations of citizens in the Old World.

Sullivan's poor esteem for immigrant genius is also evident in the contrasting portrayal of his personal character, even as a child, against that of his native Irish father and nanny. It is clear that he privileges his Continental heritage above his Irish background, an attitude he emulates from his mother, who Anglicized the family name (from O'Sullivan) before moving to Chicago. More importantly, Sullivan uses physiognomic depictions of native ethnic features to visualize the relatively low status of Irish Catholic immigrants. This is apparent in the notorious description of his father's animalistic features:

> It seems strange at first glance that these highly virile and sensitive powers should be embodied in one so unlovely in person. His medium size, his too-sloping shoulders, his excessively Irish face, his small repulsive eyes—the eyes of a pig—of nondescript color and no flash, sunk into his head under rough brows. . . . Naturally enough he had not found time to acquire an "education" as it was then called and is still called . . . he was no gentleman as that technical term went, but essentially a lackey, a flunkey or social parasite. Perhaps it was for this reason he revered book-learning and the learned. He knew no better.[38]

The trope of the piglike Irishman was a common caricature of Irish immigrants that conflated farmers with the animals they tended, including the pigs and dogs that were nurtured in the fields.[39] Sullivan's biographers have often struggled to account for the aggressively negative depiction of his Irish father, especially since there is no existing record of actual discord between the two during his lifetime.[40] A political explanation for Sullivan's distrust of Old World traits, however, provides a clear intellectual framework for interpreting this hostility.

Stereotypical depictions of pastoral Irish character continues in *Autobiography* with the portrayal of Julia Head, the nanny employed by Henri and Anna List on their country farm. Julia's lack of education is linguistically marked by the mannered inflection of her speech and her constant recollection of Gaelic phrases and traditional Irish yarns. The comparative characterization of Irish and Irish American stock emerges very clearly in these passages, with Julia typifying the common plight of first-generation immigrants and young Louis illustrating the second-generation citizen's path toward assimilation. Initially, the playfulness between these figures betrays a familial tone, although the gap in intelligence suggests that this relationship is one between siblings or friends instead of mentor and mentee. Young Louis asks Julia to comment on a recent parade for a battalion of Irish soldiers returning from serving in the Civil War. In a frenzy of Irish pride, Julia relays the only explicit references to African Americans found in all of Sullivan's writings outside of his rejection of slavery in *Democracy*: "From the shawls the women wore and the dirty childer, I know the whole crowd was Irish and poor; and as everyone knows, the Irish won the war. Think of it! Holy Virgin!—the Irish fighting for the naygers! What will it be next time?"[41] It is interesting that both Julia's negative perception of black citizenship in *Autobiography* and Sullivan's indictment of slavery as a feudal institution in *Democracy* are told within the context of post–Civil War platitudes of freedom. Since each context reveals a purported support of abolitionism, what is the ultimate status of the black subject in these situations? While it is clear that Julia is incapable of considering African Americans to be her equal, or even fit for citizenship, the views of young Louis are held in abeyance. Are we to believe that Sullivan harbors a higher opinion of African Americans than Julia does, being a more enlightened assimilated subject, or are we to take his silence as condoning his nanny's perspective?

As Nell Irvin Painter discusses in her work on Emerson, one cannot automatically take a rejection of slavery as legitimation of the social potential of black citizens, as many abolitionists rationalized, as stated above, the Civil War as a war for the soul of white America instead of one that affirmed the humanity of its black subjects.[42] The ambiguity raised by Louis and Julia's exchange can only be addressed if one takes into consideration his overall political philosophy. The troubled status of black subjects reflects the historical difficulties that African Americans experienced as an abject group striving for assimilation within the body politic. While it is tempting to attribute some positive motive to Sullivan's silence—a potentially hidden optimism that rarely surfaced in the nineteenth century—it is more reasonable to assume that his indirect reference to black subjects is meant to reveal the social and class antagonisms that conditioned the lives of Irish immigrants in the United States.

Much of the racial and class tension that persisted between Irish immigrants and African Americans during the 1840s and 1850s was predicated on the notion that free black labor threatened Irish social mobility.[43] In this historical context, a freed slave represented a patent absurdity to Julia Head, a working-class Irish woman, precisely because it worked to disenfranchise her labor as a marginal white ethnic subject. Studies of Irish labor conditions such as Noel Ignatiev's *How the Irish Became White* and David Roediger's *The Wages of Whiteness* recover some of the perceived economic stakes of ethnic identity for Irish immigrants in this period. Ironically, the defamation of black citizenship and labor did not always guarantee Irish social mobility, but did work to improve Anglo-Americans' perceptions of Irish Americans as fellow white ethnics. As a group, Irish Catholic immigrants fleeing the potato famine of the 1840s were of humbler means that the immigrants who had migrated to the United States just a few generations before.[44] Ignatiev argues that poor Irish immigrants responded to their new political contexts by rejecting the reforms endorsed by native Irish abolitionists such as Daniel O'Connell to secure favor (and employment) with employers in US territories where slavery was routine.[45] Sullivan's recollections of his nanny's broken path toward assimilation poetically reveal the self-aggrandizement that accompanies her desire for racial normativity ("as everyone knows, the Irish won the war"), and the racial strategies Irish immigrants used to solidify their assimilation of whiteness ("Think of it! Holy Virgin!—the Irish fighting for the naygers").

Sullivan's retreat into the ennobling effects of democracy on Irish American citizenship provides him with a refuge against the seemingly static manifestations of racial and national genius inherent to Old World citizens. This respite, however, was contingent upon one's ethnic heritage in the New World: Sullivan is not only an Irish American but a hybrid American, and thus is conditioned by more than just his Irish heritage. If he dreaded being born an Irish immigrant, he feared still more being born a black man in nineteenth-century America. As a result, his spiritual reading of American character did not fully embrace the intellectual and creative potentials of nonwhite social minorities recently freed in the Civil War—an event that could conceivably be taken as a national referendum on the feudal legacies of slavery. The relative decline of African American life in the Jim Crow era historically paralleled the rise of Irish American assimilation, which complicates Sullivan's pregnant silence on the status and potentials of African Americans in the body politic.

The racial themes of *Autobiography* were informed by Sullivan's exposure to physiognomic theory and the evolutionary models of history that proliferated in art history, anthropology, and sociology. As mentioned above, many critics

N° 844. Prix du numéro : 35 centimes. 2 Novembre 1872.

Dans les gares des Départements : 40 centimes. (25e ANNÉE.)

20, *Rue Bergère.* LE *Rue Bergère,* 20.

JOURNAL AMUSANT

JOURNAL ILLUSTRÉ

Journal d'images, journal comique, critique, satirique, etc.

PRIX : 3 mois. . . . 5 fr. 6 mois. . . . 10 » 12 mois. . . . 17 »

PRIX : 3 mois. . . . 5 fr. 6 mois. . . . 10 » 12 mois. . . . 17 »

POUR TOUS LES GOUTS, DU CHARBON, DES POÊLES, DES JAMBONS, DES BAINS DE SIÉGE, DES PEIGNES, DES CHEVEUX, DU BEURRE; LE TOUT ENTOURÉ DE VERDURE AVEC DE LA BONNE MUSIQUE AU MILIEU.

10854

LE MONSIEUR. — Ça n'a pas mauvais goût.....! Et quelle est la vertu de cette source?

LE MARCHAND. — Oh! monsieur, c'est une eau purgative d'une promptitude surprenante; dans deux secondes, vous m'en direz des nouvelles.....

Figure 3.2. Cover of *Journal Amusant,* November 2, 1872. Bibliothèque Nationale de France, Gallica Collection.

Figure 3.3. "Le Tramp," *Journal Amusant,* March 24, 1877. Bibliothèque Nationale de France, Gallica Collection.

believed that national character and architectural style constituted two parallel and empirical manifestations of progress in cultural history. The equivalent status of race and style in nineteenth-century ethnographic histories also contributed to the interchangeability of these categories in architectural theory. One example of this practice can be found in Gottfried Semper's representation of cultural differences in *Der Stil,* which uses illustrations of material culture as a physical proxy for racial and national characters.[46] These conventions laid the groundwork for Sullivan's organic interpretation of architectural physiognomy as the visual expression of the cultural particularities of an artist.

Since the late seventeenth and early eighteenth centuries, physiognomic theory had provided artists with an aesthetic lens for representing the physical and intellectual characters of different national groups.[47] Architectural theorists such as Jacques-François Blondel used the geometrical profiles of human figures to communicate the moods associated with the architectural orders.[48] Sullivan was exposed to this brand of physiognomic theory in the 1870s through his Beaux-Arts curriculum at MIT and later while traveling abroad in Paris.[49] The influence of physiognomic theory is also apparent in his freehand drawing. Sullivan made copies of caricatures found in the satirical French magazine *Journal Amusant* and continually sketched people and landscapes throughout his career in ways that were suggestive of their inner characters (fig. 3.2). The editors of *Journal Amusant* used caricatures to visualize the constituent elements of French national culture; popular and literary depictions of Jewish peoples regularly appeared in its pages, including discussions of bourgeois French interests in the 1852 opera *Le Juif errant* (*The Wandering Jew*). Several issues of this magazine contained illustrations of Jewish stereotypes, such as depictions of Jewish businessmen with prominent noses, or ink sketches of Jewish peddlers roaming about the city (fig. 3.3).[50] Since Sullivan used this

Figure 3.4. Alfred E. Willis, "The Jewish Nose." Alfred E. Willis, *Illustrated Physiognomy* (Chicago: Alfred E. Willis, 1879), 39.

journal to familiarize himself with French cultural norms, he would have been familiar with these representations of Jewish character during his personal travels.

The use of physiognomic principles to describe the moral and intellectual character of human beings formally reached the United States by the twentieth century in the form of handbooks on the subject. A brief survey of the 1909 auction catalog of Sullivan's personal library shows, he owned several handbooks on the subject, including Johann Caspar Lavater's *Essays on Physiognomy* (1804), Max Nordau's *Degeneration* (1895), and an eight-volume illustrated set of Alfred E. Willis's *Treatise on Human Nature and Physiognomy* (1880). Nordau was an enthusiastic reader of Cesare Lombroso's criminal anthropology and applied his ethnographic principles toward readings of artistic character as "positive" forms of social degeneracy.[51] Willis was commonly cited in the nineteenth century for his physiognomic explanations of facial features, especially the relative importance of the eyes, ears, and nose.[52] Each illustration is accompanied by short textual explanations of the cultural origins and psychological import of each physical trait, including explanations for the Florentine and Jewish noses, two physiognomic forms explicitly referenced in Sullivan's *Autobiography* (fig. 3.4).[53] He used the former to characterize his mother's character and the latter to describe that of his business partner, Dankmar Adler (fig. 3.5).[54] More important than a compartmentalized analysis of facial features, however, were Willis's claims that physiognomic principles were universal properties of form that could be used to analyze morphological development in both organic and inorganic entities.

In the 1879 text *Illustrated Physiognomy,* Willis claims that the general laws of physiognomy could be applied to all material forms, including the morphology of the physical landscape.[55] His sentiment that "geology was really the physiognomy of the earth" was very suggestive to someone like Sullivan, whose interest in physiognomy was often related to the built environment.[56] An analogical reading of physiognomic traits explains Sullivan's personification of inanimate objects in *Autobiography,* including the buildings and landscapes recorded during his travels. He notes his youthful intuition for developing physiognomic readings of Gothic architectural interiors and a strong impression of the dignity of mountainous and wooded terrain. As young Louis ages in the memoir, he learns to apply these elemental readings to wider spectrums of phenomenon in the built environment: "As they moved into the little harbor of Dieppe, what was

Figure 3.5. Portrait of Dankmar Adler, n.d. Richard Nickel Archive, Art Institute of Chicago.

Figure 3.6. Louis Sullivan, character studies, December 7, 1874. Sullivaniana Collection, Art Institute of Chicago.

left of Louis gazed at the quaint city with acceptance and delight. How different from England. What a change in physiognomy."[57]

Archival evidence of Sullivan's visual experimentation with architectural character appears in the form of personal sketches. One drawing held at the Art Institute of Chicago demonstrates his interest in documenting vernacular type forms as well as understanding the surrounding effects of environment on human character (fig. 3.6).[58] In this image, a modest country cottage in a pastoral landscape hovers above caricatures of local residents done in a manner emulating the style of caricature found in *Journal Amusant.* The quaintness of country life is communicated by portraying the range of personal characters that emerged in proximity to this architectural setting.[59] The resulting figures are more social types than portraits of actual people. This was perhaps due to Sullivan's greater ability to copy caricatures than to realistically capture the likeness of actual subjects. He also created what can be called physiognomic illustrations of geographical landscapes from the bird's-eye view that captured its defining characteristics. Two examples include the squiggly lines of a map that essentialize the saturated wetlands along the coast of Maine, dated 1868, and the network of arable lands hugging the coast of continental Africa in a map dated 1878.[60]

Hints of Sullivan's organic interpretation of character can be found as early as his 1885 address to the Western Association of Architects, titled "Characteristics and Tendencies of American Architecture."[61] In this essay he outlines the complementary functions of "type" and "character" in design. Both of these terms mirror the biological language scientists used to refer to immutable physical characteristics that were common among all peoples (type), and the psychological, moral, and intellectual capacities of a specific person or group of people (character) in time. In "Characteristics and Tendencies," Sullivan claimed that architectural style could not be passed down through history as ready-made formulas of formal typologies, but must organically emerge from their historical moments by expressing the essential characteristics of its people.

The type/character epistemology of Sullivan's speech persists in later works, which is most succinctly summarized in his *Kindergarten Chats* (1918). In this text, Sullivan produces a comparative analysis of the objective and subjective elements of architectural form in order to explain their organic relationship to surrounding cultural contexts. He considers the objective formal models of historical typologies to be soulless, literally without character, because they were expressive of "no time, no people, [and] no race."[62] The abstract masses and profiles of historical styles were meaningless when disconnected from a particular place and time. However, once the architect made specific use of an actual type form, they begin to express his subjective character and in turn reflect the local contexts that informed their intellectual development. In this sense, the construction of abstract forms was not possible in Sullivan's architecture theory, only characteristic expressions of contemporary life: "From the character of a pier may we not discern the character of a race: and from the slowly changing character of a developed pier may we not discern the temperamental changes taking place in a race: its growth, its fulfillment, its decay! Has man at any time, can man at any time, can he now lay his hand upon anything, can he focus his mind upon anything, without leaving upon that thing the impress of his character?"[63] This conception of architectural character extended the physiognomic concepts Sullivan learned while studying in Paris toward a bona fide theory of architectural invention. The organic principles that inherently linked the artist to his cultural artifacts established an anthropological basis for a living architecture that continuously evolves in the present. Sullivan's belief that an artist cannot help but materially communicate his inner life through creative activities constitutes what can be called his theory of architectural physiognomy.

Sullivan's conception of architectural characters was an organic extension of the universal laws that seemingly regulated social character and racial variation in nature; they mirrored the "organic" principles of natural evolution and guaranteed the authenticity of material culture in the present. This reading is equally borne out in Adler and Sullivan's collaborative designs for Jewish immigrant houses, civic spaces, and synagogues in the 1880s and 1890s. At this stage of his career, Sullivan experimented with transforming historical architectural types by strategically implanting his botanically inspired architectural ornament into the surfaces of each project. As an ornamental figure, these botanical grafts figuratively took root within the faces of nineteenth-century building types to reform the feudalist ideals that such historical borrowing represented to the American public. This creative process extended the parallels between Sullivan's earlier lessons in physiognomic theory at the Beaux-Arts and the beginning of his mature phase of architectural experimentation.

The Architectural Character of Kehilath Anshe Ma'ariv Synagogue, 1888–1891

Sullivan's theoretical studies of character and physiognomy bore fruit in his role as lead designer for Kehilath Anshe Ma'ariv Synagogue on Chicago's South Side. As a result of Adler's relationship with the Jewish community—he was a lifetime member of Kehilath Anshe Ma'ariv and the son of the prominent orthodox rabbi Liebman Adler—their firm received regular commissions for Jewish synagogues in Chicago. The division of labor between each partner made Adler responsible for determining the structural and spatial schemes of the firm's designs, leaving Sullivan to determine the overall massing of the exterior and the decorative schemes of each building.[64]

Adler and Sullivan's first proposal for Kehilath Anshe Ma'ariv Synagogue was a modern, secular building in a Richardsonian style (fig. 3.7). In physiognomic terms, the Romanesque profile of this proposal visually expressed the volumetric massing of the main worship space contained within the building. The north, south, and west façades were relieved with deeply set semicircular openings at the second-story and clerestory levels. The external massing and

Figure 3.7. Worms Synagogue, 1174–1175. Postcard, 1914; photo by Christian Herbst, item 49153, Yad Vashem Archives, Jerusalem.

profile of the building's form outlines the main volume of the worship hall inside. A rendering of this 1889 scheme portrays a heavy rectangular base clad in granite with an intermediary hip roof connecting to a clerestory level above. The entire composition is capped by a pyramidal hip roof clad in terra cotta. The façades of this design emulate those found in medieval watchtowers and nineteenth-century urban armories.[65] Despite Sullivan's claims that his building "has no historical style," architectural historians have located a precedent for his use of a Romanesque style in Worms Synagogue (1174–1175) (fig. 3.8).[66] Identifying this precedent suggests that Sullivan's design was the result of a synthetic formal operation: he was capable of transforming the architectural elements and symbolic emblems of the traditional Jewish synagogue in order to make a new statement about the contemporary function of this religious space.

Sullivan's business partnership with Adler prospered in response to their ability to address the cultural needs of their German Jewish clientele. In the case of the Kehilath Anshe Ma'ariv Synagogue, for example, Adler and Sullivan collaborated with rabbi Isaac S. Moses and the building committee of Kehilath

Figure 3.8. Adler and Sullivan, Kehilath Anshe Ma'ariv Synagogue, 1889, perspective of first Richardsonian scheme. Richard Nickel Archive, Art Institute of Chicago.

Anshe Ma'ariv to respond to the practices of Reform Judaism—Sullivan's 1889 design produced an expression of this religious movement that idealized Reform Judaism's secularism and gave it an assimilationist form. The Jewish Reform movement first flourished in Germany at the turn of the nineteenth century under the leadership of rabbi Abraham Geiger.[67] Geiger and his supporters introduced a gradualist model of divine revelation that aligned religious practices with emerging modern practices. Reform leaders consciously experimented with secularizing religious principles for moral behavior to arrive at a universal standard capable of binding believers and nonbelievers.[68] They turned to German Enlightenment principles such as *Bildung* (self-education) to liberalize Jewish political identity.[69] By the 1840s, German-speaking migrants brought Reform ideals to Chicago. The Reform movement expanded in the United States as a broad search for appropriate forms of worship within American culture.

The cultural politics of the Jewish Reform movement affected the design and construction of American synagogues throughout the nineteenth century. While prominent Reform leaders were ideologically motivated to find architects capable of expressing their secularizing philosophical beliefs in visual terms, congregants tended to conceive of synagogue architecture as means of easing social tensions between fellow members and nonbelievers by concealing the building's function or tamping down on its exotic formal elements. Turn-of-the-century Reform synagogues consisted of three interior zones: the main worship hall; a nearby school or educational center; and a vestry for social activities.[70] In the typical floor plan for American Reform synagogues the entry hall does not lead directly into the worship hall as might be expected, but to the vestry and classroom spaces that support the public functions of this building typology (figs. 3.9 and 3.10).[71] Worship halls were situated above grade to mark their separation from the profane activities occurring on the street below.

In addition, the location and orientation of key interior elements of the worship hall such as the bimah, the ceremonial ark for holding the Torah, and the platform for sermons reveal much about the shifting role of the rabbi in Reform Judaism. In Orthodox synagogues the bimah was centrally located to situate the rabbi within the flock, which elevated the reading of scripture as the most important activity of the men in the congregation. By contrast, Reform synagogues locate the bimah and the ark on or near a central stage and a podium reserved for the rabbi or cantor to deliver sermons, as in Adler and Sullivan's design for Kehilath Anshe Ma'ariv Synagogue. To accommodate a choir, Adler and Sullivan created recessed alcoves on either side of the stage, which integrated all the sound elements of the interior (organ and singers) into the physical framework of the auditorium (fig. 3.11). The most progressive congregations entirely eliminated the bimah and ark from their worship hall, as was the case in Adler and Sullivan's 1892 renovation of Sinai Temple (fig. 3.12). The new visual focus on the podium reflects the growing importance of rabbis, who became modern scholars leading the way toward enlightened forms of contemporary worship. Jeanne Kilde notes the popularity of theater arrangements for Reform congregations and Baptist churches due to the egalitarian leveling of sightlines between attendees and the rabbi or preacher.[72] The sense of community formerly

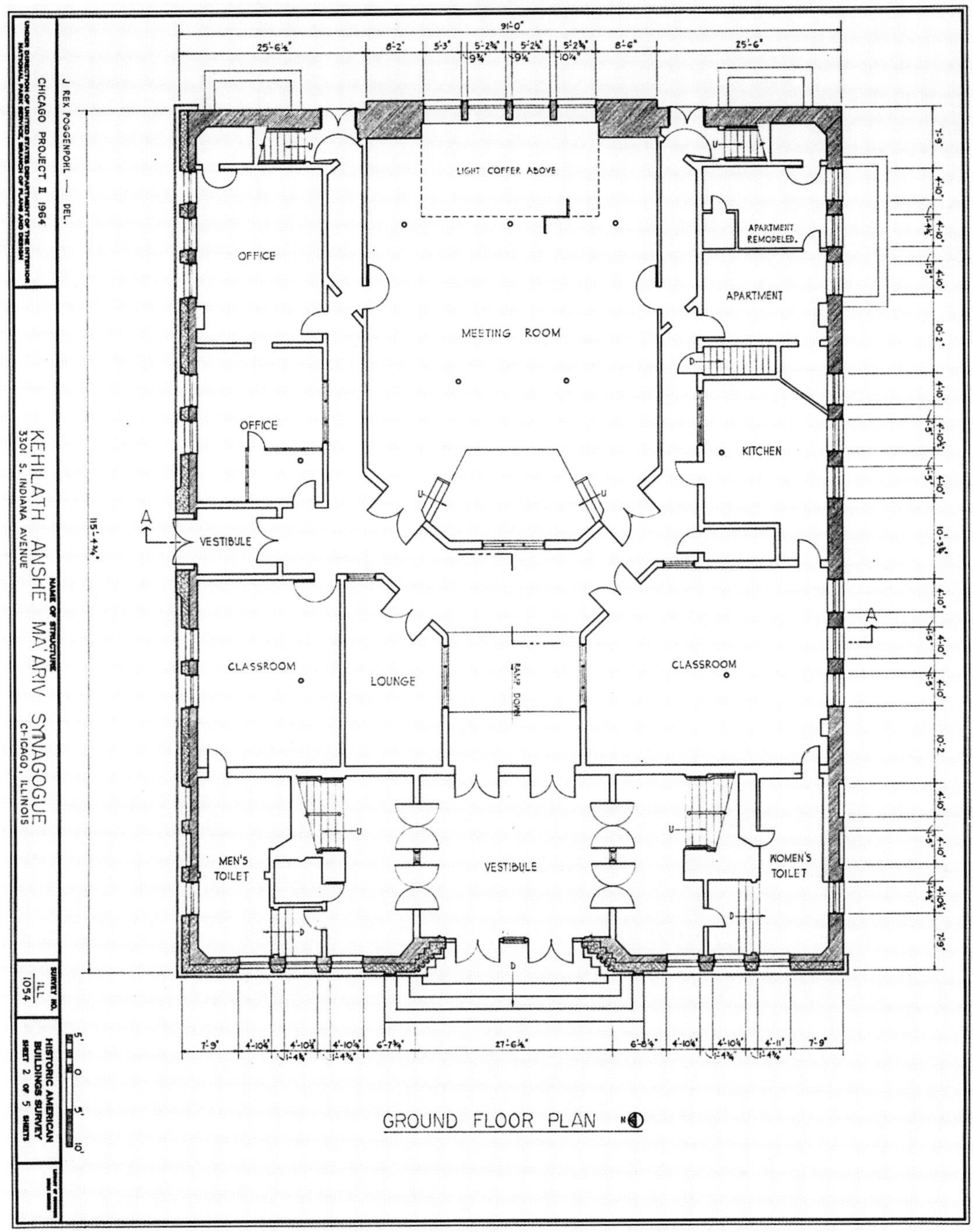

Figure 3.9. Adler and Sullivan, Kehilath Anshe Ma'ariv Synagogue, Chicago, 1891, ground-floor plan created by the Historic American Buildings Survey, 1964. Historic American Buildings Survey, HABS ILL, 16-CHIG, 56, sheet 2 of 5, Prints and Photographs Division, Library of Congress, Washington, DC.

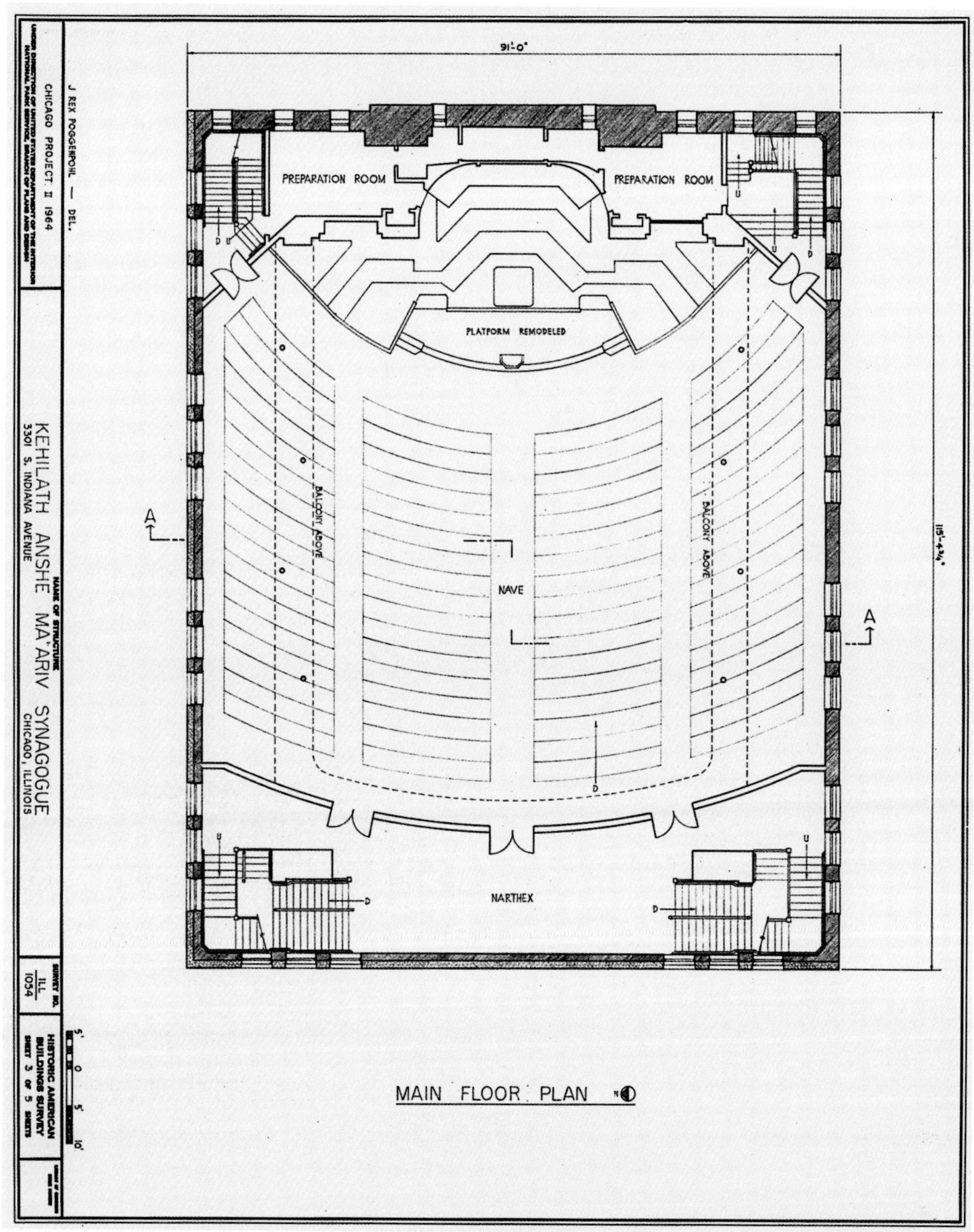

Figure 3.10. Adler and Sullivan, Kehilath Anshe Ma'ariv Synagogue, Chicago, 1891, first-floor plan created by the Historic American Buildings Survey, 1964 (Historic American Buildings Survey, HABS ILL, 16-CHIG, 56, sheet 3 of 5, Prints and Photographs Division, Library of Congress, Washington, DC.

INTERIOR VIEW, SYNAGOGUE, CHICAGO, ILLINOIS.

ADLER & SULLIVAN, ARCHITECTS.

Figure 3.11. Adler and Sullivan, Kehilath Anshe Ma'ariv Synagogue, 1891, interior of auditorium. Inland Architect and Builder 18, no. 1 (1892), 20. Richard Nickel Archive, Art Institute of Chicago.

Figure 3.12. Adler and Sullivan, Sinai Temple, Chicago, 1892, renovated interior. Richard Nickel Archive, Art Institute of Chicago.

Figure 3.13. Adler and Sullivan, Zion Temple, Chicago, 1884–1885, building exterior. Inland Architect and Builder 6, no. 2 (1886): 31. Richard Nickel Archive, Art Institute of Chicago.

Figure 3.14. Adler and Sullivan, Sinai Temple, Chicago, 1892, renovated exterior. Richard Nickel Archive, Art Institute of Chicago.

built by a common reading of texts among the men of an Orthodox congregation was now created between men and women engaged in building a contemporary Jewish worship.

Two other designs for Reform synagogues—Zion Temple (1885) and Sinai Temple (1892)—use a very similar floor plan and building section as that found in Kehilath Anshe Ma'ariv, but differ from this latter case in ornamentation and stylistic articulation (figs. 3.13 and 3.14). In both the renovation of Sinai Temple and the construction of Zion Temple, Sullivan used Moorish ornament to denote the historical roots and religious symbolism of Judaism. These Orientalist motifs had been popular in the 1830s because they recalled the prominence of Jewish culture in medieval Spain and the Middle East. Adler and Sullivan used of the Star of David, the tablets of the Mosaic Law, and other religious emblems on Zion and Sinai Temple to designate the Jewish liturgical function of its interior spaces. For example, the Star of David marks the main worship space on the façade of Zion Temple. Adler and Sullivan also brought these buildings closer to Anglo-American religious spaces by emulating some of the compositional features of Protestant churches in the area. For example, Adler's centrally planned worship hall for Sinai Temple did away with the central nave and side aisles of traditional Protestant churches. On the façade, however, he maintained a tripartite organization that emulated the paired tall, ornamented towers that fronted many Gothic designs in the neighborhood. In contrast to these designs, Sullivan's 1889 scheme for Kehilath Anshe Ma'ariv Synagogue altered the religious associations of the reform synagogue by purposefully omitting the overt display of key religious emblems and Moorish ornamentation from its exterior. A comparison between Sullivan's Kehilath Anshe Ma'ariv Synagogue and Henry Hobson Richardson's Trinity Temple shows that Sullivan emulated Richardson's constrained massing for urban civic spaces (fig. 3.15).

The secular character of Sullivan's Romanesque design can be read as a physical embodiment of the civic function that he believed religious spaces could perform in America if they shed their exclusive ecclesiastical functions. The association of the religious with the civic in his synagogue design aligns with principles in Jewish Reform literature. Reform leaders such as Isaac Mayer Wise believed that Judaism could serve as the fundamental basis of a contemporary ethics, which would demonstrate to all American citizens the political value of religious thought.[73] Interdenominational cooperation became common among Jewish Reform and Christian leaders, exemplified by Kehilath Anshe Ma'ariv's custom of inviting Christian preachers to speak in the congregation on ceremonial occasions.

By March of 1890 the design for Kehilath Anshe Ma'ariv Synagogue reflected significant changes to Sullivan's Romanesque design that made the

Figure 3.15. Henry Hobson Richardson, Trinity Temple, Boston, 1885. Historical Architectural and Landscape Image Collection, Art Institute of Chicago.

correlation between the external character of the building and the liturgical function of its interior spaces more explicit (fig. 3.16). The architectural massing of the resulting new design had two distinct compositional forms: a strong rusticated base that preserves the original Richardsonian design topped by a new wood-framed, copper-clad clerestory level that more plainly expressed the religious nature of the worship hall within. The structural framework and visual detailing of the clerestory recall several features of the Ark of the Covenant—a historical religious object that Jewish congregants would have known was made of wood and inlaid with precious metals. The parallels between these two forms is quite striking. The combination of the copper banding along the monumental frieze of Kehilath Anshe Ma'ariv that prominently displays the Star of David and the perimeter molding above the Chinese railing of the parapet appear to imitate the decorative cabin and lid to the ark. Four metal piers on each corner of Kehilath Anshe Ma'ariv's clerestory also complete the rectilinear geometry

Figure 3.16. Adler and Sullivan, Kehilath Anshe Ma'ariv Synagogue, 1891, detail of clerestory level. Richard Nickel Archive, Art Institute of Chicago.

of this religious referent. Architectural historian Joseph Siry even describes the tripartite windows of the clerestory as abstractions of the tablets that contain the Law of David, yet another nod to Judaic custom.[74] The hip roof of Kehilath Anshe Ma'ariv formally emulates the orientation and placement of the two inward-facing cherubs that crown the original ark. These alterations to the clerestory level collectively reduced the secular connotations of the 1889 design, but were only partially successful in fully exerting the ecclesiastic character of the design. Schuyler remained critical of the secular character of Sullivan's design for the synagogue in 1891: "It is an interesting scheme but it cannot be said to have been fairly carried out in the exterior, which not only fails to convey any ecclesiastical impression, but which appears rather as a sketch than a completed design."[75]

While the exterior of the new 1890 scheme for Kehilath Anshe Ma'ariv did not create an organic synthesis out of the structural and ornamental elements of the building, as Sullivan initially intended, the disjunctions of its final form better express the tensions that existed between the nationalist and religious tendencies within the Reform movement. Historians have long noted the compositional dissonance within this second design, but have only considered it in terms of Sullivan's idealized view of an organic architecture.[76] However, it is more productive to interpret the second scheme as a revision of Sullivan's ideas of American character and its translation into architecture. This was a moment when the architect seems to have been forced to rethink his assimilationist conception of American character to render a representation of a marginal people's hybrid identity. Ironically, the earlier Orientalist façades of Chicago's Reform Jewish synagogues also expressed the hybrid identity of this ethnic minority, although these were still associated with an exoticism that characterized Jewish Americans as an "other." Sullivan's organic solution of 1889 overcorrected this situation with an architecture that emulated the anonymous character of Worms Synagogue—a precedent completed during an intolerant regime in Europe—in order to help them fit in. He represented Jewish American character through both the sacred and secular components of the building program instead of assimilating them into an expression of a unified national character.

Character Building and the Alteration of Kehilath Anshe Ma'ariv Synagogue, 1915–1970

African American migrations into Chicago's South Side precipitated the fragmentation and displacement of Jewish enclaves at the turn of the century. The Baptist and Methodist congregations that flourished in these neighborhoods repeated the communal patterns of their Jewish predecessors: new congregations reused existing religious structures before constructing their own, and all religious spaces were interpreted as self-representational objects of community

Figure 3.17. Congregants leaving Pilgrim Baptist Church, Chicago, on Easter Sunday, 1941. Photo by Lee Russell. Farm Security Administration Collection, Library of Congress, Washington, DC.

values (fig. 3.17). While certain structural and stylistic features of inherited buildings could not be easily changed, this pattern of migration established the framework within which new congregations provided innovative clues of their new religious faith and their relative levels of assimilation within the American body politic. Demographic changes and white flight made African Americans the final stewards of Kehilath Anshe Ma'ariv Synagogue beginning in 1921. It was only through these historical migrations that blacks were finally given a chance to contribute to the democratic aims of Sullivan's political discourse; their inheritance of former Jewish enclaves placed them at the center of the historical transformations of Sullivan's American architecture, which occurred at a time when many commercial clients were abandoning Sullivan's vision for the commercialization of skyscraper design.[77] Subsequent urban renewal policies and the strategic neglect of Chicago's poor black neighborhoods made African Americans one of the few groups willing to continue developing Sullivan's unique brand of democratic architecture. These efforts were coterminous with

Sullivan's experiments with designing rural banks and they continued beyond this period during the geographical emergence of the "Black Metropolis" that gave birth to the earliest forms of gospel music in the early twentieth century.

Historical evidence suggests that the African American tenants of Kehilath Anshe Ma'ariv alternated their reading of Sullivan's ornamentation from nationalist to localized terms over the course of nearly fifty years. According to articles published in the *Kansas City Sun* and the black-owned *Broad Axe* newspapers, a committee of eight prominent black and white civic leaders in Chicago created a business organization to purchase and renovate Kehilath Anshe Ma'ariv upon Booker T. Washington's death in 1915 to establish a vocational school for educating black professionals.[78] The building committee's symbolic intentions for their renovation project included the creation of a "Practical Memorial" to honor the legacy of Washington that provided "a social center and industrial training school for Negro children in Chicago." This transformation would have successfully exploited the monumentality of Kehilath Anshe Ma'ariv for building a decidedly black institution that was based on the religious and moral principles of Tuskegee Institute.[79]

Washington was no stranger to the role of monumental buildings in uplifting the character of the black race. He summarized a series of moral lessons he delivered to Tuskegee students on Sunday evening at the turn of the century in the text *Character Building* (1902), in which he uses architectural metaphors to reinforce the communal function of civic buildings in black communities. This function would be fulfilled by the parallel construction of individual and architectural character, which took place when communities directly participated in the building up of common spaces: "We can succeed in putting up good buildings only in proportion as everyone performs well his part in the erection of each building."[80] These words suggest that community buildings embodied the labor and values of the community, and Washington's emphasis on a practical and humble aesthetic reflected his desire to shape African American character in a decidedly Christian image.

Washington also praises the utilitarian aesthetic of the buildings on Tuskegee's campus, many of which were of the Romanesque style, for communicating what he called "the virtue of simplicity" to a generation of laborers just out of slavery: "We do not expect to have fine, costly buildings, nor do we want to have them. But we do expect to have well-constructed buildings, and attractive buildings; and, if we can go on in this simple, humble way, the time will come when we shall have all the buildings we need. Just in proportion as our friends see that we are worthy of these good things, they will come to us."[81] Like Sullivan, Washington praises the culture of "the New England character" for building wealth in the New World and considers the relative position of black peoples in comparison to their white peers.[82] Though he was open to urban life, he paints a romantic image of primitive black life in the rural south that was manifest in the condition of poor blacks' "cheap lands, a beautiful climate and a rich soil."[83] For Washington, the humility of urban civic buildings must be expressed by its simplicity, which was sympathetic to the simple dress and grooming of rural southern migrants that represented the origins of blacks in the United States.

The character lectures given at Tuskegee set a spatial precedent for the adaptive reuse of Kehilath Anshe Ma'ariv in Chicago both for their religious moral sensibility and because they were delivered in the campus chapel. If it were constructed as planned, the Practical Memorial would have produced a major public statement regarding the presence and importance of black labor in Chicago. Although a public subscription was started for the memorial with the Chicago Title and Trust Company to raise the $85,000 asking price for the Kehilath Anshe Ma'ariv Synagogue—nearly $40,000 lower than the market value of the structure—the deal for the project never materialized.[84] It is not clear why the project was scrapped, as newspapers remain silent on this change and no building plans have ever been located of the renovation project.

The executive council for Pilgrim Baptist Church (PBC) eventually purchased Kehilath Anshe Ma'ariv Synagogue on January 12, 1921, and the property was turned over to the church's leadership later that same year for renovation and occupation.[85] The continued religious function of this space reinforces the transdenominational use of ecclesiastic spaces on Chicago's South Side. And in line with this historical pattern, PBC's congregation developed a local interpretation of Adler and Sullivan's original design that accommodated the direct representation of black Christian faith in the form of spatial and ornamental renovations.

This process began with the range of social services the congregation provided for new migrants that implicitly reinforced Sullivan's secular interpretation of religious space. As Michael W. Harris explains in his study of black urban churches in Chicago, rural migrants were just as often attracted to the secular services congregations provided as they were to continuing their religious worship.[86] In some cases, however, these two forces ran in direct opposition to one another: rural congregants sought ways of assimilating into northern cultures without giving up their long-established religious practices. The poorest migrants explicitly disliked the conservative tenor of religious services that discouraged any speaking from the audience during sermons and prayers. This form of call-and-response between the clergy and his congregation was more common in the rural South. In time, however, as the numbers of rural migrants grew during the Great Migration, established congregations moved from outright suppression and later toleration of rural practices to greater forms of accommodation. The growing reception of this audience was achieved by two important innovations to religious services: the clergy's emulation of southern preachers' oration patterns, and the tolerance of call-and-response behaviors through the introduction of gospel choirs. This change in music was an important cultural sign of the growing importance of vernacular culture as classical traditions learned at seminary schools gave way to southern musical traditions, including the fusion of gospel and blues music. Thomas Andrew Dorsey helped to introduce this shift in taste to black churches in Chicago, and his selection by Reverend Austin of PBC to lead their choir in 1932 represented an explicit attempt to assimilate rural and urban patterns of black worship.

The acceptance of a gospel choir in Baptist services pluralized the class character of PBC by incorporating the rising number of rural black migrants then attending religious services. This shift in turn also changed the spatial dynamics of the main religious space (see plate 7). The call-and-response practices of rural religious services were no longer relegated to the basement levels of the church but were now on full display in the central auditorium. By the 1960s a formal transformation of the stage concretized a long-standing spatial transformation within the church: instead of standing alone behind a podium facing the congregation, the clergy of Pilgrim Baptist found themselves sharing the stage with more and more people as the interchange between speaker and audience gradually increased. Alongside the deacons and other fellow clergy that traditionally shared this stage, members of the choir soon performed solos or played musical instruments on stage as well.

The growing importance of the gospel choir implicitly challenges the physical separation of stage and audience that was appropriate for Kehilath Anshe Ma'ariv, even before any physical changes had to be made to this structure. Adler and Sullivan's final design for Kehilath Anshe Ma'ariv created two auxiliary stages alongside the main bimah to accommodate a choir and other elements of musical performances. The pipes to a large organ were hidden behind the main stage to give the impression that the walls produced the music that supported religious services—an occult-like phenomenon that preserved a religious aspirant's belief in the divine while equally referencing Sullivan's belief in the secular power of nature to order the built environment. In the time between the black acquisition of Kehilath Anshe Ma'ariv and the physical modification of its central stage, Austin and other PBC leaders experimented with placing the choir in different places in the auditorium, including the area directly in front of the lectern. This practice led to the eventual closure of the access door to the choir room as they were no longer needed; the oral connection between preacher and congregant had already moved beyond the walls of the main stage.

Ironically, the eventual alteration of the stage area in PBC increased the secular function that Sullivan hoped might emerge for religious spaces in the late nineteenth century. This was especially the case as gospel music gained popularity as a commercial art form. By the close of the interwar period, it

Figure 3.18. William E. Scott, *Last Supper*, 1936–1937. Oil on plaster, 20′ × 6′. Pilgrim Baptist Church, Chicago. Photo by Jeanine Oleson, ca. 1997.

was not uncommon for one to hear gospel music in church on Sunday and the "gospel blues" on the radio at home during the twilight hours.[87] The only difference consisted in the lyrics of each song, which was holy in one context and profane in the other. The popular dissemination of gospel music is one of the most prominent features of social and cultural histories of black religious spaces and an aural sign of the reformist politics of the civil rights movement. The critical importance of this aural tradition in PBC needs to be written into contemporary Sullivan studies. The growing popularity of the gospel blues continues the secularization of religious culture that Sullivan first established at Kehilath Anshe Ma'ariv. Yet there is very little indication in Sullivan's writings that African Americans were ever meant to be included in this secularization. This is a major oversight in the architect's interpretation of American character. Kymberly Pinder's study of William E. Scott's painted murals provides evidence of African American congregants' explicit struggles with conceiving of themselves as fully fledged Americans (fig. 3.18).[88] Scott's murals depict Jesus Christ and other biblical characters as black subjects of different hues, which pluralizes the racial discourses associated with white Anglo-Saxon Protestant elites.

The changes that PBC introduced to Adler and Sullivan's original designs for Kehilath Anshe Ma'ariv presented a dilemma for the preservation of this structure in 2006. A fire erupted in the main hall of the building during a routine renovation, which burned down everything except for the brick and masonry perimeter walls along the east and west façades. Efforts to rebuild began almost immediately, and the church leadership decided that the building should be restored to its historical status. However, instead of deciding to reconstruct this space as it was originally constructed in 1890, the reconstruction committee considered its state during the birth of gospel music as the most important historical configuration of the building. This claim is of course based on the cultural importance of music in the history of the black church, as well as the local importance of figures such as Dorsey and Mahalia Jackson in popularizing this music within the church and beyond.

While architectural historians are generally trained to preserve the integrity of an architect's original vision, the proposal for preserving the black reinvention of Adler and Sullivan's design might be an advantageous way of crediting the work of social minorities that has until now remained invisible to most people. The formal changes to the PBC building by black congregants pluralized Sullivan's pessimistically narrow vision of who constitutes a real American. Constructing a historical narrative that preserves the black appropriations and renovations to this space directly challenges canonical histories that pretend the user of a building makes no important contributions to the meaning of modern architectures.

The most ubiquitous illustration created for the first phase of restoration efforts at PBC suggests the secondary importance of the clerestory in the day-to-day function of the main hall (see plate 8). In this photograph, which was reproduced in several press stories, the clerestory level is ghosted in with steel structural members in a manner that recalls the slow neglect of the clerestory's exterior treatment in historical photographs. The most obvious and least interesting interpretation of this situation is one of economics, as all institutions have to make decisions about where to spend their money in the life cycle of a building. Yet given the central importance of the clerestory level in Adler and Sullivan's original design and the radical transformation of this feature in the 1890s construction, it is more interesting to consider the meaning of this exterior feature in the context of the South Side neighborhoods, where the physical form of a church can visually represent the character of black Christian faith to outsiders.

The nearly superfluous nature of the exterior surfaces of the clerestory is powerfully illustrated in a 1960s photograph that treats this upper story as a nearly blank exterior element (fig. 3.19). The denuded surface ornamentation of

Figure 3.19. Pilgrim Baptist Church, Chicago, 1960s, with asphalt shingles covering the clerestory level. Richard Nickel Archive, Art Institute of Chicago.

this façade is a radical aesthetic bracketing of the architect's original intentions for this space. In the language of architectural organicism, it translates as a disconnection between the spatial function of the interior, the structural system that ties the interior to the exterior and the ornamental surface that reveals the integration of these elements in a living architecture. Is the religious function of the interior calling for more expression on the exterior of the building, perhaps in a way that reveals the identity of its new Christian denomination? Or does the building wish to reflect the secular impulses of its lower stories in a restoration of the original Richardsonian solution for this space? A third contextual alteration exists that transcends Adler and Sullivan's original intentions. If one looks from the rooftop of PBC to some of the two-story houses surrounding it on Chicago's South Side, the use of asphalt ceiling tiles reflects a mirroring of the common aesthetic used by homeowners in the area. At one level, the black tiled finishing of PBC is a lay interpretation of the clerestory as a glorified "roof" for the building. At a deeper level, however, it reinforces the indeterminacy of Adler and Sullivan's original design solution in the "make-do" aesthetic of its surrounding context. The denuded treatment of this exterior element sits as a bandage or cast that covers the scars left by the layers of dead skin that have fallen from this structure over the years. In very poetic terms, it is a posthumous call to its architect to provide an appropriate exterior aesthetic for its new residents—one that can restore its organic wholeness with a new visual language. The ambiguity that haunts the exterior treatment of the clerestory level does not continue on its interior. In fact, it was the church's efforts to restore the interior hall that led to the 2006 fire that leveled the building in the first place. If the restoration efforts ever take place, the aesthetic masking of the clerestory level will finally be revealed by new construction that seeks to memorialize the limitations of the original design in an updated physical language.

The racial politics of Louis Sullivan's democratic vision for American architecture were manifest in his dual interpretations of physiognomic character of national peoples and the buildings they created, as well as in his struggle to accommodate an Anglo-American interpretation of national character in US politics. Sullivan believed that the everyday life patterns of the average person would produce an indigenous local culture that was reflective of broader democratic ideals. However, his assimilationist conception of American citizenship bracketed the racial and ethnic composition of this common man, which in turn limited the application of his political theory for new waves of white immigrants and nonwhite peoples then living in the United States.

The practical and aesthetic limits of Sullivan's self-labeled democratic architecture become evident in the design and renovation of Kehilath Anshe Ma'ariv Synagogue. Adler and Sullivan's desire to create a living architecture led them to integrate the spatial, structural, and aesthetic dimensions of Kehilath Anshe Ma'ariv into an organic whole. However, their final design did not completely resolve the contradictions inherent in the sacred and secular requirements of the architectural program. While the ornament for this synagogue elevated the singularity of Jewish life in Chicago, its Richardsonian ornamentation and profile imposed a secular-assimilationist model of national belonging onto this religious space. The final program of the space was also split between secular and communal spaces in the basement level, which are somewhat hidden from sight and the auditorium space, which is sacred in function but rendered secular in its Richardsonian guise.

The acquisition of this synagogue for PBC in the 1920s and its subsequent renovations posthumously challenges the political and aesthetic limits of Sullivan's architecture theory for African Americans, a group he failed to consider in his writings. Though PBC did not directly commission a building from Adler and Sullivan, their renovations of Kehilath Anshe Ma'ariv suggest the problematic aspects of their inherited space, in terms of both its changing religious affiliation and the limitations of Sullivan's secular interpretations of religious spaces. PBC leadership introduced two prominent changes to the building, which included the expansion of the stage area in the main worship space and the denuded surface ornamentation of the exterior clerestory. A close examination of the spatial changes precipitated by the black choir demonstrates a gradual weakening of the formal separations Adler and Sullivan established between the clergy and the laity in their original nineteenth century design. The changing ornamentation of the clerestory also brings new meaning to the exterior as it better reflects the common aesthetic used in surrounding neighborhood housing, which parallels the "make-do" aesthetic of many black homeowners in the area. These shifts subtly destabilized the synthetic integration formerly achieved between the spatial, structural, and ornamental elements of organic architecture. Collectively, the Jewish and African American material contributions to Kehilath Anshe Ma'ariv Synagogue, later Pilgrim Baptist Church, complicate the assimilationist framework of Sullivan's political theory both theoretically and formally.

Two contrasting intellectual forces struggled for dominance in Sullivan's political theory. On the one hand, his belief in the eventual formation of a unifying common culture expressed faith in an assimilationist ideal of American nationalism. This aspiration was fueled by anthropological speculations on the type of American citizen being produced by cultural hybridizations occurring between European immigrants in the United States. Irish and Jewish immigrants were only contingently accepted as worthy of such integrations because of the notion that their social differences constituted an entirely separate race of white peoples in the nineteenth century. The Irish did not experience general acceptance as an ethnic people of a shared white race until late in the nineteenth century; Jewish Americans would not be accepted in this way until the first half of the twentieth century. This social transformation is poetically dramatized by the physiognomic descriptions of white subjects in Sullivan's *Autobiography.*

A second dominant force in Sullivan's democratic theory of architecture lies in his interpretation of artistic genius. He favored an image of exceptional individualism for the artistic avant-garde that exceeded the limits of minority group status. Sullivan's aggrandized self-image as a prophet of modern architecture must be seen as a rhetorical strategy that distinguished him from the plights of Irish immigrants struggling for acceptance into the American body politic. As an Irish American, he challenged the hegemonic ideal of Anglo-American character that defined national genius in his lifetime. Ironically, Sullivan's romantic portrait of individualism may have compelled marginalized racial and ethnic minorities to see themselves in Sullivan's struggles for acceptance. At the very least, it is clear that the semiotic confusion between Sullivan's notion of "exceptional genius" and Reform Jewish minorities' feelings of distinctness in America was especially present in Adler and Sullivan's designs for Reform Judaism synagogues in the 1880s. In the final analysis, Sullivan's political theory necessitated the adaptation of a secularist majority perspective, despite the inclusive rhetoric that masked the inequalities perpetuated by such a position. It still remains difficult to conclusively determine how conscious Sullivan was of the social implications of his architectural practice.

The Jewish clientele of Adler and Sullivan's business served as a bridling influence on Sullivan's protracted view of the American body politic. This partnership forced him to respond to the needs of Jewish immigrants, even as he insisted on making architectural ornament that represented the dominant Anglo-American image of national genius. African American appropriations of Jewish buildings during the 1920s and 1930s constitute yet another challenge to Sullivan's exclusive conception of American citizenship, which has yet to be incorporated into contemporary Sullivan studies. A multicultural interpretation of Sullivan's "American architecture" was not possible under the assimilationist framework he used to develop his architectural theory. However, a multicultural ideal was constantly debated among the white ethnic and nonwhite social minorities who challenged and expanded the boundaries of hegemonic definitions of citizenship in the public sphere. An initial wave of revision was manifest by the Reform Jewish congregations that employed Adler and Sullivan to create public housing and religious spaces for their communities. This tradition continued with the efforts of African Americans who inherited and renovated previously Jewish-owned spaces for new uses. By the 1920s and 1930s, Adler and Sullivan's multiple contributions to Chicago's South Side neighborhoods became progressively dependent on the creativity and resilience of African Americans. Not only had Sullivan's philosophy fallen into disfavor among the bankers and businessmen of his native Chicago but the South Side was on its way to becoming a segregated enclave. Only with the black appropriation of Sullivan's civic architecture was a truly expansive conception of American architecture finally realized. This ideal would be reached only after the architect's death and without any direct commissions from African American civic or cultural groups.

Historical efforts to reconstruct PBC raise the issue of which version of Adler and Sullivan's building offers the most authoritative interpretation of their architectural ideals. While canonical histories of modern architecture and the principles of connoisseurship will privilege the original state of construction, a counterargument can be made from the perspective of cultural history that restores the building's state of occupation during the birth of the gospel choir of PBC in 1932. This latter option recognizes the importance of the black oral tradition that was finally manifest in a physical transformation of the central stage of this structure in the 1960s. Recovering the African American contribution to Sullivan's democratic conception of American architecture is important for reassessing his legacy in Chicago. The democratic values at the heart of his architecture theory were only fulfilled by the minority occupation and renovation of spaces that were originally designed to fit the social mores of the late nineteenth century. A full accounting of Sullivan's democratic architecture theory requires us to acknowledge its limits and revisions, and to continually reassess its relevance for contemporary audiences.

Figure 4.1. PSFS building, Philadelphia, George Howe and William Lescaze, 1929.

4

WHEN PUBLIC HOUSING WAS WHITE

William Lescaze and the Americanization of the International Style

> To plan housing, to plan federal government buildings, to coordinate all the building enterprises of the government in its praiseworthy efforts to act as a "primer" and thus revive private work, to organize nationwide public-works surveys—all this is necessary. Yet it is not enough. The choice of a definite architectural theory must be made, a clear-cut position must be taken. Who knows if, in investing its and our millions functionally, economically and aesthetically, the government would not be laying down the foundation of an American architecture, of modern architecture for a modern nation?
>
> **—William Lescaze,**
> **"New Deal Architecture"**

OVER THE LAST TEN YEARS, architectural historians have turned their attention back to the architectural legacy of William Lescaze—the native Swiss designer who emigrated to the United States in the 1920s. By 1932 Philip Johnson and Henry-Russell Hitchcock had canonized Lescaze in their *Modern Architecture: International Exhibit* at the Museum of Modern Art as a popularizer of European modernism in the Northeast. This reputation was built on his collaboration with George Howe on the Philadelphia Savings Fund Society (PSFS) building—a project that is identified as the first International Style skyscraper in the United States (fig. 4.1).[1] Lescaze was later approached in 1932 to design the site plan and exteriors of the most expensive International Style public housing project then built in New York City—Williamsburg Houses (fig. 4.2). Despite a persistent record of designing public housing in the States,

Figure 4.2. Williamsburg Houses, Brooklyn, Courtyard Garden View, ca. 1938. La Guardia and Wagner Archives, LaGuardia Community College, New York.

Lescaze's reputation had dwindled by the 1960s to that of a minor architect whose career peaked with the PSFS building.[2] Architectural historians have recently attempted to recuperate his professional contributions to the birth of American public housing. Gaia Caramellino has persuasively argued that a major factor behind Lescaze's reputation as a housing expert was his status as an émigré capable of adapting the technical and aesthetic standards of European social housing to American life.[3] Williamsburg Houses was a major achievement in this regard: it borrowed the "towers in the park" approach of European planners but employed a regional material palette that made it unique to the city. According to Samuel Zipp and Nicholas Dagen Bloom, administrators of the New York City Housing Authority chose Lescaze because they "imagined Williamsburg as a testing ground for Modernist planning ideas from the start."[4] The transatlantic trajectory of this process intimates a further study of the racial politics that affected two parallel groups of immigrants at Williamsburg Houses: those of its architect and those of its residents. As Caramellino notes, Lescaze experienced a prolonged process of Americanization that compelled him to synthesize the aesthetic ideals of his European training with the social and cultural demands of American practice.[5] This process was likely also a conditioning factor for the Eastern and Southern European immigrants who would later call Williamsburg Houses their home.

Historical studies of Americanization note the ways this process imposes a singular definition of national identity upon all immigrants arriving to the United States at the end of the nineteenth century. The term *Americanization* first emerged in the 1880s as the label for the process of assimilation that new immigrants underwent to emulate the cultural values of the so-called American race.[6] Proponents of this process relied upon a number of institutional programs—including the educational, medical, and commercial programs established at Williamsburg Houses—to ensure that working-class immigrants became familiar with and learned to acculturate the "Anglo-Saxon conception of righteousness, law and order and popular government" that defined white elite culture in the states.[7] As many of the first residents for Williamsburg Houses were working-class European immigrants, it seems reasonable to ask how Lescaze's European aesthetic for the building reflects the various national origins of its residents and their status as immigrants in the United States. This chapter analyzes the critical role of racial segregation policies on the cultural pedigree of International Style public housing during the interwar period. It argues that the racial segregation policies of public housing authorities deterministically channeled the cultural meaning of International Style public housing toward a visual representation of the white diaspora then living in the United States. This narrow cultural focus unwittingly transformed exclusively white projects such as Williamsburg Houses into a material emblem for white working-class character in the United States. While Lescaze's efforts were concentrated on the outside of the building, a host of housing reformers used the interiors of this material context to precipitate the assimilation of new waves of Eastern and Southern European immigrants. In this way, the interior and exterior spaces of Williamsburg Houses performed complementary functions in the racial codification of public housing, with the architectural style providing a visual sign of the social norms encouraged by the civic dimensions of the architectural program.

In order to examine the critical influence of racial segregation and Americanization theory on the meaning of Williamsburg housing, we must first challenge some of the myths that continue to skew our understanding of public housing today. One such myth is the notion that public housing has always been associated with low-income people of color in the twentieth century. This perspective is the result of negative political campaigns to pathologize the people living in public housing as welfare queens or chronically unemployed. Such efforts continue to shape public attitudes of the historical legacy of public housing in the states. Another source of confusion comes, ironically, from scholarly studies of the antiblack attitudes that led to the underfunding and mismanagement of public housing during the postwar period. This research has revealed the patterns of de facto segregation that were perpetrated by state and federal housing authorities to maintain a high concentration of black Americans in segregated urban enclaves while working-class whites were offered subsidized home loans to move away from the city and into segregated suburbs.[8] Of course, these studies are of great benefit to us when we contextualize its findings within a broader history of housing initiatives in the states. However, if they are considered in isolation they can promote the assumption that "race" has only operated in physical settings where people of color reside. But the antiblack attitudes of the postwar period are only part of the story. Another part consists of the white racial privileges that were put in place by housing authorities in the 1930s. American public housing was racialized from its birth through the "separate but equal" laws that shaped urban demographics and the placement of public infrastructure around the nation. These very laws set the tone for the antiblack attitudes of the postwar period by normalizing public housing as an experimental context for shaping white working-class character.

The close relationship between whiteness and public housing has become so seamless that its historical function remains invisible to even those of us who are trained to be architects. And this is no accident. As Martin Berger notes, the aesthetic practices of white elites in the nineteenth century was normalized for both white and nonwhite members of society in order to ensure that this visual economy became the dominant paradigm that structured all viewers experiences of the built environment.[9] A similar critique should be made of the racial politics of American public housing. A complete narrative of American public housing can be achieved only by considering the assimilationist functions of the interwar years as a précis for the institutional abandonment that prevailed once whites no longer constituted the majority of residents of these spaces. This narrative for public housing would enable us to account for the relative abandonment of public housing by American avant-gardes in the 1950s and 1960s when it was no longer a fashionable topic for research.[10]

While federal and state authorities made careful studies of the living conditions that both whites and nonwhites enduring the living conditions of tenement slums, the plight of the white immigrant was held above that of their peers as a result of public debates on Americanization. Scientists, politicians, government administrators, and social reformers all questioned whether the historical patterns of "old" white immigrants "made up mainly of Swedes, Norwegians, English, Irish, Scotch, and Germans" were predictive of the future assimilation patterns of new waves of white immigrants arriving from Eastern and Southern Europe.[11] The white immigrant's path toward assimilation was closely documented and romanticized by social scientists, photojournalists, and even

Figure 4.3. Jacob Riis, "Old Mrs. Benoit in her Hudson St. Attic." From *Children of the Tenements* (1904), 202.

modern architects responsible for constructing a typical model of the needs and requirements of contemporary Americanization.[12] Publications such as Jacob Riis's *How the Other Half Lives* were representative of the types of images that people were trained to associate with the living conditions of the poor (fig. 4.3).

They opened readers' eyes to the class structure that then divided the nation. While these images were popularized as simple documentary photographs they became important ideological tools for motivating federal and state bureaucrats to act. Public campaigns for housing reform used this aesthetic portrait of urban poverty to measure the empirical impact of new programs on white uplift in the post-Depression years.

Within this social and political context, modern designs for public housing presented a concrete answer to the dilemma of white ethnic assimilation. The smooth white surfaces of International Styled housing in Western Europe presented a stark contrast to the soiled and derelict tenement structures new immigrants were forced to occupy—a contrast that suggested an immediate change for the better.[13] And of course, this was entirely the point. As Lescaze hints in his 1933 essay "New Deal Architecture," the payoff for spending millions of dollars on national public works programs was to lay a foundation for modernizing "American architecture."[14] While a broader recognition of Lescaze's contributions to American public housing is a good start to correcting the myopic assessments of his postwar biographers, we have yet to account for the ways his work was complicit in the racial politics of its day. The concept of Americanization provides a productive lens for analyzing the ways that Williamsburg Houses functioned as a physical instrument for shaping white working-class character during the interwar period. As a result of this civic function, it became a material emblem of the shifting state of whiteness in the American body politic. The racial discourses that conditioned Lescaze's design for this structure originated from at least two complementary institutional contexts: the first was the European pedigree of the International Style exhibit at the Museum of Modern Art (MoMA), for which Lescaze was a reluctant representative; and the second was the restrictive racial policies that US housing departments used to regulate the demographic composition and physical placement and form of public housing. Since Williamsburg Houses was located in New York City, this location will provide the geographical context of the following analysis.

Nathan Strauss, the first director of the US Housing Authority in Washington, DC, explicitly praised American architects and critics for helping him to summarize the principles of British and Western European models for social housing.[15] One figure slated for special praise was the American critic Lewis Mumford, who curated the housing section of *Modern Architecture: International Exhibit*, which first introduced New Yorkers to European trends.[16] A consistent ideal to emerge from Mumford's writings was his hope that architects could use the organic rules that regulated historical human settlements to establish new social housing typologies for advanced Western economies.[17] His notion of an organic architecture was predicated on a socially based approach to design that treated the visual aesthetic of social housing as a functional reflection of the social and cultural demands of mass culture then influencing major centers of Western Europe.[18] This ideal was repeated in several other seminal texts, from Carol Aronovici's *Housing and the Housing Problem* (1920), Edith Elmer Wood's *Housing Progress in Western Europe* (1923), and Louis Pink's *The New Day in Housing* (1928) to Catherine Bauer's *Modern Housing* (1934).

Ironically, it was the homogenous character of European social housing that gave some conservative American politicians pause, precisely for the confusion this might introduce for a new American type: a vocal lobby of bankers, real estate investors, tenement owners, and Congressional leaders expressed concern that the socialist associations of a European building style might taint the public reception of American public housing as deviating from the capitalist and free market basis of the nation.[19] This situation presented a unique conundrum for American critics: how were they to convince American legislators that a domestic program for public housing could be visually distinguished from European models while still emulating the social and technical standards that made them desirable in the first place?

Mumford, Bauer, and Clarence Stein were among the most prominent figures to assuage these conservative fears by theorizing the possibility of a homegrown system for regulating public housing that organically emerged from the social values and economic basis of American democracy.[20] The content of Lescaze's "New Deal Architecture" suggests that he was fully supportive of employing the principles of architectural organicism to produce new vernacular forms. Not only was he familiar with the writings of leading American critics on this subject, he was also exposed to European theories of architectural organicism that were based on the natural metaphors for design, outlined in previous chapters.[21] Within this politicized context, Lescaze's proposal that Franklin Delano Roosevelt's New Deal should constitute the social basis of a modern American architecture should not be taken as an incidental statement.[22] These words represent his first steps toward creating a "definite architectural theory" that he believed would shape the meaning of American public housing.[23]

Governmental efforts to reform working-class character were an institutional response to public perceptions of the sociological causes of urban poverty. The general influence of scientific debates on racial character are apparent in some of the advertising the New York City Housing Authority (NYCHA) used to build support for its public housing programs. One poster from 1936 draws an explicit connection between the dilapidated living conditions of New York's slums and the high rate of criminality measured in poor white demographics (see plate 9). Turn-of-the-century studies conducted by the Prison Association of New York supported the view that a stable home life was the key to minimizing criminality in working-class communities.[24] In response to this model home ideal, the diagonal text of this poster promises that a "cure" for juvenile delinquency will be found in the modernization of working-class housing stock. This image visualizes the class-based fears many harbored of poor whites living in neglected districts of the city, and in terms of its visual economy, contains a simultaneous message of hope and despair: the crime that is born out of need can be entirely eliminated if one's natural environment is functionally considered.[25]

It is interesting that the ominous male figure of this image is stigmatized only for his poverty, not for his race. This option for redemption was not open to every racial group. Khalil Gibran Muhammad notes in *The Condemnation of Blackness* the role of sociological studies of racial character in normalizing a pathological image of black criminality in the late nineteenth century.[26] According to Muhammad, a consensus on the irredeemable state of black racial character was used to legitimize the separate-but-equal policies in the states.[27] However, the racial character of poor whites was routinely perceived as redeemable if caught at an early age or pathological in a small aberrant minority. Emulating the structure of these sociological studies, this NYCHA poster offers a road to reform for the white working classes negatively affected by the poor state of their surroundings. This scientific perspective on racial character fed the race-based fears of residential integration programs that motivated an enforcement of separate-but-equal laws in official housing policy.[28]

Another paradigm of working-class character to influence housing policy originated from architecture in the form of Garden City planning theory. Some of the most famous writers in this field romanticized images of the medieval English cottage for recalling a premodern era when the needs of a population were perfectly harmonized with the means of local construction.[29] Modern architects used this reference to vernacular forms to inspire their own version of functional simplicity in working-class environments. Such rhetoric also contributed to the popularity of Garden City principles among housing bureaucrats in the early years of the NYCHA.[30]

After public housing became an official component of municipal budgets, the moral language surrounding its use grew on several fronts: the "efficient" use of public funds became a moral issue for politicians, as did the selection of the right types of residents to live within these modernized public housing units. Even the aesthetics of public housing was up for debate, as many reformers desired architectural forms capable of communicating the symbolic cleansing that this modernization represented for the nation's working classes. The contentious battles over the moral rhetoric of these debates was also visualized by the diagrams modern architects used to substantiate the superior "efficiency" of their functionalist housing programs. Lescaze mastered this language for public presentation of his early ideas, which compared the proportion of land use left open by his cruciform plans and those remaining from courtyard-oriented plans (fig. 4.4).

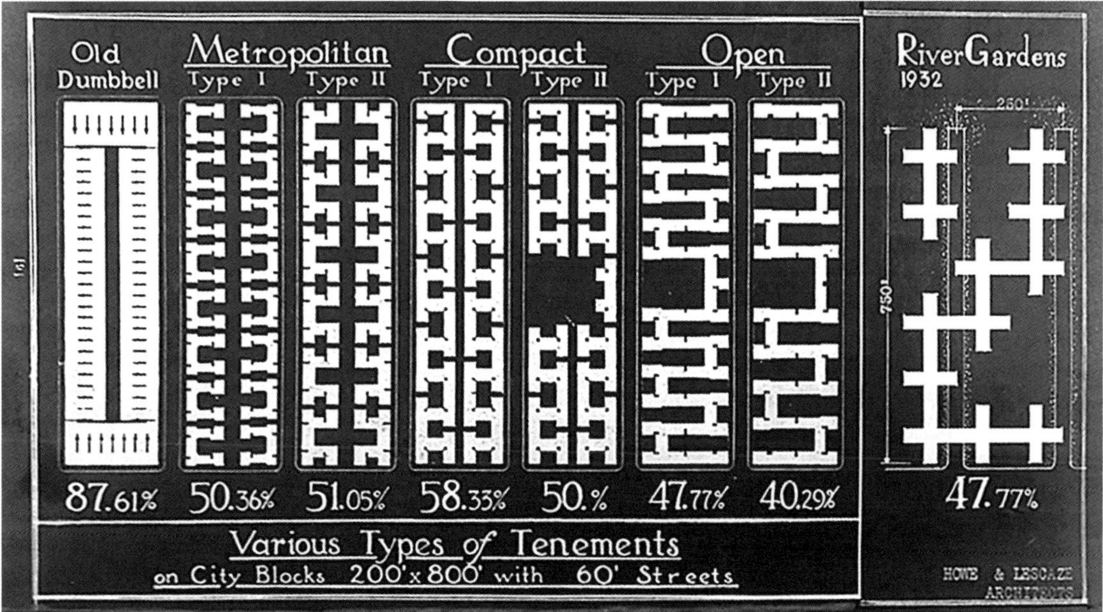

Figure 4.4. A comparative diagram of the efficiency of William Lescaze's solution for River Gardens Housing, an unbuilt project for Manhattan's Lower East Side, and other housing types of the late nineteenth century. WELA, Special Collections Research Center, Syracuse University.

The historical movement to institutionalize public housing in New York City resulted in an uneven synthesis of middle-class interpretations of public morality, from the lingering Victorian notions of domestic propriety and decency to modernist notions of rationality and efficiency. Resolving these ideological tensions was no simple task. Yet people found a way of collaborating in the new institutional landscape that emerged to manage this public trust. The debates on working-class character became a subject of intense interest for all the parties responsible for managing American public housing during the interwar period.

The Architectural Reform of Working-Class Character

Leading avant-garde architects in France, Germany, Britain, and the United States were engaged in researching the topic of public housing to find ways of creating a new vernacular building typology that established a visual analogue between international norms of working-class character and the functional and technological demands of working-class life. These figures collectively speculated on the best ways to determine what principles guided mass culture in advanced modernized nations and diagnose the most pressing problems of low-income communities in order to be successful. It was in this spirit that the

US government began to commission documentary surveys of urban poverty to provide an empirical baseline for assessing the social problems generated by contemporary urban living conditions. Riis's turn-of-the-century study of poverty in New York's tenements is perhaps the most famous example of this genre of literature that first raised public interest in the urban poor. As a reporter, Riis was dedicated to elevating public discourse, but as a reformer he knew that he must directly address "the half that was on top" of the class ladder if he wanted to initiate the institutional momentum to change the living conditions of "the other half" at the bottom.[31]

In retrospect, Riis's survey of working-class poverty is an important visual documentation of the beleaguered state of white racial character as it was experienced by Eastern and Southern European immigrants. While he records the lives of many different racial groups—the table of contents lists the Italians, Jews, Chinese, and African Americans specifically—a good degree of his primary subjects were members of European immigrant groups or the "submerged middle classes" of white citizens still suffering from the economic downturn of the Depression years.[32] Riis's survey brought wider visibility to the living conditions of white urban poverty, as did Mumford's narration of documentary films that directly contrasted the poorly designed tenements of New York City with the healthful environments of Radburn, New Jersey—a suburban community designed by his peer Clarence Stein.[33] These visual surveys reveal the extent to which the public imaginary of New York's urban poor was figured by a vulnerable but seemingly redeemable class of white foreigners. Riis's documentary attitude toward photography parallels the interests of nineteenth-century ethnographers who previously used pencil and paper to capture the essential traits of the world's racial and national characteristics. The only difference was that the world seemed to come directly to Riis through the gates of Ellis Island. His study rarely detailed the specific functions of the physical objects associated with the expressive or material cultures of recent immigrants. He kept his focus on the conditions of squalor that seemed to arise from one's class status. This narrow framework treats these objects of culture as a mere visual extension of the rubbish and filth that hindered the immigrant's acquisition of greater comfort and stability. Abandoning any trace of the foreign elements of their past life was one of the costs of assimilation.

The critical assumption that race and place were organically integrated in vernacular architectural styles likely elevated the public's interests in modern architectural debates. If the clean white spaces of private modern housing prototypes provided a visual proof of this elite class's fitness for modern society, then perhaps a physical transformation of the urban ghetto into an equally clean and neat space might be enough to transform the moral character of the city's forgotten working classes (fig. 4.5). Such a line of reasoning was implicit in museum

Figure 4.5. A family of six pose in their new living room at Williamsburg Houses, November 4, 1938. Photo #02.006.1161, La Guardia Archives, LaGuardia Community College, New York.

exhibits, journal articles, and magazine essays of the time. At least one *New York Times* article covering MoMA's 1932 exhibition on modern housing made this suggestion to readers. The unnamed author textually compels future tenants to measure up to the modest sense of decorum and reserve that is required of a truly modern citizens: "Each of these last projects, by the way, is represented by an elaborate model and each is doubly interesting—first, as a piece of ingenious machinery and second, as an index of what the standardized tenant of the future (the fellow who has to pay minimum rent) is expected 'internationally' to be like. In New York, as in Germany, he is expected to be tame and neat. In Germany he has three times as much space to be tame and neat in."[34] This article intimates that the "tame and neat" characteristics required of modern tenants was physical proof of a transformation of working-class character; a visual ideal that was meant to saturate both the upper and lower ends of the housing market in the modernized world.

Progressive Era philanthropists first pushed the idea in the United States that social housing was an invaluable tool for reforming the morality and intellectual capacities of working-class residents during the late nineteenth century.[35] This social instrumentalization continued into the twentieth century with government-funded public housing, most of which was rendered in some variation of Williamsburg Houses in New York City in the 1930s and 1940s.[36] Yet the social and economic opportunities these residences opened up for working-class Americans was not applied equally among those in need. State and federal policies mandating the segregation of public housing initially constructed the greatest number and the most progressive housing experiments in white working-class neighborhoods.[37] When race riots and public protests in black neighborhoods caused New York City mayor Fiorello La Guardia to finally relent and construct new spaces for black residents, the participants who were chosen were purposefully gleaned from families with the most financial and material resources to prevent any backslides into poverty so as not to taint the public's perception of the future promise of public housing.[38]

The first federally funded and state-managed International Style public housing project in New York City was Williamsburg Houses in North Brooklyn. Its planning began in 1932, the same year that Henry-Russell Hitchcock and Philip Johnson cocurated the International Style exhibit at MoMA that introduced this universal mode of building to New York audiences. The modern aesthetic of Williamsburg Houses helped inaugurate a new phase of New Deal housing policy in New York state. Administrators of the recently formed NYCHA decided to abandon their former policy of renovating existing tenement structures or subsidizing limited-dividend projects for the full-scale implementation of a municipally funded and managed housing system. Two prominent modern architects were chosen to spearhead the design for Williamsburg Houses. Richard Shreve of Lamb & Shreve was selected as the chief architect because of his contributions to the construction of the Empire State Building, which became an emblematic monument to New York City's strength to ride out the Depression years. William Lescaze of Howe & Lescaze was chosen as the lead designer, however, for his contributions to *Modern Architecture: International Exhibition*, including his design of the Chrystie-Forsyth public housing complex that was intended to become a public housing structure for working-class residents on Manhattan's Lower East Side (fig. 4.6).[39] Both Shreve and Lescaze were actively reforming the aesthetics of New York City's architecture in the first half of the 1930s to reflect new modes of design, with Shreve as a representative of art deco and Lescaze of the international style. Each served in their own way as translators of the hopes and dreams embodied in Roosevelt's New Deal

Figure 4.6. Model of Chrystie-Forsyth Housing Development, *Modern Architecture: International Exhibition* (New York: Museum of Modern Art, 1932), 146.

policies at the federal level, La Guardia's reform efforts in New York City, and nearly three generations of housing reformers across the country. Lescaze was so convinced that public housing would become an important building typology that he invented the phrase "New Deal Architecture" to identify the range of new building types that would emerge from Roosevelt's political activism.[40]

La Guardia's inauguration as the ninety-ninth mayor of New York City announced a new era of political reform in the city.[41] Although he had been involved in city politics for many years, even serving as the deputy attorney general of New York and a representative in the US House of Representatives, La Guardia was an outsider to the Irish-led bureaucrats of the Democratic machine that had directed local governance for nearly eight decades.[42] La Guardia was also a member of the Fusion party, a political group that emerged in order to clean out the nepotism and corruption facilitated by Tammany Hall politics. In addition, he was a Republican in a traditionally Democratic stronghold. His close association with Roosevelt, a prominent Democrat and president of the United States, is generally attributed to their common interests in reform instead of any common party affiliation. In cultural terms, La Guardia represented a departure from the traditional biographical profile of New York City political candidates: a loud, brash son of an Italian father and an Italian Jewish mother, he emerged as an unlikely alternative to the old-monied WASP and Irish establishment candidates of the 1910s and 1920s. His victory was in no small part enabled by voter dissatisfaction with Tammany Hall's response to the Depression and the rise of white ethnic working-class communities in New York, including the radical Jewish and Italian laborers who formed socialist labor unions. These communities developed strong political alliances with reform movements while maintaining ties back home through local newspapers published in their native languages, such as the *Jewish Daily Forward* and the Italian *Il Progresso*. While each group inherited distinct ethnic and cultural traditions from the Old World, they were forced to work with other groups of nonnatives in the United States to secure fair wages and rent controls.

A prominent example of the white immigrant cooperation mentioned above was the formation of interethnic labor unions that performed communal activities on the behalf of new immigrant populations. During the 1920s and 1930s the Amalgamated Clothing Workers of America (ACWA) actively recruited members from a broad base of European immigrants living in New York at the turn of the century. Its founder, Sidney Hillman, had a long history of establishing Jewish cultural and business organizations.[43] Hillman served on federal committees such as the National Recovery Administration in Roosevelt's administration, which contributed to organized labor being a major force in Democratic elections. Such connections enabled Hillman to advocate for Jewish immigrants and Jewish American citizens' rights locally and federally. In 1927, under the leadership of then president Abraham E. Kazan, the ACWA extended its purview from organized labor to collective housing with the construction of a cooperative housing complex in the Bronx.[44] This structure was situated on an entire block of Sedgwick Avenue between Saxon and Dickinson Avenues. The overall site plan maintained the tradition of perimeter block housing with subdivided interior courtyards that was established by philanthropic organizations during the Progressive Era.[45] The ACWA formed a corporation to manage the construction of this project, which became the first limited-dividend company to operate under the Limited Dividends Housing Companies Act that Governor Alfred E. Smith signed into law in 1926. In order to raise the funds necessary to begin, the ACWA performed outreach to potential residents through their credit union, which enabled members to directly contribute a part of their savings or to take out a loan in order to become a partial owner in this endeavor.[46] Funds from prospective tenants were advanced to secure one-third of the construction

Figure 4.7. "Eastside Dwellings, Hillman Housing"—Courtyard with empty fountain. Photo by Wide World Studio, 289 West 43rd Street, New York City, n.d. Kheel Center, Cornell University.

costs, with the Metropolitan Life Insurance Company advancing the remaining two-thirds of the $2 million budget.

In 1930 the architects George W. Springsteen and Albert Goldhammer were commissioned to design a second cooperative housing structure for ACWA—the six-story, 236-apartment Amalgamated Dwellings—on the Lower East Side of Manhattan (figs. 4.7, 4.8). It was fitted with several communal functions, including "a monthly bulletin, nursery school, forums, [and] recreational facilities" as well as a collective means of purchasing "milk, electricity and food."[47] The creation of a monthly newsletter provides evidence of the importance of the media in establishing neighborhood cohesion: it was common for housing administrators to cooperate with existing resident-run newsletters, or create new ones, to foster a sense of community.

Figure 4.8. "Grand St., Manhattan- Amalgamated Dwellings Inc.—Limited Dividend Co-operative Apartments." Doorways into building. Photo by Albert Rothschild Photographer, 324 W. 42nd Street, New York City, n.d. Kheel Center, Cornell University.

Figure 4.9. "Architects sketch of the Sidney Hillman Development under construction on the New York East Side." Drawing of apartment buildings. Photographer and date unknown. Kheel Center, Cornell University.

Another important aspect of these early ACWA projects is how closely they presaged the diverse aesthetic components of Williamsburg Houses. Both Williamsburg Houses and Amalgamated Dwellings combined the traditional brickwork of Progressive Era housing structures with the carved art deco ornamentation reminiscent of local commercial buildings and the naked concrete detailing of European social housing experiments. Amalgamated Dwellings projected a relatively minimalist building façade toward the street edge, which is in keeping with later developments in International Style public housing in New York City. However, there are some key differences, in both the architectural detailing of these buildings and their site orientations. For example, Amalgamated Dwellings is activated by a greater sense of historical revivalism than its successor, including its use of architectural ornamentation. A key point of comparison is the imposing entry archways that recall romantic medieval imagery in Amalgamated Dwellings, as do the brick quoins that trace the corners of each projecting volume (figs. 4.9 and 4.10). The use of art deco surrounds in Amalgamated Dwellings is visually heavier than that found at Williamsburg Houses as well, which in the latter case soars above the doorways as ornamentation for stainless steel marquees instead of being anchored to the

Figure 4.10. "Amalgamated Housing Lower east Side, New York City." Arch. Photographer's stamp: Sam Reiss, 2907 Kingsbridge Ter. Bx. 63, N.Y., n.d. Kheel Center, Cornell University.

ground as stone carvings. Despite these differences, however, Lescaze expressed a desire to preserve Amalgamated Dwellings in his 1930s speculative designs for a River Gardens development on Manhattan's Lower East Side, a project that was never built (see plate 10). Amalgamated Dwellings and Williamsburg Houses represent two explicit attempts to visualize the collective character of working-class communities in New York City, which was especially important for the white ethnic immigrant communities gaining new power to physically shape their living environment. They balanced similar historical and aesthetic factors, including the popular associations of brick, art deco ornamentation, and the public reception of European modernism.

At least one period guidebook describes Williamsburg as the home of a "polyglot population" of white ethnic immigrants that included native Italians, Germans, and Jews, among others.[48] The 1903 construction of the Williamsburg Bridge precipitated the infusion of many white working-class families from the Lower East Side into what was previously a wealthy suburban enclave. These demographic migrations resulted in a dramatic physical transformation of the area. While there was always a persistent African American minority living in Williamsburg's Southside neighborhood between 1900 and 1940, this population thinned out over time and the area quickly became associated with white working classes until the influx of Puerto Rican immigrants in the 1960s.[49] The NYCHA worked both officially and unofficially with neighborhood entities to insulate this demographically shifting area from further black integration by segregating nonwhite communities in Central Harlem and building separate public housing complexes in this area. When asked by black activists as to whether the NYCHA would racially integrate new public housing projects around New York City, Mary Simkhovitch, a prominent housing activist and the vice-chair of the NYCHA, stated that the socially progressive efforts of the authority would be unduly endangered by an integrationist stance on public housing.[50] Instead, the authority focused its attention on promoting class uplift for white and black residents by constructing segregated housing projects in distinct enclaves. However, the distribution in early years favored the construction of white residential units. In this way, the NYCHA used the inclusive language of class uplift to mask the divisive racial politics that was situated at the heart of this movement.

If Williamsburg Houses came to represent the most progressive image of International Style public housing in the late 1930s, then the restrictive racial covenants regulating its construction almost guaranteed that the racial character of this structure would remain white, monolingual, and aspirationally middle-class in the eyes of the public. A survey taken by the National Association for the Advancement of Colored People and the American Civil Liberties Union shows only slight progress on reforming this vision by 1947: of the 1,622 residents living in Williamsburg Houses, only 34 were "Negro," and the residents of these units were carefully selected by the authority to be the most politically moderate and economically middle class of all the applicants.[51] These late concessions were primarily due to worries of pending judicial decisions that threatened to outlaw segregation in federally funded projects, and even then such prompts only elicited minimal efforts from the NYCHA to ensure that the percentage of black residents to gain access to predominantly white housing projects remained as minimal as possible.

The US housing department's official policy of racial segregation reflected the abject characteristics that modernist architects associated with black culture in modern architectural debates. European designers such as Le Corbusier simultaneously praised the primitive or instinctive genius of blacks to create the modern idiom of jazz while insisting that black Americans were too limited to engage with the rationalist principles that were required to create a modern architecture.[52] The combination of these institutional factors resulted in the upward mobility and the social mixing of white ethnic subjects at the expense of nonwhite social uplift. This perspective is confirmed by the path through which African Americans historically secured public housing in New York City; namely, through consistent public protests and the moral critique of the racial exclusivity of public housing policy in newspapers, speeches, and other venues available in the counterpublic sphere.

New York City was racked by two prominent race riots during La Guardia's term as mayor, once in 1935 and again in 1942.[53] While each incident was precipitated by interactions between police and private citizens, the issue of public housing stoked the fires of protest before and after these two riots.[54] La Guardia did not fully capitulate to black demands for new public housing until the race riot in Harlem in 1935, leading to the design and construction of Harlem River Houses in 1936–1937.[55] In 1942 he approved the construction of Stuyvesant Town on the basis that black residents not be permitted to apply at all. Before the construction of Harlem River Houses, minority reporters for the black newspaper *New York Amsterdam News* feverishly covered the issue of public housing for their readers.[56] Not only were reporters made aware of the construction of new building projects but the exclusion of African American applicants to Williamsburg Houses was the subject of several articles published in 1937: "Although under construction for nearly two years and more than one-third filled, the New York City Housing Authority continues to bar Negroes as tenants in the Williamsburg Houses. No attempt has even been made to investigate the eligibility of the Negro families that have made applications for apartments, it was learned."[57]

In some cases, the very words of Langdon Post, NYCHA's first chairman, were used to challenge the NYCHA's assessment that Harlem was not an ideal location for experimentation. In a *New York Times* article published in 1935, Post legitimized the need for social housing with three main criteria: the introduction of fireproof construction in new developments; the reduction of crime (and thus, the improvement of moral character) in low-income neighborhoods; and the elimination of disease. By virtue of low land values, overcrowding living conditions, and annual crime statistics, Harlem seemed to be one of the areas in most urgent need of public housing.[58] Yet the NYCHA selected a predominantly white neighborhood to construct its most expensive public housing project. The $12.5 million price tag of the building construction (as well as the land acquisition costs and the economic stimulus it prompted in Williamsburg) was also proudly reported upon in the *Brooklyn Daily Eagle*, a neighborhood newspaper for the largely white ethnic residents of Williamsburg.[59]

In contrast to the pointed racial character of the news coverage in the *Amsterdam News*, the only exclusion that seemed to worry white Brooklynites was the possible omission of family pets in new public housing units. In an article that spread across three-quarters of the front page, titled "Fido's Locked Out of Uncle Sam's Williamsburg Houses," the issue of pet ownership was heavily discussed. This article was accompanied by before-and-after images of the district and a close-up of the modernized interior of a model apartment.[60] Given the lack of coverage on the racial segregation policies of the NYCHA, it is understandable that black activists and political leaders considered International Style public housing to be the relative privilege of white ethnic groups in these early years.

The tone of protest found in the articles published in the *Amsterdam News* explicitly demonstrates the lengths to which black Americans would go in order to participate in the progressive modernization of New York City. The Brooklyn Urban League offered to screen residents from "Brownsville, Williamsburg, Bedford, Stuyvesant and Navy Yard districts" in order to ensure there were enough qualified candidates to enter Williamsburg Houses.[61] However, Harold Ickes, the commissioner of the federal Public Works Administration (PWA), announced that only whites would be queried for inclusion in this space. The fact that Harlem River Houses was only included as an afterthought to the NYCHA's construction program lends weight to the notion that a pan-European conception of the International Style provided yet another ideological legitimation for reserving the most modern environments for white ethnic communities in New York City. This makes the eventual turn to the interwar conception of public housing as a permanent black space that much more ironic—it took only twenty years for the consolidation of the white working class to mature enough to accrue the social and economic capital necessary to flee these housing projects. By this time the eventual inclusion of black residents into International Style public housing was one of the major factors to finally unravel the optimism that marks the introduction of Lescaze's "New Deal Architecture." The Supreme Court's elimination of segregated federal housing alongside newly established segregationist policies for federally subsidized veterans' home loans guaranteed that the struggle to integrate public housing would continue in detached suburban home developments. It seemed that racial integration was destined to continue haunting the modernization of American housing well into the postwar period.

The European Pedigree of *Modern Architecture: International Exhibition*

The pan-European intellectual framework for the *Modern Architecture: International Exhibition* at MoMA evolved from the discrete interests of its two cocurators: the American architect and critic Philip Johnson and the architectural historian Henry-Russell Hitchcock. When Johnson was appointed as the first secretary of the newly established Department of Modern Architecture within MoMA in the early twentieth century, he consciously envisioned that this department would serve as an institutional headquarters for propagandizing the dissemination of European aesthetic ideas to the American public. Johnson reached out to Hitchcock in 1930 to plan the museum's first exhibit on modern architecture. This process took nearly two years as Johnson traveled across the United States and Western Europe with family and friends to create a list of works to be included in this exhibition.[62] Hitchcock was an important addition to this exhibition, as he had become one of the most respected scholars of modern architecture at this time. His first book-length study of the subject, *Modern Architecture: Romanticism and Reintegration* (1929), constructs a linear and progressive narrative of the gradual transformation of distinct national architectural styles into a commonly shared international building culture.

Part 1 of this monograph outlines "The Age of Romanticism," which examines the picturesque representation of organic concepts through architectural ornament. According to Hitchcock, the architect's emulation of painting and poetry unduly elevated the aesthetic function of architectural ornament above all other factors of building. This phase of development is interpreted as an interruption of the structural principles of modern architectural style later exemplified in Gothic architectures:

> For the phases through which European architecture has passed since the culmination of the High Gothic in the thirteenth century are not to be considered as constituting successive independent styles comparable to those of the earlier past, the Greek or the Egyptian for example, but rather as subsidiary manners of one Modern style. Those architects and builders who have worked within this Modern style have had on the one hand more or less conscious intellectual interests in abstract form and have frequently preferred experiment to the continuance of tradition. But on the other hand, their free tendencies have until the last few years been balanced by a sentimental desire to recall one or several styles of the far past and by an inertia which has caused a considerable retention of the features of style of the near past.[63]

Hitchcock's rejection of Romanticism, or the "organic" rhetoric of the nineteenth century, is slightly confusing for a contemporary reader because it is primarily used to describe the picturesque representation of naturalistic forms. In contrast to this philosophy, several nineteenth-century architecture theorists used organic concepts in a direct attempt to metaphorically emulate the generative principles of nature, not just its external forms. Such an interpretation was manifest by nineteenth-century theorists such as Eugène Emmanuel Viollet-le-Duc and Gottfried Semper, who equally celebrated the integration of form and function in medieval forms, especially the ecclesiastical structures of France. Thus, Hitchcock's defense of the synthetic integration of all building elements dovetails with an alternative approach to "organic" design during the height of Romanticism.[64]

Part 2 of Hitchcock's *Modern Architecture* examines the historical emergence of "The New Tradition" that gave birth to a style of architecture that is finally free of all forms of eclecticism, or what he called sentimental revivals of exterior ornamentation. Part 3 isolates "The New Pioneers" of this movement, with France, Holland, and Germany leading the way. According to Hitchcock, International Style architectures began in Western Europe and were disseminated by a few key figures to lands as far away as North America, Russia, and Japan.

The European pedigree of International Style architecture was most firmly established by the coauthored exhibition catalog *The International Style: Architecture since 1922* (1932), which Hitchcock published with Johnson. This text continues Hitchcock's formal interpretation of modern architecture, but establishes a starker contrast between the Romantic traditions of the past and present by providing the impression of a more radical shift in contemporary developments. This change results in a more unified interpretation of the International Style, which was outlined by three formal criteria: the visual expression of interior volumes, the visual expression of interior structure, and the rejection of applied ornament.

In the eyes of most architectural historians, the latter criterion undoes the synthetic relationship established between space, structure, and ornament by nineteenth-century theorists of architectural organicism. However, despite the avowed rejection of applied ornament, *International Style* does in fact discuss the manner in which aggregated building materials such as brick and tile can be applied in the modern fashion. Thus, any explicit attempt to emulate the embodied or monolithic character of stucco or concrete is offered as a proper modern aesthetic. These options are discussed openly in the section titled "Surfacing Materials." After outlining the demerits of brick as a traditional building material, Johnson and Hitchcock claim, "Nevertheless, much can be done to emphasize continuity of surface. If the color of the mortar be near that of the brick, and the bricks relatively even in value and texture, the bonding pattern need not be strikingly evident. The actual material of a wall surface of considerable area is then relatively inconspicuous. . . . Since brick is permanent in color and not subject to cracking and streaking, it is in the long run actually superior aesthetically to stucco for large-scale constructions."[65] Four architectural precedents are offered as evidence of the modern potential of brick as a monolithic material: the Jakob Kolb Soap factory in Zurich (1930), by Theodor Merrill; the Konigsgrube Mine Works in Bochum, Germany (1930), by Kellermüller and Hofmann; the Lange House in Krefeld, Germany (1928), by Mies van der Rohe; and the city employment office in Dessau, Germany (1928), by Walter

Gropius. Tile is discussed immediately thereafter: "In the range of constructions of medium cost and medium size glazed tile laid with continuous vertical as well as horizontal joints provides a material that vies in aesthetic effectiveness with plate sheathing. . . . The shape of the units may be such that all suggestion of the traditional masonry block is lost. The texture is smooth and permanent; the color possibilities are wide. . . . Tiles properly laid give even more surely than bricks a continuous surface pattern like the texture of a fabric. They also quite avoid the suggestion of a supporting masonry wall."[66] The façade of J. W. Lerh's Volksstimme Building in Frankfurt (1929) is offered as a precedent for the modern potential of tiled surfaces.

Lescaze would apply the aesthetic principles of these very passages in his design for Williamsburg Houses, completed just seven years after the International Style exhibition. This can be taken either as a compromise of strict stylistic standards due to budgetary reasons or as an aesthetic attempt to create the illusion of a bounded volume, just as was prescribed by the exhibition catalog. Either way, the synthetic relationship between space, structure, and ornament that bound architectural organicism in the past is clearly relevant in the design of Williamsburg Houses.

Architectural historians have long hinted at Lescaze's critical role in bridging the aesthetic positions expressed by social housing in Western Europe and the United States, though few have fully accounted for the white racial politics that regulated the transatlantic dissemination of ideas.[67] The European pedigree of the MoMA exhibit establishes a discursive relationship between the achievements of Western European avant-gardes and the relative social status of white ethic diasporas living in the United States. Upon closer examination, the political commitments of the International Style were not theoretically universal, as many have claimed, but instead constructed new alignments within the existing patterns of international cultures that influenced the Euro-American modernist avant-garde. The shifting alignments of this cultural legacy affected its reception in the United States by serving as a class-equalizing agent for white ethnic immigrants that could claim a distinct kinship with European cultures. When interpreted through the lens of character, the racial polarization of New York City's public housing market merely deepened the cultural pedigree already implicit in the 1932 International Style exhibit. The transatlantic character of this formulation was a fundamental aspect of the tensions that emerged between national and international interpretations of modern culture and its expansion around the globe.

By the time African Americans became full beneficiaries of modern public housing in the postwar period, the avant-gardist wave behind this amenity had given way to the new frontier of suburban housing. As public housing became the rear guard of official state and federal housing policies, it more explicitly reflected a racially stigmatized—and class-stigmatized—context. White middle classes, now uplifted by older public housing environments, moved on to the newly modernizing suburbs, while poor blacks remained segregated in ghettoes and were forever out of step with mainstream architectural modernism. In this sense, the specter of integration continued to haunt the universalist claims of International Style public housing in New York from its inception in the 1930s to late in the postwar period. The racial associations of postwar US public housing can be traced back to the racial politics of International Style architectures during the 1930s.

A fully fledged organicist interpretation of International Styled public housing appears in the third and final section of *Modern Architecture: International Exhibition*. The homogenous character of brick and concrete housing projects constructed in Germany and the United States was interpreted as an aesthetic index of the collective modern lifestyle that became possible by means of mass production techniques. Mumford describes what he believed was an inverse relationship between the homogenous character of modern architectural environments and the eventual liberation of an individual's personality: "As the background becomes more standardized, so that it no longer applies to a single caste but a whole community, no longer to a single community but a whole civilization, so will the foreground become more individuated. Here we have in architectural taste that necessity for combining the intimate and the individualized, which we find in the region, with the generic and universalized, which we shall find only in the widening of the processes of culture to our whole planet. The common ground will thus become broader."[68] The architectural projects used to illustrate this modern aesthetic included Clarence Stein and Henry Wright's Sunnyside housing project in Long Island (1924) along with a second in Radburn, New Jersey (1928); Springsteen and Hammer's Amalgamated Dwellings (1939); Otto Haesler's Rothenberg Housing in Kassel (1930); J. J. P. Oud's Kiefhoek Housing Development (1928); and Ernst May's Römerstadt Housing Development in Frankfurt (1927). The European projects all consisted of white monolithic *Siedlungen*, while the American projects consisted of minimalist two-to-three-story brick volumes.

Though the housing section of this exhibit is generally attributed to the writings and theory of Mumford, he contributed very little to the final catalog and composition of the show. Instead, three of his closest associates—Bauer, Stein, and Wright—contributed works that kept to the broader principles of his thought.[69] Sample text was also taken from previous writings of Mumford or exposés on public housing in the national press.[70] Mumford was principally known as a contemporary critic of city and urban development. Trained by Patrick Geddes, the Scottish biologist and town planner, Mumford interpreted cities as an organic outgrowth or exponent of local cultures and customs. His theory appeared in massive anthologies, newspaper columns, and even documentary films such as *The City*, which appeared in 1939.[71] The organicist language he used to describe city development became a common element of interwar housing debates. Reformers such as Bauer and Louis Pink likewise attributed the formal character of modern social housing experiments found in Germany, France, and Great Britain to an organic connection between the lifestyle of mass-produced culture and the development of a new standard in housing. This socioaesthetic relationship was thought to parallel those obtained in earlier forms of Heimat culture, including the medieval cottage architectures of the English and German countryside.

Pink and Bauer spent a considerable amount of time visiting and documenting built examples of social housing in Great Britain and Western Europe. Their travels across the Atlantic helped them establish the political and aesthetic rhetoric that housing reformers used to direct the movement in the United States as well as popularize European avant-garde designs with nonprofessional audiences. One common criterion they both used to assess the success of modern housing was the organic character of each design, or the visual expression of the social integration that was achieved in each project. In Pink's *New Day in Housing* and Bauer's *Modern Housing*, the social cohesion of working-class residents was represented by an overriding visual aesthetic that overtly expressed the new vernacular standard for modern living. This modern vernacularism was littered with comparative moralistic readings of premodern and modern housing settlements, especially when these environments were designed for the working classes. A neopastoralism was prominent among British designers of Garden City communities, which were directly inspired by medieval housing fabric. Such projects explicitly revived the visual aesthetic of the cottage house situated within its bucolic landscape while introducing a unified urban fabric for composing newly aggregated housing units in satellite new towns on the city's periphery.

Bauer believed that the natural progression from this pastoralism to "a new kind of order in the human environment" would be manifest by the integrated visual aesthetic of modern housing at the level of the superblock.[72] She translated this search for holism into a general principle of design: "A single building is not a painting hung in a gallery—it is rather an arm or a leg or a spinal column of a larger organism which, if it is healthy, we may call architecture. If buildings do not express an integrated society (or at least a desire for such society) they merely state the fact that society is discordant—and little more."[73] This sentiment continues and revises the stylistic implications of nineteenth-century architectural organicism. By claiming that architecture is a social art, Bauer emulates nineteenth-century paradigms of architecture as a direct exponent of social order, which required national character and architectural character to mirror one another in human civilization. Yet the organic principles that formerly directed the visual articulation of a building's tectonic features in architectural ornament were now stretched to regulate the visual integration of an entire urban district.

In this sense, the scale for patterns of a site plan for a Siedlungen apartment block in Germany or the plan geometry of a Garden City district in the United Kingdom replaced the scale of Louis Sullivan's elevational studies for botanical ornament. These interwar revisions to architectural organicism effectively displaced the strategic importance of visual ornament in modern architecture in service of unifying the visual aesthetic of a building to represent the growing anonymity of mass culture. In order to better express the collective character of an entire district—the scale that Sullivan and other Chicago Style architects had yearned to reach in the nineteenth century—the modern architect turned his gaze away from ornamenting the individual object to regulating the visual cohesion of the city block. This left the architect to express the truth of materials by overtly displaying them to the eye. If concrete could not be used to produce a monolithic aesthetic, then brick and tile could be combined with colored mortar to preserve this effect from the building scale to the block.

Williamsburg Houses and the Physical Embodiment of Whiteness

As a Swiss émigré to the United States, William Lescaze epitomized both the European pedigree that the International Style came to be associated with in New York in the 1930s and the Americanization that political elites desired for new immigrants. Lescaze had trained across the Atlantic with the protomodernist Karl Moser in Switzerland and Henri Sauvage in France before migrating to the United States and naturalizing as a citizen. Yet despite the international roots of his design philosophy, Lescaze strove to refine the American character of his architectural practice. By 1942, in his autobiography *On Being an Architect*, he was convinced that modern man must have both national and international traits to live in contemporary society: "There is nothing more or less 'international' about 'modern' architecture than there is about 'modern' man. They are both international and national. Man, wherever he has appeared, has followed the same general design. The Prussian general, the Spanish fisherman, the Eskimo, the cowboy, the American tycoon are basically international and national. The nationalism always shows up in the details, in the way of walking, talking, language, the food eaten, the clothes worn—and so it does in buildings. Modern architecture is as international and as national as was Gothic architecture."[74] This viewpoint departed from the most polemical claims of international style theorists that praised the homogeneity of the new art. These claims limited the presence of nationalist factors to nonarchitectural elements such as furniture, language, clothing, and other specimens in the practical arts.

While Lescaze rejected the use of applied ornament and recognized the critical function of the practical arts for exhibiting local flourishes, he held on to the possibility that a building still contained the capacity to express formal particularity in its own right. Like Sullivan before him, Lescaze continued to define style as a visual exponent of the cultural condition that produced period forms. The latent romanticism of this position is manifest in the continued relevance of particularity, although it is now restricted to "the details" that were not outlawed by international style debates: the underlying spatial and material constituents of architectural form. Lescaze's interpretation of functionalism revised the central claims and assumptions of aesthetic nationalism in a new and decidedly expanded political context.

It is not surprising that Lescaze rejected Johnson and Hitchcock's stylistic interpretation of contemporary design. As Lorraine Welling Lanmon notes in her biography of Lescaze, his journey across the Atlantic helped him to appreciate the ways national boundaries still exerted an indelible force on architectural production.[75] He struggled tremendously with adjusting his organicist architectural training under Moser to a new professional context, and he abandoned many aesthetic lines of inquiry in painting and graphic design that did not prove immediately relevant to the US national context. Robert Bruce Dean has even suggested that Lescaze went through the trouble of casting himself as a businessman-architect to better reflect the pragmatism of American capitalism—a step that many of his European migrant peers rejected outright in order to maintain their mystique as a foreigner with international roots.[76] These experiences likely increased his belief that the regional character of a place could not be completely erased by a universal (i.e., functionalist) approach to design. But the problem of materializing national differences remained. What relationship existed between the seemingly universal procedures of functionalism and the visual expression of architectural characters? Lescaze would address this issue by investing in the political commitments of his new homeland, especially in the form of public housing.

In his essay "New Deal Architecture," Lescaze explicitly equates the progressive and pragmatist aims of Roosevelt's New Deal policies with the functionalism of European modern architectures. According to Lescaze, the parallels between these two forces suffered from some confusion insofar as the phrase "New Deal" had become a neologism for updating what he considered to be outmoded architectural practices. This historical conception of form, which discussed buildings in terms of their visual appearance only, mistook the results for the cause of new forms in architecture. Such discussions should remind us of Viollet-le-Duc's distinction between historical styles and "style," the latter of which was understood to be a process of design and not a visual model. After outlining the range of infrastructural projects that were to be constructed with federal monies, one-third of which would consist of public housing, Lescaze goes on to discuss the appropriate aesthetic expression of this modern construction effort. He characterizes North America's existing public housing stock as a hodgepodge of historically eclectic works, or what he called "'picture' architecture," which was out of sync with Roosevelt's vision: "A government with a forward-looking and planning attitude toward agriculture and industry should not be so retrogressive as to weigh down the country with such a baroque collection of bastard buildings."[77]

By contrast, Lescaze portrays modern architecture as a natural response to man's contemporary needs, making it a visual diagram of his current mode of existence. In this sense, the scientific organization of man's interior and exterior environment was an ergonomic extension of himself. Lescaze's view of a New Deal architecture was reinforced by a civilizational narrative of past styles, which legitimized the notion that the large-scale building effort now facing the nation should reflect the contemporary character of American life:

> The first successful attempts made recently in European cities to clear away slums to build decent housing on a large scale were undertaken by modern architects. Modern architects rediscovered that man is the scale, that what counts is man and his activities, that man had been actively engaged in digging oil wells, developing railroads, automobiles, harvesting machines, electric lights, telephones, wireless, and that all these activities had modified his point of view, his requirements, his very life. . . . It is to the acceptance of man as the scale for architecture, instead of a king of Versailles, God as at Mont St. Michel, or a tomb as in the Pyramids, that we owe the present tendency in housing.[78]

In this historical parallel, the physical replacement of the slums of New York was an epochal event that visually expressed the maturation of modern life in the United States. Any remnant of nineteenth-century man, with his tenements, lack of indoor plumbing, poor education, and insanitary existence would literally be disciplined and transformed into a citizen fit for the industry and purposes of the modern nation-state. In an implicit critique of the NYCHA's previous solutions for public housing, Lescaze condemns their nostalgic use of "walled-in courts," a planning feature that became a staple of early tenement reform and limited-dividend housing projects that predated the establishment of a local authority.

Lescaze ends his article with the direct suggestion that a principled investment in public housing should lead to the development of a unique form of American architecture: "Who knows if, in investing its and our millions functionally, economically and aesthetically, the government would not be laying down the foundation of an American architecture, of modern architecture

Figure 4.11. Aerial view of Williamsburg Houses with Gaynor Junior High School in the foreground, ca. 1938. Photo no. 02.016.390, Sheba Ziprin collection, La Guardia Archives, LaGuardia Community College, New York.

for a modern nation?"[79] Yet Lescaze never fully explains how this American variant would be different from the movements inaugurated in Europe. He left such subtleties to his architectural practice. The clearest example of what this might look like was presented in the planning and architectural detailing of Williamsburg Houses (fig. 4.11). This project was the most expensive design put forward by the NYCHA at the time, with a combined land acquisition and construction cost of nearly $13 million (in 1930s currency).[80] Lescaze was put in charge of determining the architectural character of the exterior façades as well as the overall site planning of the complex. His innovations were slight, but very effective in elevating the modern features of this project. First, he replaced the enclosed perimeter block courtyard plans of the limited-dividend projects that he criticized in his article for of a series of smaller outdoor spaces

Figure 4.12. Construction photo of Williamsburg Houses, ca. 1937. La Guardia Archives, LaGuardia Community College, New York.

aligned alongside of individual midrise buildings. His tower in the park scheme included a few U-shaped green spaces, which resulted in a more open and asymmetrical plan arrangement. The entire complex sat within a vast superblock collected from several smaller city blocks, with each building plan shifted fifteen degrees from the orthogonal street grid. The exterior of each volume was minimally detailed with concrete spandrels visibly displayed along the exterior, which in turn supported a series of brick infill panels with punched windows above. Period construction photos verify the primacy of the concrete frame in the final design (fig. 4.12). Lescaze's solution purposefully combined the bare concrete finishes that were reminiscent of Western European social housing with the brick finishes that were characteristic of philanthropic social housing experiments in the United States. This combination of brick and concrete was preceded by his solution for the Chrystie-Forsyth housing project, designed for the Lower East Side.

Figure 4.13. Harlem River Houses under construction. Box 14: New York State; folder 13/14, Record Group 135-SAR: Prints: Photographs rejected for use in the Photographic Report to the President: "Survey of the Architecture of Completed Projects of the PWA, 1939," National Archives.

Two of the NYCHA's most visible demonstration projects, First Houses and Harlem River Houses, directly employ the red brick that "was the most frequently used material in housing developments" of the 1920s and 1930s.[81] Yet there are some important distinctions regarding the formal treatment of this material in comparison to International Style ideals. For example, the brick finish of First Houses was not based on any formal idea but was the economic result of speculative housing models of the private market. Administrators at the NYCHA decided to demolish the interior and keep the exterior in place, which merely revitalized the existing treatment of this tenement structure. By contrast, Harlem River Houses was intentionally designed to be a physical emblem of black social uplift, as it was meant to house predominantly African American residents. The lead architect, Archibald Manning Brown, decided to pursue a site plan organization that emulated the exterior courtyard schemes of the limited-dividend schemes of the previous generation. This produced one long and contiguous building mass that was more fixed, and thus seemingly heavier than the tower-in-the-park organization of European housing models (fig. 4.13). The architects for this building employed brick corbelling along prominent exterior walls leading through the entry to an exterior courtyard. The zig-zag patterns of this surface emulated the aesthetic treatment of brick surfaces in Amalgamated Dwellings much more than the bold and minimalistic finishes found at Williamsburg Houses. The entry walls of the courtyard were capped on one end with an ashlar-based brick pier that held up statues of black figures and animal specimens to enliven the space.

Heinz Warneke, a German American artist appointed to be the lead sculptor of this project, was made responsible for designing the two most iconic figurative sculptures for the exterior courtyard: a black male laborer titled "Man, the Provider" and a black female matron titled "Woman, the Mother and Housekeeper"[82] (see plate 11). Warneke's work was inspired by the undulating curves of organic forms and his study of primitivism. Each sculpture celebrated the themes of labor and work that were prominent in most of the social realist art commissioned by the WPA. However, several members of a committee representing the residents complained that Warneke's sculptures created a degrading and exaggerated portrait of black features.[83] Instead, the residents preferred a sculpture of a black male "remodeled as a businessman dressed in jacket and tie" that would have brought the image of black masculinity into the twentieth century. There was a black sculptor on Warneke's team, Richmond Barthé, who developed a concrete frieze containing an alternative portrait of blackness. Barthé's *Green Pastures: The Walls of Jericho* would have introduced a contrasting portrait of black personhood to Williamsburg Houses if it had been installed as originally intended (fig. 4.14).[84] The heroic lines of his two-panel decorative frieze, titled "Exodus" and "Dance," respectively, were inspired by Biblical themes and Egyptian architecture. The art historian Margaret Rose Vendryes interprets some of the gestures of Barthé's black subjects recalling the poses taken by members of the Black Panther Party.[85] As a participant of the Harlem Renaissance, Barthé was invested in an artistic culture that challenged stereotypical portraits of African Americans. Such limited conceptions were put forward by leading architects such as Le Corbusier, who viewed black racial character as too primitive or premodern to grasp the rational principles required to create modern architecture.[86] Mayor La Guardia added an African American architect, John Louis Wilson Jr., to the design team for Harlem River Houses after the project was officially started; however, the apparent racism of his colleagues prevented him from serving as the lead architect of this project.[87] He was thus unable to channel the project in a material direction that updated disciplinary norms for representing minority character.

Figure 4.15. Richmond Barthé, "Green Pastures: The Walls of Jericho." This decorative frieze was originally designed for a black housing project but was relocated to a white housing project in 1941.

The institutional history of the limited-dividend projects that served as a model for their design came from a tradition of creating charitable spaces for the poor that celebrated the generosity of its sponsor more than the cultural legacies of its residents. These cultural factors complicate the ultimate meaning of this housing project. Perhaps the combination of social realist and International Style conventions found in Harlem River Houses was the result of its being completed nearly a year before the end of construction on Williamsburg Houses. There may not have been enough time to update the visual aesthetic of this building to reflect current trends. Given the primitive themes of its figurative sculptures, however, it seems much more likely that this design was created to reflect the contemporary perceptions of black racial character as perpetual primitive subjects of the modern world.

Lescaze chose to reference the brick tradition of New York's limited-dividend social housing, but with a twist: he selected a tan brick instead of the stock red of earlier projects to soften its overall effect on the form. This specification brought the color of the brick closer to the concrete used in the project, which made it even more distinct from other projects completed by the NYCHA. This visual aesthetic did not evoke any of the dread that such solutions have come to represent today. From the perspective of the white ethnics living in 1938 they likely represented a bright liberation from such circumstances. Historical reviews in local newspapers and in papers published by the NYCHA note the gentrification that occurred around the neighborhood in response to this development. Period images of residents moving into the apartments, as well as staged model living room and bedroom arrangements suggest that many whites believed this setting would be instrumental in promoting their upward social mobility. When one compares the interior living patterns of white ethnics living in tenements torn down to accommodate Williamsburg Houses and the model photographs of these new interiors, it is apparent that some of the material cultures that marked individual white ethnic groups as distinct cultures falls away for a more homogenous image of white personhood.

A visual comparison of the artistic principles regulating the interior murals sent to this public housing project and the artworks hanging in many of the upper middle-class interiors included in the 1932 MoMA show suggests the instrumental function of public art. The architectural program for Williamsburg Houses directly contributed to the modernization of working-class character through the public amenities and leisure activities that were set aside there. One of the most conspicuous examples was the construction of community meeting rooms in the basements of each housing block. The weekly PTA meetings and resident board meetings of Williamsburg Houses were often held in these rooms, and these flex spaces were also the sites where local children learned on how to get along with others, presumably of a different ethnic background than themselves.[88] The rooms were decorated with murals created by modernist artists (see plate 12). Though not formally in charge of these interior details, Lescaze requested that abstract modernist paintings, instead of art using the figurative style of social realism produced by most other PWA artists, be included in the basement recreation rooms. The reason he gave was that abstract paintings might help day laborers relax when they came home from toiling jobs, whereas social realist works were likely to remind them of work. However, Lescaze's personal experiences with Americanization made him intimately familiar with the acculturating function of high art. This was likely also a factor in his suggestion, as abstract art introduced an upper middle-class aesthetic to the domestic milieu of Williamsburg Houses. In this way, the communal spaces of Williamsburg Houses were transformed into a physical laboratory for assimilating white ethnics into the American body politic, and the avant-garde artwork literally connected this process of racial amalgamation with the pan-European aesthetic of modernist art and architecture. Lescaze's intuitions on the acculturating function of high art seemed to be on target: the second edition of the resident newsletter, the *Projector*, reported plans to establish a larger art-lending program that would permit residents to place works of art on loan from local museum to decorate their homes for parties, community meetings, and other gatherings that merited a formal air.[89]

In 1938 Talbot Hamlin called Lescaze a champion of "a new vision of democracy" for the ways that Williamsburg Houses materialized the social values of Roosevelt's New Deal politics. While the minimal aesthetic of the project expressed the new repose expected of the globally aware modern citizen, Lescaze's formal departure from the white concrete aesthetic of the 1932 MoMA International Style exhibit visualizes an Americanization of the style in the United States. Yet this stylistic hybridization was burdened by two primary issues in the interwar period: the Eurocentric cultural frameworks used to market the MoMa exhibit in New York City and the official segregationist policies of state and federal housing agencies in the 1930s.

There were at least three institutional bodies that strategically worked to define the racial character of public housing in the early twentieth century. The first set of institutions were the governmental agencies intent on materializing the cultural ideals of Roosevelt's New Deal politics. These included the federal PWA and the state-run NYCHA. Their interests in defining American character were evident in the social gains for working-class residents that they claimed would come with the construction of public housing, as well as the funded social programs they added to housing complexes in order to reform the lifestyles of these residents. These latter programs included daycare centers, public schools, local clinics, and semipublic meeting rooms that served as social condensers to encourage the communal mixing of white immigrants from eastern and southern Europe. These social integrations were not always common among the white ethnics that settled in New York, especially when language and material customs revealed deeply rooted cultural differences. These spaces also provided didactic exposure to middle- and upper middle-class cultural norms, such as the art lending program that was started in Williamsburg Houses and the founding of a community newsletter, the *Projector*, which advocated saving for homeownership and other notions of private property.

A second institution that was invested in defining the American character of public housing was the Museum of Modern Art, which sponsored "*Modern Architecture: International Exhibition*." This exhibit was divided into three sections, the first concentrating on the work of individual modern architects; the second illustrating the national tendencies and international extents of this style; and the third highlighting the innovations made to public housing in the United States. Despite the inclusion of Russian and Japanese practitioners in the first and second sections of the show, the pan-European geography of most of the exhibit established a Eurocentric cultural framework for interpreting the relevance of International Style architectures in the United States. In New York City, this Euro-American conception of internationalism served as the perfect ideology for promoting the unification of new waves of European immigrants entering the United States; while new immigrants may not have had the cultural capital to immediately succeed in the American context, they could conceive of themselves as working toward the types of modernity that had already taken root back home.

This cultural imaginary was articulated to an even greater degree in the third set of institutions that helped define the character of public housing in the United States: the local and national press. Local newspapers proliferated in the racial and ethnic enclaves of New York City in order to discuss the social, political, and economic happenings in each district. This phenomenon helped neighbors to feel that they belonged to a particular neighborhood, as well as to an extended diasporic community when local conditions were compared to those in other major cities. Even the physical construction of Williamsburg Houses prompted the creation of a newsletter that was meant to serve this complex alone. Analyzing the racial politics of local newspapers alongside those of housing authorities and the architectural discipline allows us to better understand the impact of internationalist discourses on the character of public housing.

While the polemics of the International Style debates defined this aesthetic as theoretically universal in extent, the legalization of separate-but-equal policies of federal and state housing authorities made a universal application of this style a practical impossibility. On the one hand, the European pedigree of the International Style debates enabled a conceptual relationship to be drawn between "old" and "new" waves of European immigrants to the United States that promoted the Americanization of white working-class communities into the American body politic. The social utility of public housing for this group was empirically demonstrated by their ability to flee these contexts during the postwar period and move to the suburbs with the aid of new federal legislation for subsidized home loans. On the other hand, the white cultural pedigree subtending these debates hindered its applicability for incorporating the cultural legacies of African Americans also desiring to live in public housing projects. In contrast to the pan-European pedigree that helped the white working classes contextualize themselves within the process of Americanization, the cultural pedigree of International Style architectures was never imagined to specifically embrace the cultural legacies of black Americans during the interwar or postwar periods. This was not the case for visual representations of black modernity created by participants in the Harlem Renaissance, a parallel artistic phenomenon in New York City. The racial politics of the period prevented the visual construction of an alternative cultural legacy for International Style public housing in the early years of the NYCHA.

The institutional patterns of racial segregation had an inevitable effect on the public perception of Williamsburg Houses in New York City. Evidence of this racial codification can be found in local newspapers and municipal records: articles in the black press detailed the ways the budget and location of this project—the most expensive project to that date for the NYCHA—exemplified the secondary status of African Americans in this citywide modernization effort;

while the white press in Williamsburg celebrated the new levels of social and economic investment that were occurring in their neighborhoods. A social history of Williamsburg Houses also reveals the critical function of these spaces for shaping the character of working-class European immigrants. The architectural programming of this project introduced a string of civic programming that was designed by the state to homogenize the language patterns and even shape the bodily habits of new residents. A public school was the first program ever completed on the site, which guaranteed that white ethnic children of different language groups would learn to speak English from a young age. In addition, the introduction of a PTA enabled the mothers of different language groups to learn to settle disputes in a common forum that encouraged group cohesion. Basement clinics were also included to address the race-based fears of poor white ethnic diseases through a comprehensive program of communal inoculation. Other features of the interior program were designed to elevate the public taste of new residents to enable an acculturation of middle-class aesthetic sensibilities. The community newsletter, the *Projector*, details an art lending program created to enable residents to decorate their homes in ways that emulated the opulence of middle-class families. Basement activity rooms were also decorated with murals of cubist art, an abstract precedent that departed from the social realist idioms of other working-class projects.

The exterior form of Williamsburg Houses was shaped to promote an American interpretation of the International Style. In both aesthetic and political terms, Lescaze's design for Williamsburg Houses placed two competing models for social housing in conversation with one another. The first is represented by the common brick material and courtyard-oriented plans of American limited-dividend projects, a solution that was very popular among philanthropists and union-organized housing at the turn of the century. This model grew from a tradition of public-private partnerships that combined the strengths of the private market with publicly funded projects. As Bloom notes in *Public Housing That Worked*, this combined approach was somewhat unique to New York State.[90] Its success in times of lean governmental financing explains its continued use there for nearly two decades after public housing had officially begun in the 1930s. By contrast, the second aesthetic tradition employed in Williamsburg Houses is represented by the monolithic concrete aesthetic of Siedlungen housing units completed in western Europe during the 1910s and 1920s. The most famous examples of this tradition are Ernst May's pioneering designs for municipal housing in Frankfurt, and Weissenhof Siedlungen organized by Mies van der Rohe in Stuttgart. Progressive housing reformers in the United States revered these models of social housing for materializing the radical socialism that many believed was implicit to FDR's New Deal policies, which used the powers of the federal government to expand the social safety net for the nation's working classes.[91] By combining elements from these two national building traditions, Lescaze produced a hybridized design that was politically expedient for mitigating the socialist (and thus "un-American') associations of European social housing but enabling the political instrumentalization of public housing as a material context for assimilating first-generation European immigrants into the body politic.

The social and disciplinary histories of Williamsburg Houses reveal the shifting role of character judgments in twentieth-century architectural organicism. The organicist rhetoric American critics employed to describe European social housing considered this building type to be a transparent reflection of rising international norms for mass culture. American architects hoped these standards would enable them to create a new vernacular aesthetic at home. In contrast to nineteenth-century paradigms of architectural organicism, American critics did not employ explicit references to natural metaphors of design to integrate the principles of race and style theory in modern architectural debates. Instead, they interpreted the historical continuity of organic relationships that regulated vernacular settlements in premodern societies as a material precedent for contemporary designs. Mumford was a leading proponent of such thinking in the United States. Lescaze was exposed to both traditions of architectural organicism: first from his European mentors Moser and Sauvage and later through the writings of leading American theorists. While Lescaze continued to use the formal idioms of International Style architecture to visually represent the essential traits of racial and national character in the twentieth century, the institutional contexts of the interwar period required a contextualist response to national debates.

In the final analysis, Lescaze's most pioneering design for American public housing—Williamsburg Houses—established a contemporary style of organic architecture that shored up the authenticity of a modern American architecture against the homogenizing culture of an international avant-garde. His personal experiences with becoming an American citizen likely made him sympathetic to the plights of working-class European immigrants arriving during the interwar period. Unfortunately, the racial politics of his day conspired to prevent him from extending this accommodation to most other minority communities desiring to participate in this new American experiment.

Figure C.1. Le Corbusier, model of Plan Obus for Algiers, 1930. Fonds Guillaume Jullian de la Fuente, Canadian Centre for Architecture, Montreal.

CONCLUSION

Race, Nature, and Nation in Postwar American Architecture

> The new European architecture opened our eyes, stimulated our minds and finally did materialize as an important influence on the American scene, but in conjunction with two other factors: first, a strong new interest in Frank Lloyd Wright, encouraged by his renewed creative activity in the middle and latter 'thirties; and second, a revaluation of that very dark horse—traditional vernacular building.
>
> —**Elizabeth Mock,**
> **"Built in USA—Since 1932"**

ONE WAY TO TRACE THE continued racialization of architectural styles in the years following William Lescaze's designs for public housing is to examine the efforts of the Museum of Modern Art's curators to further "Americanize" International Style architectures of the interwar and postwar periods. A common reference to organicist language can be found in the curation of exhibits on modern architecture at MoMA, especially in catalog essays and press materials that attempted to judge the corporate and political programs that defined the extent of American international power during this time. These curatorial themes collectively attempt to correct the perceived Eurocentric character of the 1932 *Modern Architecture: International Exhibit* by articulating a specific American genius at work in completing the most iconic buildings of the international avant-garde. Of particular interest is the racial and nationalist charge of Henry Russell-Hitchcock's revival of American pragmatism in the description of the American architect Wallace K. Harrison's work. For Hitchcock, Harrison seemed to replace Lescaze as the new representative of the "businessman-architect" practitioner in the 1940s. This narrative portrait rhetorically substitutes the process of Americanization associated with the social experiences of the European émigré (in the figure of Lescaze) with those of the native-born citizen (in the figure of Harrison). Several architectural historians have noted the increased popularity of International Style architectures within the interwar United States, with several generations of Harvard-educated architects believing they had developed their own version of the style to think of it as a homegrown approach to design.[1]

The racial content of Harrison's career can be teased out by examining the perceived organic principles of his design approach in the postwar period. He has been credited with actively modeling a humble and deliberative approach to designing some of the most iconic projects of the postwar period, including the conceptual design for the United Nations Headquarters in 1947. However, this building in particular was developed by combining the proposals of several leading architects into one coherent design—a synthetic process that redirects the design strategies of organic architects in the nineteenth century. As George Dudley recalls in the book *A Workshop for Peace: Designing the United Nations Headquarters*, Harrison was forced to operate as a peacemaker between the international celebrities appointed to serve on the board of design, including the French architect Le Corbusier, whose frustrations with losing the League of Nations project made him more determined than ever to obtain credit for authoring an international design.[2] Harrison's ultimate skill was formulating a process for combining the distinct formal characters of several competing designs into one unifying scheme. As the consummate pragmatist, he was perceived to have the personal and professional pedigree that prepared him to embody the essential characteristics long associated with successful American businessmen and entrepreneurs in the United States, from the white settlers on the frontier to the speculators of the industrial revolution. A contextual analysis of Hitchcock's postwar revival of American pragmatism as the ultimate design expertise of the domestic architect will enable us to articulate the shifting racial and nationalist associations of architectural talent after World War II. The disciplinary stakes of this label parallel the broader stakes of American international power as it was figured by national figures who sought to increase their role as leaders of a growing international community.

The geographical scope of American power after World War II complicates the individualized nationalist themes that have thus far been the focus of my analysis in *Building Character.* While I have consciously restricted my study of race and style to the racial and nationalist implications of architectural organicism in France, Germany, and the United States, the political impacts of modern architecture were never fully contained within the transatlantic geographies recorded in this book. The physical and economic infrastructures of European and American imperialism actively supported the outmigration of national ideas to outlying areas, including the colonial territories that were physically but rarely legally incorporated into the fabric of the nation-state. As Amy Kaplan notes in her study *The Anarchy of Empire in the Making of U.S. Culture*, the closing of the American frontier compelled many domestic politicians to consider the prospects of securing American power and territory beyond the geographical extents of North America.[3] The annexations of Hawaii and the Philippines as official protectorates and the construction of military bases and treaties for trade are just two products of national efforts to secure America's presence within the Asia-Pacific. The Panama Canal also helped secure an American presence in South America, an effort that would repeat itself in the form of the international design expositions and business collaborations during the interwar period. In addition to these US developments, most of the independent nation-states of Western Europe maintained colonial outposts in what is now called the Global South to provide, among other things, testing grounds for new experiments in architectural formalism and urban design.[4] The infrastructural networks that connected the European metropole to colonial satellite cities were exploited by modernist architects such as Le Corbusier, who campaigned to complete urban designs for colonial Algiers and Brazil, among other places (fig. C.1).

By the mid-1950s and early 1960s, a wave of independence movements resulted in the liberation of previous colonial territories and the establishment of postcolonial powers. These political events forced designers to think of the remnants of European modernization and the social, cultural, and political meanings of Euro-American modern architectures in a new light. The appointment of non-Western architects to the role of lead designers for postcolonial projects, sometimes for the very first time since colonization, further complicated the semantic registers of International Style architectures as a stable sign of Western technology and progress. Would it be possible to design and build with modern materials and emulate Euro-American forms of the 1910s and 1920s without inherently reflecting or reinforcing the social norms and cultural practices of oppressive Western political regimes? Could postcolonial African, Indian, and Asian architects generate a new set of material emblems that were an appropriate fit for the social conditions of their home territories in the postwar period? The curatorial debates for a uniquely "American" historiography of modern architecture perhaps anticipated the cultural fragmentations to emerge later within modern architectural debates of the 1930s, 1940s, and 1950s by revealing the latent potential for cultural pluralization within the international style that was masked by the Eurocentric focus of *Modern Architecture: International Exhibit*. A more expansive history of the International Style debates will expose the inherently paradoxical portrait of racial and national character that was endorsed at that time. The resulting complexity of this alternative history will enable us to better account for the conflicting portraits of American power within the discipline that alternated between distinctly nationalist projects of design and a set of material practices that were mutually identifiable with the efforts to abandon the promotion of nationalist content in an international design culture.

A brief exploration of the shifting curatorial themes at MoMA from *Modern Architecture: International Exhibit* in 1932 to the *Built in USA* exhibits of 1946 will provide us with a discrete institutional framework in which to reinterpret the racialization of architectural character in the International Style debates. In an effort to render the United States an untainted champion of democracy and freedom around the world, even within its own protectorates, some MoMA curators interpreted the reductive aesthetic character and programmatic flexibility of modern architecture as a visual sign of the inherent character of laissez-faire capitalism.[5] This democratic-capitalist interpretation paradoxically renders international style architectures as simultaneously apolitical by virtue of belonging to the entire Euro-American avant-garde and inherently "American," a further indication of the semantic flexibility that Johnson and Hitchcock interpreted in this architectural style during their first surveys in the 1930s. When the European pedigree of this style consciously evoked a socialist tinge in the United States, such as when progressive American critics touted the benefits of European social housing, MoMA curators responded by constructing a decidedly nationalist root for American modernism as a countermeasure to such negative readings.[6]

Frank Lloyd Wright and the Refinement of American Character

In her 1945 essay for the exhibit, "Built in USA—Since 1932," Elizabeth Mock constructs a series of alternative historical narratives to displace the European historiography of International Style modern architectures established at MoMA in 1932: the first strain consisted of the historical tradition of architectural organicism that Frank Lloyd Wright inherited in the 1930s and 1940s and the second consisted of a longer anonymous vernacular building tradition that proliferated in the United States through the use of readily available raw materials such as wood and stone. Mock's first narrative revives the historical innovations of the Chicago School of Architecture that established a unique aesthetic for the office towers of the Gilded Age. She credits John Wellborn Root and Louis Sullivan as the first architects to completely harmonize the functional and aesthetic requirements of the skyscraper typology in Chicago.[7] Wright had become the most famous inheritor of the Chicago school tradition within this domestic historiography for modern architecture, both for continuing the organicist ideals of his mentor and for the documented interests of European practitioners in his architectural writings at the turn of the century. Other historical figures such as Frank Furness and Henry Hobson Richardson were included in this pantheon for their theoretical and architectural contributions during the nineteenth century. While Wright's Prairie Style represents the most avant-garde strain of a postwar American architectural organicism, the anonymous architects of early American history also provide an alternative origin point for the efflorescence of a unique national building tradition. The two trajectories—the Chicago school and the revival of vernacular principles of design—fostered competing forms of white cultural nationalism that explore the singularity of American modernism within the international avant-garde.

As discussed in chapter 3, Sullivan's architectural writings collectively establish an interpretive framework for reading the embodied racial character of his buildings. The clearest articulation of this line of thinking is captured in the narrative progression of his *Autobiography of an Idea* (1924), a bildungsroman for the central idea of his architectural practice. As I have argued, Sullivan's emulation of physiognomic theory establishes a racialized human body metaphor in his architectural practice that can be traced back to his architectural writings in their textual representations of Anglo-American character. Sullivan's interpretation of physiognomy transforms the interpretive practices of eighteenth-century art into a set of generative principles for manipulating the external character of modern buildings. Like the eighteenth-century practice of judging the hidden motivations of a subject by reading their exterior characteristics, the most expressive element of Sullivan's buildings—his floral ornament—is a superficial sign of the liberated democratic ideals that enabled him to create ex nihilo architectural ornaments without being burdened by historical precedents. For Sullivan, liberating the ideation of form from historical precedents is the architect-poet's primary occupation, and it is what makes his or her work an emulation of the democratic spirit of the nation.

There are several key similarities between Sullivan's and Wright's theories of architectural style. For example, Wright's architectural ornament is not meant to be a direct mimetic imitation of the flora or fauna found in nature or the ornamental features of a historical building precedent but is instead a freely structured geometrical expression of the creative forms that the human mind can create when it is no longer bound by the rules of classical composition. In an ontological sense, Sullivan's floral ornament extends the picturesque beauty of the American prairie into the city of Chicago, which was structurally reliant upon the raw materials of its surrounding contexts to establish itself as a major industrial center of development. Wright would pursue a similar path in his emulation of the American frontier in his Prairie Style architecture.

The democratic spirit of freedom embodied by Sullivan's architectural ornament was also expressed in the overall character and programmatic function of his buildings: from the identical cellular organization of the rooms contained in his office towers to the secular and utilitarian external appearance of his religious structures, Sullivan's architecture was molded from the inside out to condition its users to think of themselves as one part of the collective movement to define American democracy. Yet there were some apparent limits to who was representative of these efforts and who was best suited to directly contribute to its progress. These social and cultural limits become clear when we examine the racial politics of Sullivan's autobiography, which reveal a negative estimation of the creative potentials of first-generation immigrants too solidly molded by the Old World to fully assimilate the practices of the New World, as well as non-white peoples deemed too inherently limited by their biological temperaments to ever operate as autonomous individuals within the American body politic. The saving grace for Sullivan as the child of an Irishman comes in the form of his innate appreciation of America's promise, which he achieves through the direct observation of nature on the family farm and an early regimen of artistic training. *Autobiography of an Idea* sets a clear precedent for Wright's memoir, which was titled simply *An Autobiography* and released in 1932.[8] Both Wright and his mentor were fond of their memories of nature on the family farm. Wright's account is also a bildungsroman, although it lacks the poetic pretensions of its predecessor, which makes it much simpler to read and digest as a document. We also find similar intellectual references to proponents of European architectural organicism, such as the Welsh architect Owen Jones's *Grammar of Ornament* and Eugène Emmanuel Viollet-le-Duc's *Habitations of Man in All Ages*, the latter of which is explicitly discussed in chapter 1 of *Autobiography*.[9]

In *Autobiography*, Wright uses physiognomic descriptions to communicate the inner characters of his family members, his associates, and other people he meets during his career. At a crucial point in this narrative, he physiognomically describes the inner character of Dankmar Adler, the Jewish entrepreneur and business partner of his mentor Sullivan, whom he credits with being "a strong personality, short-built and heavy, like an old Byzantine church."[10] We are likely meant to translate the mutual civilizational associations of the Byzantine style—nominally of the Western tradition, but perceived to be mired by the synthetic integration of Eastern elements—as a visual representation of Adler's intellectual position in the United States; he is a member of a white ethnic minority that must learn to assimilate the hegemonic rules of the Anglo-American tradition. We can infer that Wright believes this is a good quality when he reassures us that he "felt comforted" by Adler's presence; something that is not true of the Jewish peers he meets in Adler's office. Wright builds upon his mentor's rhetorical strategy of physiognomic description, however, by embellishing these passages with meticulous accounts of the spatial dynamics that structure his interactions with others. This combination of physiognomic and spatial description results in a more visceral accounting of the interracial and interethnic competitions that are merely hinted at in Sullivan's *Autobiography of an Idea*.

An obvious example of this enriched narrative approach occurs in book II of *An Autobiography* with an account of the various staff members employed in Adler and Sullivan's office: "Next table to mine Jean Agnas, a clean-faced Norseman. To the right Eisendrath—*apparently stupid*. Jewish. Behind me to the left Ottenheimer—alert, apparently bright. Jew too. Turned around to survey the group. Isbell, Jew? Gaylord, no—not. Weydert, undoubtedly. Directly behind, Weatherwax. Couldn't make him out—probably Jewish. In the corner Andresen—Swedish. Several more Jewish faces."[11] This scene is a literal example of what we would call racial profiling today, in a gesture that emulates Immanuel Kant's instructions on physiognomic description.[12] Wright believes that a person's psychological character is transparently rendered by their external appearance. Although we are never given enough information to participate directly in this practice ourselves, the reader gets a sense of the mental activities required to take stock of one's surrounding environment. According to Wright, the general sense of antipathy between himself and his Jewish peers was overtly articulated to him in the office: "The gang had evidently combined to 'get' me. Their phrase."[13] This situation takes a turn from a war of words to literal combat in the form of a boxing match. Wright develops the strategy of punching the first combatant, Isbell, in his "abnormally large nose," which allegorically draws blood by calling attention to the physiognomic feature of the Jewish face that was associated the racist stereotypes during this period. The final straw consists of a faceoff with the Jewish "ringleader" of the office, Ottenheimer, who assaults him with a cutting blade while the principals are out to lunch.[14] Wright's description of the primal scream this otherwise "intelligent" man emits as he prepares to strike transmogrifies the Jew into an animal-like creature, that is compared to an inarticulate drunken Japanese person: "With a peculiar animal scream—I've heard something like it since from a Japanese mad with *sake*, but never else—he jumped for a knife, the scratch-blade with a wood handle lying on his board. Half-blinded, he came at me with it."[15] This bestial characterization appears again and again but is only reserved for nonwhite people the architect meets during his career. The most scandalous example appears in the form of a Barbadian servant who torches Taliesin and attacks his family and the staff with "superhuman" strength.[16]

Of all of the racial groups to appear in direct conflict with Wright in *An Autobiography*, the Japanese are the most striking to consider given Wright's historical fascination with Japanese art and his longstanding praise for their "ancient-modern" culture.[17] Wright developed a reputation shortly after the turn of the century as an expert in Japanese woodcuts, which contributed to his being considered a sympathetic ally of the Japanese people. This perception, in part, contributed to his selection as the design architect for the Imperial Hotel in Tokyo. Yet his views of Japanese subjects are not entirely positive. At one point, he makes an implicit distinction between "a good Japanese" and a bad one.[18] In characteristic fashion, this early perspective coheres through a physical struggle between races, this time with a former employee who was "fired for cause" from Wright's office. His perpetual return to speak with his peers results in Wright kicking him down a flight of stairs while wearing a pair of equestrian riding boots: "A well-directed intimate kick landed him well down the half-flight on the main public stair running from directly in front of the entrance door down the half-landing below. He lay there in a whimpering heap and I turned back into the office and sat down—waiting."[19] Wright's domineering posture in this passage is suggestive in this narrative: his upper middle-class mode of dress and the unequal status between employer and employee within the office reflect a power dynamic that privileges the architect. The racial and class separations illustrated by this event anticipate what I call an aesthetic imperialism in the architect's synthetic integration of Japanese motifs in his Prairie Style houses. Like the secularizing character of Sullivan's Romanesque design for the Kehilath Anshe Ma'ariv Synagogue discussed in chapter 3, Wright's Prairie Style is a visual sign of his clients' level of acculturation of worldly experiences, a soft indication of their status as pioneers in the definition of American character.

While the legal and social definitions of the American body politic are slightly more expansive in Wright's memoir than those recoded by his mentor a generation earlier, the Japanese subject is perpetually marginalized from the center of American culture. As Claire Jean Kim notes in her study of Asian Americanization, even Asian American citizens of the United States struggle to fit within the country's white-black binary of race relations, which leads to them being stereotyped by white and black Americans alike as too foreign to ever become fully assimilated subjects.[20] This chronic perception of otherness was likely reinforced by the political conflicts that existed between the United States and Japan in the South China Sea leading up to World War II, as well as the physiognomic features of whites and Asians that superficially rendered them visually distinct racial groups. We get a sense of the deeply felt incompatibility with which Asians are viewed by white elites in Wright's comparison of Japanese and American housing types. He begins by praising the inherent modularity of the tatami mats in the Japanese home:

> There are some things so perfect that nothing justifies such curiosity. By heaven, here was a house used by those who made it with just that naturalness with which a turtle uses his shell. It is as like the natives as the polished bronze of their skin, the texture of their polished hair or the sly look in their slant and sloe eyes. We of the West couldn't live in Japanese houses and we shouldn't. . . . The ethnic eccentricity is too great. The West can copy nearly everything easier than it can copy the Japanese house or Japanese things for domestic uses.[21]

As a perpetually marked primitive being, each Japanese subject is praised or jeered at in *An Autobiography* for how well they become a cultural representative of a non-Western lifestyle that confirms Wright's organic conception of spatial order. His conflation of the distinctiveness of Japanese bodies and their housing forms not only returns to the bodybuilding metaphors that structure architectural organicism but also reifies the notion of American exceptionalism as a people gifted with the ability to transparently interpret and assimilate the aesthetic principles of otherness. The Asian artist and architect, by contrast, is never seen to be capable of fully grasping the American dream in Wright's narrative: they are rarely his clients, and in the case of the Imperial Hotel, which was commissioned by Japanese diplomats, this structure was designed for the benefit of Western dignitaries visiting Japan—not for the Japanese themselves. This distanced relationship to Wright's architecture—formally integrated but phenomenologically remote—makes Japanese subjects props for denoting the worldliness of American artists without conferring equal status to nonwhite subjects as international travelers or cultural producers.

Architectural historians have struggled with Wright's claims to have never been directly inspired by any other artist or tradition outside of his own theories for architectural organicism. There are at least three book-length studies on the subject that demonstrate the incredible depth of Wright's debt to Japanese art and architecture, despite the architect's claims that these references are mere proofs for his autonomous genius. Yet all we need to do is recall his own words in *Ausgeführte Bauten und Entwürfe* from 1911—the cultural principle I referenced in the introduction to *Building Character*—to get a sense of why this disavowal is such a central feature of his modus vivendi: "His machine, the tools in which his opportunity lies, can only *murder the traditional forms of other peoples and earlier times*. He must find new forms, new industrial ideals, or stultify both opportunity and forms."[22] Directly accounting for the racial politics of Wright's Prairie Style architecture enables us to account for his persistent interest in Japanese art, while recognizing that these references can only ever be consciously acknowledged as post facto evidence of his autonomous explorations in design. This act of borrowing without recognition, what I have called Wright's aesthetic imperialism, permits him to naturalize the racial genius of white settler cultures around the world. If we view the Imperial Hotel as an example of the material culture of the midwestern prairie setting foot in Japan, then it is important from a civilizational standpoint to demonstrate the relative independence and adaptability of white ethnics around the world. In political terms, this means that Wright must maintain the social and political segregation of Japanese and Japanese American citizens from the white ethnic elite that is common practice in the United States by privileging the lifestyles and attitudes of a white ethnics in any and every context. That is the cultural objective of any imperialist, be they from the West or any other corner of the globe.

The most overt evidence of Wright's aesthetic imperialism is evident in his ornamental embellishment of the Prairie Style in several projects dating from the late 1910s to the early 1930s: these include Midway Gardens (1913–1914); the A. D. German Warehouse (1915–1920); the Frederick C. Bogk House (1916–1917); and the Imperial Hotel (1912–1923). Wright orientalizes the construction of the Prairie Style even at home in his narrative description of Midway Gardens by making himself as the young Arabian Aladdin from the romantic stories of his youth: "Well, as a boy Aladdin and his wonderful lamp had fascinated me. But by now I knew the enchanting young Arabian was really just a symbol for creative desire, his lamp intended for another symbol—imagination. As I sat listening I was Aladdin. Young Ed [Waller]? The genii. He knew apparently where all 'the slaves of the lamp' could be found."[23] Following this logic, when Wright is Aladdin his client becomes the genie that grants all of his wishes. The curious projections of slave labor onto the circumstances of the unionized worker found in this passage parallel Sullivan's ruminations on chattel slavery in the United States. Paul Mueller, the general contractor for the project, is the figure who "rented slaves from the union by making the usual terms."[24] In both Sullivan's and Wright's cases, however, the legal enslavement of black bodies is elided by a discussion of indentured servitude by virtue of "wage slavery," which places the focus squarely back onto the white ethnics more suited to ennoble the tradition of American arts and letters than nonwhites. Just in case we miss the parallels between chattel slavery and wage slavery, Mueller is subsequently described in *Autobiography* as a "slave-driver" for the duration of the construction of Midway Gardens. This makes this project a physical setting for an Arabian Nights adventure with Wright standing in for a famous primitive subject.

Given Wright's narrative focus on the groups of people he meets throughout his career, it is likely that his rhetorical substitution of blackness for whiteness is much more indicative of the segregated reality of his professional world than of his negative estimation of nonwhite subjects. To put this another way, it seems much more likely that his references to nonwhite psychological and class characteristics enable him to render the social distinctions of white ethnics in his everyday world more dramatically through proxy; in point of fact, he doesn't have to think about the actual experiences of nonwhite peoples in order to levy stereotypical depictions of their group identities for literary effect.

The concrete elements of Midway Gardens operate as an ornamental embellishment of the dominant brick facing of the Prairie Style a few years before he experiments with a more comprehensive handling of concrete in the Hollyhock house (1916–1921) and the Ennis house (1923–1924), two projects meant to serve as material signs for a lifestyle developed in the "Far West," or the West Coast. Wright describes the primary features of his Prairie Style as a conscious reconfiguration of the masonry foundation and structural frame of the Victorian house, which was very popular among upper middle-class elites living in the Midwest. In every case, the concrete or stone embellishments to the Prairie Style house direct the eye toward the formal elements of the exterior that dress the clerestory level or transitional spaces of the building.

Wright scholars have completed several careful studies of the Japanese and pre-Columbian referents found in these decorative elements. For example, the architectural historian Kevin Nute has persuasively identified the Japanese sources for many of the decorative motifs and the axial plan arrangements found in Wright's Prairie Style architectures.[25] Anthony Alofsin has also uncovered the influence of pre-Columbian art on Wright's architectural ornament in his expertly archived study of the architect's activities during the previously "lost" years between 1910 and 1920.[26] I consider now the cultural associations that Wright's architecture accrues within the international contexts of their making. Do these non-Western references make his architecture Japanese or pre-Columbian in any substantive way? And if not, do they offer Japanese and pre-Columbian residents in the United States a visual allegory for their own assimilation into the American body politic? The Imperial Hotel is perhaps the apotheosis of Wright's aesthetic progression from the midwestern origins of the overall massing for the Prairie Style house to the organic enrichment of concrete motifs that formally emulate Japanese and pre-Columbian sculptural practices (fig. C.2). Wright notes in *An Autobiography* that many of the ornamental features of the Imperial Hotel were created in consultation with indigenous workers who lived in the hotel as it was being constructed.[27] Yet the resulting architectural forms were consistently described in the project brief, in press releases, and in the architect's writings as a visual setting for American visitors to the East. That is to say, while this hotel was designed to meet the needs of the local Japanese in the event of a disastrous earthquake, it was always designed for the enjoyment of Western subjects traveling abroad and was thus purposefully oriented to anticipate, and perhaps to also extend, their social and cultural norms. If we take a note from Adrienne Brown's phenomenological study of racial embodiment in modern architecture, *The Black Skyscraper*, then it is important to think of the Imperial Hotel in terms that reconstruct the phenomenological experience of space that originates from the cultural associations of the range of people that historically used this space.[28] Such an approach prepares us to judge how well Wright met his mark for Western users, as well as to speculate on the latent potentials that existed for non-Western users as this space accrued new meanings over time.

If we return to the material composition of the exterior walls of the Imperial Hotel, we note the structural integration of its handmade brick and hand-carved

Figure C.2. Frank Lloyd Wright, Imperial Hotel, Tokyo, Japan, 1915. Box 65.5, Historic Architecture and Landscape Image Collection, Art Institute of Chicago.

Oya stone, the latter of which was a physical remnant of active volcanoes in the area. This material had sacred connotations for Wright, as he describes the cultural relationship that he believed existed between Japanese residents and the climactic conditions established by the local volcanoes: "From infancy, a sort of subjective contemplation, the minds and hearts of the Japanese are fixed upon the great calm mountain God of their nation—the sacred Fujiyama brooding in majesty and eternal calm over all. They deeply worship as the mountain continually changes moods, combining with sun and moon, clouds and mist in a vast expression of elemental beauty the like of which in dignity and repose exists nowhere else on earth. It is not too much to say that the sacred mountain is the God of old Japan; Japan the Modern Ancient."[29] From this passage, we can infer Wright's perception of a material parallel between his use of brick and Oya stone. If his material handling of brick can recall the horizontally oriented spaces of the American prairie, then perhaps he can develop the material sensibility of the Oya stone in an equally authentic manner. He goes into great detail in his autobiography regarding how the final walls of the Imperial Hotel were constructed and the seminal role of Japanese construction workers in resolving this aesthetic detail:

> The outer walls were spread wide, thick and heavy at the base, growing thinner and lighter toward the top. Whereas Tokio buildings were all top-heavy . . . The stone everywhere under foot in Tokio was a workable light lava weighing as much as green oak. It was considered sacrilege to use this common material for the aristocratic edifice. But finally it was used for the feature material and readily yielded to any sense of form the architect might choose to indicate. And the whole structure was to be set up as a double shell—two shells, an exterior of slim cunning bricks, and an interior one of fluted hollow bricks raised together to a convenient height of four feet or more. These shells were to be poured solid with concrete to bind them together. The great building thus became a jointed monolith with a mosaic surface of lava and brick.[30]

The concrete and mortar that structurally integrates the three elements of the façade together—the hollow core bricks of the interior with the brick and Oya stone modules of the exterior—create a material instance of "integral ornament" that Wright cites as an aesthetic ideal in his autobiography (fig. C.3).[31] What is most curious are not the moments of visual juxtaposition between each of these elements—which are representative of Japanese and American national genius, respectively—but the modified brick forms that synthetically integrate the formal idioms of both modules. How are we to read the significance of this form? Is it synonymous with Wright's earlier work on the Prairie house, or is this a feature that emerges from his experience with Japanese laborers?

If we develop a generous interpretation of the hybrid status of the Oya-inflected brick modules of the Imperial Hotel, then these elements constitute a material attempt to bridge the singularity of Japanese and American racial identity. Yet we get conflicting messages from other passages of *Autobiography*. As I have already stated, Wright insists upon separating the essential characteristics of Japanese and American housing because he believes that they are incompatible as a result of their unique native cultures. In other passages, however, he credits the Japanese craftsmen on the job for making aesthetic contributions to his work, which is a partial outgrowth of their experiences of making the Imperial Hotel their home during construction. Who is the final author of these hybrid brick modules, and what portrait of Japanese and American culture do they present to visitors of this space? It is possible that the archive will provide

Figure C.3. Detail of brick and pumice stone. Frank Lloyd Wright, Imperial Hotel, Tokyo, Japan, 1915. From Cary James, Frank Lloyd Wright's Imperial Hotel (New York: Dover, 1988).

some clues, although records of any explicit conversations between Wright, his American team in Tokyo, and local builders are only referenced in passing in *An Autobiography*.

In my view, the synthetic brick modules of the Imperial Hotel represent the latent potential of Wright's Prairie Style of architecture for establishing a truly relativist and synthetic social space that views Japanese and American users as coequal and commingling populations. I interpret them as having a similar capacity for change that was recognized for Sullivan's architecture in chapter 3: the synthetic logic of the system enables the built form to surpass the cultural assumptions of its maker, but only in the event that a previously marginalized community has access to physically modifying this space to better accommodate their needs. This was likely the case for the Imperial Hotel—more so than for most of Wright's other Prairie Style houses, at least during his lifetime. By virtue of his organic conception of architecture, the Imperial Hotel possesses a geometrical capacity to materially assimilate various aspects of its surrounding context into its overall material composition. Yet this can only occur when Japanese and American visitors to the hotel are able to occupy spaces on the "served" side of the entryway desk, not just from opposing sides of this divide. Only then can each party engage in the spatial experimentation that is required for a commingling society.

Perhaps the Imperial Hotel only ever fulfilled its synthetic potential when it was under construction: after all, it was in the process of managing the complexities of the local Oya stone that the conflicting standards of Japanese and American construction habits were forced to contend with one another:

> How skillful they were! What craftsmen! How patient and clever. So instead of wasting them by vainly trying to make them come our way—we went with them their way. I modified many original intentions to make the most of what I now saw was naturally theirs. The language grew less an obstruction. But curious mistakes were perpetual. It is true that the Japanese approach to any matter is a spiral. Their instinct for attack in any direction is oblique and volute. But they make up for it in gentleness and cleverness and loyalty. Yes, the loyalty of the retainer to his *Samurai*. They soon educated us and all went pretty well.[32]

Even here, Wright is unable to acknowledge the complexity of thought among the Japanese builders without degrading their achievements as loyal servants and intuitive thinkers!

By the time the hotel officially opened, its decorous interior spaces were vacated by local builders and ceded back to the American tourist. The one exception was in the case of emergency, when the 1923 earthquake forced local Japanese residents to use it, although again only as visitors. The aesthetic framework of the Imperial Hotel reveals the latent potential of the Prairie Style to accommodate more occasional moments for Japanese American cultural exchange than any other in Wright's portfolio, which is why the actual spatial habitus of this space are so important to study. Only within an "American" hotel in Japan could a diplomatic meeting of the minds become a practical goal in the immediate programmatic and spatial sense given the monoracial ideologies subtending Japanese and American character.

When the Imperial Hotel was finally demolished in the 1960s, and Japanese-American relations were finally improving, Wright's hotel was perceived to be completely out of date by Japanese decisionmakers. It represented an antique and orientalized image of Japanese identity that locals were desperate to shed in the wake of their losses after World War II. The metallic tower that would eventually replace the Imperial Hotel became a new sign of Japanese power. The romanticism of Wright's material palette, which referenced the holy mount

Fujiyama that he believed regulated the antique and modern lifestyles of the Japanese, had given way to the technological forces that first flattened but later elevated the Japanese economy to unforeseen heights. A new form was much more likely to conjure up images of proud modernist towers in the city that dotted cities like New York City in the immediate postwar period: buildings that American architects such as Harrison would complete in the International Style.

Wallace K. Harrison and the Racialization of American Pragmatism

The polemical division between functionalist and organicist interpretations of modern architectural style is manifest in the organization of the *International Style* exhibition catalog, which consists of two halves—one dedicated the formal innovations of European designers and the other to the communal principles of social housing in Western Europe and public housing in the United States. The one small patch of common ground to bridge these two sections emerges in the figure of William Lescaze, a Swiss émigré who graces both. While Philip Johnson and Henry-Russell Hitchcock praise Lescaze for popularizing the formal idioms of the International Style among business elites and local decisionmakers, social critics such as Lewis Mumford and Catherine Bauer interpret the ubiquitous brick finishes of his designs for public housing for establishing an organic formal language for mass culture in the United States. If we can admit that the polemics of the modern architectural style debates falsely bifurcates the complementary aspects of Lescaze's work, then it becomes possible to relate the organicist and functionalist content of his modern architecture during this time. Thus Lescaze, like many of his contemporaries, belonged to both worlds simultaneously, or at least benefited from the innovations of each camp.

Another aspect of Lescaze's professional identity that made him popular domestically was his naturalization as a US citizen and his reputation as a no-nonsense businessman. If Americans loved anything, they loved the consummate businessman, and Lescaze represented a well enlightened version of this urban social type. By the end of World War II a new wave of businessman-architects emerged to design the corporate and political building programs that defined the growing reach of American internationalism. The prewar and interwar emigrations of European designers to the United States was now challenged by the growth of an American brand of design expertise that was later disseminated to the rest of the world, a thematic transition that inverted the trajectory of Lescaze's career, which began after his arrival to the United States with the completion of the Philadelphia Savings Fund Society building (1929–1932) before he transitioned to public housing in the late 1930s.

Mock's 1946 apologia for organic architecture seemed to precipitate Johnson and Hitchcock's return to MoMA to pen a rejoinder in the *Built in USA:*

Post-war Architecture exhibition of 1952. While both Johnson and Hitchcock wanted to reassess the evolving state of contemporary architecture, Hitchcock especially used this opportunity to declare public housing an abandoned aesthetic project of the American avant-garde, a pronouncement he hoped would be the final word on the curatorial squabbles of the 1930s.[33] Even though the concrete lintels and brick coursework of Lescaze's Williamsburg Houses set a new standard for so-called organic municipal housing around the country, Hitchcock's pronouncement rhetorically displaces Lescaze as the contemporary representative of the businessmen-architect. In his essay, he introduces a new ethos for business that directly counters the aesthetic restraint of 1920s European modernists with a new sensibility for the commercial value of architectural beauty: "As building costs rose, architects prated only of economy, and it was assumed that a hypothetical businessman's attitude of strict accountancy and budget paring was the only proper one for a serious professional practitioner. Yet actually it has been business, interested in the advertising value of striking architecture, which has sponsored many of the more luxurious—and not to balk at the word—beautiful buildings of the last few years."[34] This consciously opulent rendering of the International Style makes the overt display of building materials a strategic element in shaping the symbolic meaning of monumental form. Hitchcock cites Harrison as the representative of this new professional attitude toward design, particularly for his design and construction management of iconic projects such as Rockefeller Center and the United Nations Headquarters (fig. C.4).

An implicit effect of Hitchcock's advertising framework for International Style architecture was the transformation of modern architectural character from a seemingly transparent embodiment of the social norms of industrial culture into a material emblem for corporate and political institutions of the period. This commodification of architectural embodiment was evident in the public dissemination of images of the UN Headquarters, which appeared in various forms of commemorative plaques, posters, and stamps of member nations within a year of its completion. The ways in which conflicting national and international meanings were negotiated through the use of a single image constitute one of the most interesting aspects of these visual reproductions. For example, there was tremendous interest in the structural composition of this building in the American press, which identified the "New Hampshire granite" and the "Vermont marble" that composed the physical body of this project. Such descriptions gave American readers the perception that, despite the UN being an international forum for political negotiations, it was the power of local commerce and design expertise that made it an important domestic project. Foreign outlets and international participants of the board of design, on the other hand, were much more likely to emphasize the worldly character of the

Figure C.4. Hugh Ferris, perspective of United Nations Headquarters, 1947. Note the square public housing project in the bottom right of the image. From George A. Dudley, A Workshop for Peace: Designing the United Nations Headquarters (Cambridge, MA: MIT Press, 1994).

UN to combat any singular political association with the United States, or to emphasize the collaborative nature of the design effort. None other than Le Corbusier came forward to claim this project for a broader geographical context by stating that this building inaugurated "a world architecture, *world*, not *international*, for therein we shall respect the human, natural, and cosmic laws" that would come to regulate future progress.[35] This global perspective was no doubt informed by the architect's personal experiments with designing political structures such as the League of Nations building (1927–1929) in Switzerland and the Centrosoyuz (1928–1936) in Russia. Yet even he was not above seeking the title of "chef d'atelier—mandate par l'U.N." if it meant that he could be given more credit for the design and placed in charge of construction management.[36]

It is entirely reasonable to attribute the perceptions of the UN Headquarters as an American project to the practicalities of the construction process. In retrospect, the collaborative nature of its design and the centralized organization of its construction management likely contributed to Harrison receiving much of the credit for its execution. With the lack of a single design architect to speak to the press, journalists routinely sought out Harrison for public comments—an explicit result of the top-down structure of many corporate and political institutions. As chairman of the board and the architect of record, he was personally identified as the "architect," "chief architect," and "director of planning" interchangeably, while other members of the board of design were merely referred to in passing. Even in Arthur Drexler's review of the project for the *Built in USA* catalog, which credits the entire board of design for the schematic parti, Drexler primarily focuses on Harrison's formal interpretations of this scheme in the final building.

Even factors beyond Harrison's professional role within the UN bureaucracy contributed to the American branding of this project. The United States' decision to become a member nation of the UN created the perception of greater stability within the organization, since it had previously decided not to take part in the short-lived League of Nations. In addition, the decision to place the UN Headquarters in New York City seemed to reinforce the international reputation of this city as the symbolic "center of the world" by virtue of its business networks, its rising rate of GDP in comparison to other developed nations, and now for its political prominence.[37] This social and political context set the stage for the trafficking of a few critical assumptions regarding the importance of American leadership at the UN, both in terms of its political management and in terms of the architectural design of its headquarters. Architectural critics interpreted Harrison's deliberative approach to design as a microscaled model of the best practices that would likely persist at the UN.

One of the most striking nationalist depictions of the UN comes directly from Harrison, who uses a series of American colloquialisms to express his feelings upon seeing the final design. He is quoted in the *New York Times* as stating that this building was "something like seeing Joe DiMaggio hit a home run or watching Bill Robinson shuffle across the stage. You just stand up and feel proud when it happens."[38] On the surface, the content of his statement might simply reflect the high level of craftsmanship required to complete this project—an effort that is comparable to the of expertise required to be a professional athlete or an entertainer. Yet it is interesting that Harrison uses DiMaggio and Robinson to illustrate the emotive force of this structure, as these figures—Italian American and African American, respectively—represent the potential of American culture to amalgamate a single body politic from its separate racial and ethnic groups. At least one aspect of the UN building design directly emulates this portrait of American character, and that was the deliberative process that Harrison used to synthetically integrate several design schemes into a single parti. A project architect in Harrison's office remembers this being an explicit goal

Figure C.5. Design team standing in front of United Nations Headquarters model, n.d. From George A. Dudley, *A Workshop for Peace: Designing the United Nations Headquarters* (Cambridge, MA: MIT Press, 1994), 220.

of the project: "From its inception, Harrison had tried in every way possible to create a truly international, truly cooperative, anonymous design, incorporating contributions of many" (fig. C.5).[39]

In Harrison's analogy, we are meant to take DiMaggio and Robinson's fame as a representative example of the inherent potential that all Americans have, regardless of race, creed, or color, to contribute to the ethos of liberty at home and abroad. However, even a casual examination of the legal status afforded white and black Americans in the 1940s forces us to confront the lack of substantive basis behind this formal equality. The interchangeable status of these two stars can only be obtained on a symbolic register that ignores the patterns of legal segregation that separated black and white Americans. Robinson is forced to operate as both the rule for and an exception to his racial identity. The paradoxical nature of American liberty in Harrison's analogy becomes even clearer if we consider Robinson's performance of Mr. Bojangles, a fictional character that was memorialized in a song by the same name. The song "Mr. Bojangles" is an updated representation of the happy-go-lucky dancing darky that was a typical character of minstrel shows at the turn of the century. As Martin Berger notes in his book *Sight Unseen*, the black themes of the minstrel show permitted proslavery and antislavery whites to sit side-by-side, despite having oppositional views on black liberties. While abolitionists found the humanity of black subjects to be acknowledged in their use as stage performers, proslavery advocates recognized the reifying power that came with retaining stereotypical depictions of blackness that are an essential part of white supremacy. If Harrison's design for the UN building emulates the structural logic of blackness in any way, then it does so by using a visual image for liberty that masks the uneven distribution of power and the naked preservation of American self-interest that prompted the physical location of the UN Headquarters. Harrison's decidedly American voice poetically reveals the nationalist themes that are embodied by this purportedly international project.

Another way to tease out the racial content of the design for the UN Headquarters is to examine the historical myth of American pragmatism implicit in Hitchcock's redefinition of the businessman-architect. Hitchcock slowly concedes the continual influence of historical discourses in his postwar estimation of the International Style in the very language he uses to describe this phenomenon. In his commentary for *Built in USA* he plainly states, in a reversal of his definition for International Style architecture in 1932, that the use of the terms such as *beauty* and *character* remains the best means of interpreting the historical progress of modern architecture: "Modern architectural criticism has tended to eschew many terms favored in the immediately preceding generations because of the unhappy connotations such words have acquired. Beauty, character, grace, and elegance have found little favor as terms of praise with a generation seeking extra-aesthetic sanctions for an architectural revolution."[40] The revival of "character" in this curatorial context establishes a link back to the discursive frameworks for architectural organicism that explicitly related racial, national, and architectural characters within the design process.

In chapter 4 I outlined the racial content associated with the communal aspirations for public housing in New York City that was outwardly expressed by the continual use of organicist language without making any explicit references to natural metaphors of design. I wish to examine a similarly charged use of organicist language in the racial content that was associated with Hitchcock's revival of the historical myths of American pragmatism. This philosophical tradition conditioned the social context for Sullivan's architecture theory, especially as it was expressed by proponents of economic pragmatism in the Gilded Age. Like Harrison's colorblind portrait of American expertise, the historical practice of American pragmatism is effused with notions of white Protestant racial genius, but mostly in the form of omission by not considering the social experiences of nonwhite peoples. In the book *In a Shade of Blue: Pragmatism and the Politics of Black America*, Eddie S. Glaude Jr. critiques the founders of American pragmatism for developing a set of problem-solving strategies for promoting democracy that fail to consider the lack of access that nonwhite citizens might have for participating in this process.[41]

If Hitchcock's identification of the postwar model of the American businessman-architect was any indication, it is not surprising that Harrison went on to experience great professional success as a result of his association with the United Nations Headquarters. This was manifest in his selection as design architect for several important bureaucratic projects, including the Carnegie Endowment International Center (1953), which was built to formally communicate directly with the UN Secretariat, and the Central Intelligence Agency Headquarters (1957–1962) in Langley, Virginia. In each case, however, Harrison's peers and critics credit his success to the pragmatic and deliberative approach to conflict resolution he pioneered in New York. These skills date back to his position as cochair of the Office of the Coordinator of Inter-American Affairs with Nelson Rockefeller, which used advertising campaigns to counter anti-American propaganda in Latin America during World War II.[42] Despite the oppositional ways that Hitchcock characterized Harrison and Lescaze's careers, however, both figures shared an instrumental role within MoMA curators' polemical depiction of American design expertise. Perhaps it is fitting, then, that the first construction documents for the UN Headquarters were completed in the empty rooms of a public housing complex that was erected on the ten-acre plot of land that would eventually serve as the building's site.[43] The lingering presence of this housing complex was still evident, though cleverly hidden in the perspective drawings that were completed for publication in major newspapers and press releases of the 1940s.

Future Research on Race and Modern Architecture

The critical approach outlined in this book opens the way for reassessing the long-term effects of racial discourses in the paradigm of architectural organicism. A few topics that could not be included in this volume but demonstrate the practicality of this new methodology are the regional expression of whiteness in Western Europe and the United States that may have offered different conceptions of the future of the nation-state. For example, the racial discourses of the Arts and Crafts movement as it was practiced in the United States likely developed along different lines as a result of the different nonwhite communities that white settlers came into contact with as they traveled across the continental United States. Modern architects such as Bernard Maybeck were heavily influenced by his location in the far west of the United States, which both reflected a remoteness from East Coast elites as well as a new orientation across the Pacific Ocean that was permitted by expanding American naval power. Maybeck explicitly expressed an interest in the cultures that coexisted in the Asia-Pacific, including the works of Māori, Hawaiian, and Japanese peoples. He even created unique stage designs for *The Mikado* and served as a consultant for other Asian-inspired productions in the area. While Maybeck's work has been included under the general umbrella of American Arts and Crafts, his vision for American identity departed from the midwestern themes of Wright and design elites on the East Coast. Taking close stock of these regional differences would help us to more accurately depict the role that whiteness played in managing the growing complexity of the United States as a new nation.

Another area of exploration within the Arts and Crafts movement is the racial discourses that were disseminated by movements in Great Britain. John Ruskin's *The Poetry of Architecture, or the Architecture of the Nations of Europe, considered in its Association with Natural Scenery and National Character* (1855) is perhaps an obvious starting point for reassessing the contributions of British architectural organicism. This research would help us to identify what one might call the "Anglo-Saxon" body personified by the naturalistic detailing of Oxford University's Natural History Museum; a Ruskinian Gothic revival structure completed by the Irish architects Thomas Deane and Benjamin Woodward. Deane and Woodward's material display of regional characters in the form of geological column shafts, ornamental carvings of local flora and fauna, and the totemic structures of native tribes from Canadian British Columbia presented a comprehensive analogical display of the racial and ethnic diversity of the British Empire. Using the lens of character helps us to account for the museum's material index of racial variation as it was reflected through scientific interpretations of the Anglo-Saxon race in anthropological debates. It also relates the disciplinary motivations for integrating race theory into architectural discourse to postcolonial critiques of the supportive function of colonial identities formulated in the British Isles. The historical influence of the Aryan migration myth examined in chapters 1 and 2 of this book opens the way for reexamining the specific meaning of the rash of Alpine architecture movements in Germany. For example, the racial import of Bruno Taut's "Alpine Architecture" has not been greatly explored in English publications on the architect. And of course, the unification of modern Germany offers many more opportunities to explore the regional expression of national identity, especially as so many visions for the nation-state were never fully realized.

NOTES

Introduction: The Racialization of Architectural Character in the Long Nineteenth Century

1. Frank Lloyd Wright, *Ausgeführte Bauten und Entwurfe von Frank Lloyd Wright*, edited by Ernst Wasmuth (Berlin: Ernst Wasmuth, 1910), 7.

2. *Ausgeführte Bauten*, x.

3. C. Robert Haywood, *Victorian West: Class and Culture in Kansas Cattle Towns* (Lawrence: University Press of Kansas, 1991).

4. *Ausgeführte Bauten*, 7 (italics mine).

5. See Anders Stephanson, *Manifest Destiny: American Expansion and the Empire of Right* (New York: Farrar, Straus and Giroux, 1996), 28–66; and Reginald Horsman's *Race and Manifest Destiny: The Origins of American Racial Anglo-Saxonism* (Cambridge, MA: Harvard University Press, 1986). Similar studies of the racial discourses of manifest destiny include James T. Campbell, Matthew Pratt Guterl, and Robert G. Lee, eds., *Race, Nation and Empire in American History* (Chapel Hill: University of North Carolina Press, 2007); Edward J. Blum's *Reforging the White Republic: Race, Religion and American Nationalism, 1865–1898* (Baton Rouge: Louisiana State University Press, 2005); Eric Love's *Race over Empire: Racism and U.S. Imperialism, 1865–1900* (Chapel Hill: University of North Carolina Press, 2004); Amy Kaplan's *The Anarchy of Empire in the Making of U.S. Culture* (Cambridge, MA: Harvard University Press, 2002).

6. See, for example, James B. Salazar's *Bodies of Reform: The Rhetoric of Character in Gilded Age America* (New York: New York University Press, 2010).

7. Anthony Alofsin uncovers the influence of Secessionist movement interpretations of "pure forms" in premodern material cultures on Wright's architectural organicism. See *Frank Lloyd Wright—The Lost Years, 1910–1922: A Study of Influence* (Chicago: University of Chicago Press, 1994), 5–9.

8. See Joseph Rykwert's *The Idea of a Town: The Anthropology of Urban Form in Rome, Italy and the Ancient World* (Princeton, NJ: Princeton University Press, 1976); and Anthony Vidler's *The Writing of the Walls: Architectural Theory in the Late Enlightenment* (New York: Princeton Architectural Press, 1987).

9. The debate over the historical validity of Aryan invasions into ancient India has been conducted by Indo-Europeanists and Indigenous Aryanists in English-speaking countries and India respectively. For a summary, see Edwin F. Bryand and Laurie L. Patton's *The Indo-Aryan Controversy: Evidence and Inference in Indian History* (New York: Routledge, 2005).

10. See Adolphe Quetelet's *Anthropométrie, ou mesure des différentes facultés de l'homme* (Brussels: C. Muquardt, 1870); and Andrew Zimmerman's summary of Rudolph Virchow's

race science in *Anthropology and Antihumanism in Imperial Germany* (Chicago: University of Chicago Press, 2001), 204–13.

11. Caroline van Eck, *Organicism in Nineteenth-Century Architecture: An Enquiry into Its Theoretical and Philosophical Background* (Amsterdam: Architectura and Natura Press, 1999), 10.

12. Benedict Anderson, *Imagined Communities: Reflections on the Origin and Spread of Nationalism* (New York: Verso, 1983).

Chapter 1. Campfires in the Salon

1. See for example the posthumously published letters of Victor Hugo in *En voyage, Alpes et Pyrénées* (Paris: Hetzel, 1890); and Percy Shelley's *History of a Six Weeks' Tour through a Part of France, Switzerland, Germany and Holland* (London: T. Hookham, 1817), 175–83. The publisher of Hugo's letters, Pierre-Jules Hetzel, was also the publisher of Viollet-le-Duc's popular novels.

2. Eugène Emmanuel Viollet-le-Duc, "On Restoration," repr. in *The Foundations of Architecture: Selections from the Dictionnaire Raisonné*, introduction by Barry Bergdoll, trans. Kenneth D. Whitehead (New York: George Braziller, 1990), 197–98. All quotations from Viollet-le-Duc's "Style" essay are taken from this translation unless otherwise noted.

3. Jacques Gubler, "In Search of the Primitive," in *Eugène Emmanuel Viollet-le-Duc, 1814–1879*, ed. Penelope Farrant, Brigitte Hermann, and Ian Latham (London: Academy Editions, 1980), 80–83.

4. Viollet-le-Duc, *Foundations of Architecture*, 229–64.

5. "In a discussion of the origins of architecture in that work, Viollet had claimed that structures built by primitive peoples were the rational expression of their needs and of the material and constructional materials available to them. Those born on wooded territory built in wood, for example. In this model, the earth was inhabited originally by geographically distinct racial groups, each producing structures reflective of their needs and capabilities. However, after the first generation, a new wrinkle is factored into the equation. Subsequent generations behave slightly differently. They do not build strictly in accordance with their needs and resources. They inherit the artistic tendencies and preferences acquired by their ancestors." O'Connell, "A Rational, National Architecture: Viollet-le-Duc's Modest Proposal for Russia," *Journal of the Society of Architectural Historians*, 52, no. 4 (December 1993): 442.

6. "Pictet on the Aryan Race," *Anthropological Review* 1, no. 2 (1863): 232.

7. Johann Friedrich Blumenbach, *The Anthropological Treatises of Johann Friedrich Blumenbach*, ed. Thomas Bendyshe (London: Longman, Green, Longman, Roberts & Green, 1865).

8. See Robert Bernasconi's essay "Kant and Blumenbach's Polyps: A Neglected Chapter in the History of the Concept of Race," in *The German Invention of Race*, ed. Sara Eigen and Mark Larrimore (Albany: State University of New York Press, 2006), 73–90.

9. "Pictet on the Aryan Race," 233.

10. F. Norman, "'Indo-European' and 'Indo-Germanic,'" *Modern Language Review* 24, no. 3 (July 1929): 313–21.

11. Viollet-le-Duc, "First Lecture at the École des Beaux-Arts," repr. in Farrant, Hermann, and Latham, *Eugène Emmanuel Viollet-le-Duc, 1814–1879*, 20–25. According to notes at the end of the essay, this version of Viollet-le-Duc's lecture is based on the French translation published in *Revue des cours littéraires de la France et de l'étranger* (1864).

12. Viollet-le-Duc, "First Lecture," 25.

13. Louis Ferdinand Alfred Maury, "On the Distribution and Classification of Tongues,—Their Relation to the Geographical Distribution of Races; and on the Inductions That May be Drawn from These Relations," in *Indigenous Races of the Earth, or New Chapters on Ethnological Inquiry*, ed. Josiah Nott and L.-F.-Alfred Maury, vol. 1 (Philadelphia: J. B. Lippincott, 1857), 25.

14. Maury, "On the Distribution," 35.

15. George Robbins Gliddon, "The Monogenists and the Polygenists: Being an Exposition on the Doctrines of Schools Professing to Sustain Dogmatically the Unity or the Diversity of Human Races," in Nott and Maury, *Indigenous Races of the Earth*, vol. 2 (1868), 402–602; and Francis Pulszky, "Iconographic Researches on Human Races and their Art, in Nott and Maury, *Indigenous Races of the Earth*, vol. 1 (1857), 87–202.

16. Viollet-le-Duc, *Foundations of Architecture*, 234.

17. Viollet-le-Duc, *Foundations of Architecture*, 231.

18. Viollet-le-Duc, *Foundations of Architecture*, 234.

19. Viollet-le-Duc, *Foundations of Architecture*, 235.

20. Viollet-le-Duc, *Foundations of Architecture*, 240.

21. Johann Friedrich Blumenbach, "Section II: Of the Causes and Ways by which the Species of Animals Degenerates in General," in *Anthropological Treatises*, 194.

22. The five race types that Blumenbach noted were the Caucasian (white) race, the Mongolian (yellow) race, the Malayan (brown) race, the Negroid (black) race, and the American Indian (red) race. In his treatise there were illustrations of five skulls that corresponded with each of his racial designations as well. For example, the Caucasian race was represented by the skull of a Georgian woman and the Negroid race was represented by the skull of an Ethiopian woman of Guinea. See Blumenbach, "Section III: On the Causes and Ways by which Mankind has Degenerated as a Species," in *Anthropological Treatises*, 237.

23. Viollet-le-Duc, *Foundations of Architecture*, 240.

24. Viollet-le-Duc, *Foundations of Architecture*, 248.

25. Viollet-le-Duc, *Foundations of Architecture*, 248.

26. Viollet-le-Duc, *Foundations of Architecture*, 250.

27. Viollet-le-Duc, *Foundations of Architecture*, 248.

28. Donald Drew Egbert, *The Beaux-Arts Tradition in French Architecture* (Princeton, NJ: Princeton University Press, 1980), 63–65.

29. Viollet-le-Duc, "First Lecture," 22.

30. Viollet-le-Duc, "First Lecture," 21.

31. Viollet-le-Duc, "First Lecture," 21.

32. Viollet-le-Duc, "First Lecture," 24.

33. Viollet-le-Duc, "First Lecture," 20.

34. Viollet-le-Duc, "First Lecture," 25.

35. Eugène Emmanuel Viollet-le-Duc, *Habitations of Man in All Ages*, trans. Benjamin Bucknall (London: James R. Osgood, 1876), v. All English translations of *L'habitation humaine* are taken from the Bucknall version unless otherwise noted.

36. Viollet-le-Duc, *Habitations of Man*.

37. See Martin Bressani, "Notes on Viollet-le-Duc's Philosophy of History," *Journal of the Society of Architectural Historians*, 48, no. 4 (December 1989): 327–28. Bressani notes that Viollet-le-Duc's racial categorization follows Gobineau's tripartite division of man, which was itself a revision of Blumenbach's early quintipartite division of man.

38. Viollet-le-Duc, *Habitations of Man*, 8.

39. Viollet-le-Duc, *Habitations of Man*, 51.

40. Viollet-le-Duc, *Habitations of Man*, 45.

41. Viollet-le-Duc, *Habitations of Man*, 45.

42. Viollet-le-Duc, *Habitations of Man*, vi.

43. Viollet-le-Duc, *Habitations of Man*, vii.

44. "Taken together, ethnography and archaeology allowed nineteenth-century anthropologists to construct cultural evolutionary schemes in which descriptions of prehistoric artifacts were 'fleshed out' with descriptions of present-day 'primitive' peoples whose artifacts looked similar. This use of ethnography to supplement archaeology was called the 'comparative method.' In the early twentieth century, influential anthropologists criticized the comparative method as too speculative, and cultural evolutionism fell out of favour as an anthropological theory. In the late 1940s, it was revived by another group of anthropologists who called themselves neo-evolutionists and labelled their nineteenth-century predecessors 'classical.'" Paul A. Erickson and Liam D. Murphy, eds., *Readings for a History of Anthropological Theory*, 5th ed. (Toronto: University of Toronto Press, 2016), 26.

45. Eugène Emmanuel Viollet-le-Duc, *Histoire d'un dessinateur* (Paris: J. Hetzel, 1879), 249–73.

46. Viollet-le-Duc, *Habitations of Man*, 381–82.

47. Jacques Gubler, "Viollet-le-Duc et l'Architecture Rurale," in *Viollet-le-Duc. Centenaire de la mort à Lausanne* (Lausanne: Musée historique de l'Ancien-Evêché, 1979), 396–410.

48. Gubler, "Viollet-le-Duc," 403.

49. *Viollet-le-Duc au Chateau d'Eu, 1874–1879* (Eu, France: Musée Louis-Philippe, 1979), 56–57.

50. Viollet-le-Duc, *Habitations of Man*, 25–26.

51. Most of what is currently known about La Vedette comes from Jacques Gubler's publications and descriptions. See Gubler, "In Search of the Primitive." A reprint of the photos of this structure, both immediately after construction and subsequent changes before its demolition, accompanied an exhibition on Viollet-le-Duc's interests in geology in 1988. See Armand Brulhart and Pierre Frey, *E. Viollet-le-Duc et le Massif du Mont Blanc, 1868–1879* (Lausanne: Payot, 1988). Gubler has consistently characterized the chalet in Lausanne as a physical case study of the primitive in Viollet-le-Duc's work.

Chapter 2. Beyond the Primitive Hut

1. Gottfried Semper, *Style in the Technical and Tectonic Arts; or, Practical Aesthetics*, trans. Harry Francis Mallgrave and Michael Robinson (Los Angeles: Getty Research Institute, 2004).

2. Rykwert, *On Adam's House in Paradise: The Idea of the Primitive Hut in Architectural History* (Cambridge, MA: MIT Press, 1981).

3. For a summary of Semper's knowledge of anthropological theory, see Harry Francis Mallgrave, *Gottfried Semper: Architect of the Nineteenth Century* (New Haven, CT: Yale University Press, 1996), 157–64.

4. See, for example, Joseph Rykwert, *The Dancing Column: On Order in Architecture* (Cambridge, MA: MIT Press, 1999), 13–16. Most of this analysis accounts for the historical challenges to human-body metaphors in Vitruvian architecture theory, not the general role of human-body metaphors in eighteenth- and nineteenth-century modern architectural theory more generally.

5. "Organicism is based on the conviction, generally held in artistic theory from antiquity to the end of the nineteenth century, that art should imitate nature, not with the aim of producing perfectly faithful copies but with the aim of creating the illusion of life, of conferring the qualities of living nature upon the products of man, in the hope of effectuating the metamorphosis of dead matter into a living being. Since such metamorphosis will never be complete, we have to content ourselves with the use of metaphor: to speak of architecture as if it were part of living nature, shared her qualities of organic growth and unity, and could copy her methods." Caroline van Eck, *Organicism in Nineteenth Century-Architecture: An Enquiry into Its Theoretical and Philosophical Background* (Amsterdam: Architectura and Natura Press, 1999), 18.

6. See Robert Bernasconi, "Introduction," in *The Idea of Race*, ed. Robert Bernasconi and Tommy Lott (Indianapolis: Hackett, 2000), i–xviii.

7. Immanuel Kant, "Of the Different Human Races," in *The Idea of Race*, 8–22.

8. Even Georges Cuvier, a pre-evolutionary theorist who directly inspired Semper's theory of the four elements of architecture, believed in the scientific validity of race types. See Robert Bernasconi and Kristie Dotson, eds., *Race, Hybridity, and Miscegenation* (Bristol: Thoemmes, 2005).

9. There are several studies, although they are divided into discrete studies of national traditions or those of a single architect. Studies of the Viennese architect Adolf Loos that have explicitly examined the role of race science are Anne Cheng, *Second Skin: Josephine Baker and the Modern Surface* (New York: Oxford University Press, 2011); and Jimena Canales and Andrew Herscher, "Criminal Skins: Tattoos and Modern Architecture in the Work of Adolf Loos," *Architectural History* 48 (2005): 235–56. More general studies of the role of eugenics or scientific race theory on national architectural movements also exist. See Fabiola López-Durán, *Eugenics in the Garden: Transatlantic Architecture and the Crafting of Modernity* (Austin: University of Texas Press, 2018); Luis Carranza and Fernando Luis Lara, *Modern Architecture in Latin America: Art, Technology, and Utopia* (Austin: University of Texas Press, 2014); Mark Crinson, *Empire Building: Orientalism and Victorian Architecture* (New York: Routledge, 2013); Christina Cogdell, *Eugenic Design: Streamlining America in the 1930s* (Philadelphia: University of Pennsylvania Press, 2013); and Barbara Miller Lane, *National Romanticism and Modern Architecture in Germany and the Scandinavian Countries* (New York: Cambridge University Press, 2000).

10. The most explicit studies of the racial content of Semper's style theory are Harry Francis Mallgrave, "Gustav Klemm and Gottfried Semper: The Meeting of Ethnological and Architectural Theory," *RES: Anthropology and Aesthetics* 9 (1985): 68–79; and Mari Hvattum, *Gottfried Semper and the Problem of Historicism* (Cambridge: Cambridge University Press, 2004), 29–47, 64–86.

11. See, for example, Joseph Rykwert, "Gottfried Semper: Architect and Historian," in *The Four Elements of Architecture and Other Writings*, by Gottfried Semper (Cambridge: Cambridge University Press, 1989), vii; and Mallgrave, *Gottfried Semper*, 371–81.

12. While Semper was concerned with mining the historical origins of the German nation-state, even speculating on which Saxon tribes migrated from the peaks of the Bavarian Alps to first settle in the region, his form of nationalism was rarely as strident as that of his peer Richard Wagner. For a study of Aryan thinking in Nazi German architecture, see Barbara Miller Lane, *Architecture and Politics in Germany, 1918–1945* (Cambridge, MA: Harvard University Press, 1985).

13. Mallgrave cites Cuvier as an intellectual influence for Semper's pre-evolutionary conception of style. See Mallgrave, *Gottfried Semper*, 157–58, 163, 332.

14. There are many biographies of Sara Baartman, who was popularly known as the Hottentot Venus. See Clifton Cray and Pamela Scully, *Sara Baartman and the Hottentot Venus: A Ghost Story and a Biography* (Princeton, NJ: Princeton University Press, 2009); and T. Denean Sharpley-Whiting, *Black Venus: Sexualized Savages, Primal Fears, and Primitive Narratives in French* (Durham, NC: Duke University Press, 1999). There are also many texts in the history of science that recall Cuvier's role in analyzing Baartman after her death. See Michael Banton, "Race as Type," in *Racial Theories* (New York: Cambridge University Press, 1998), 44–68; and Stephen Jay Gould, *The Mismeasure of Man* (New York: W. W. Norton, 2006).

15. See Mitchell Schwarzer, *German Architectural Theory and the Search for Modern Identity* (Cambridge: Cambridge University Press, 1995), 49–54.

16. Contemporary studies of the biopolitics of German colonial architecture include Itohan Osayimwese, *Colonialism and Modern Architecture in Germany* (Pittsburgh: University of Pittsburgh Press, 2017). General histories of German colonialism include Bradley Naranch and Geoff Eley, eds., *German Colonialism in a Global Age* (Durham, NC: Duke University Press, 2014); Sebastian Conrad, *German Colonialism: A Short History* (New York: Cambridge University Press, 2012); Michael Perraudin and Jurgan Zimmer with Katy Heady, eds., *German Colonialism and National Identity* (New York: Routledge, 2013), to name just a few.

17. See Semper, *Style*, 685.

18. See Osayimwese, *Colonialism and Modern Architecture*, 61–104.

19. Suzanne Zantop, *Colonial Fantasies: Conquest, Family, and Nation in Precolonial Germany, 1770–1870* (Durham, NC: Duke University Press, 1997).

20. Semper, "Four Elements of Architecture," in Semper, *Four Elements of Architecture*, 122.

21. Semper, "Four Elements of Architecture," 122.

22. Semper, "Four Elements of Architecture," 109.

23. Semper, "Four Elements of Architecture," 102.

24. Semper, "Four Elements of Architecture," 102.

25. Semper, "Four Elements of Architecture," 103.

26. Semper, "Four Elements of Architecture," 102.

27. Semper, "Four Elements of Architecture," 112.

28. Semper, "Four Elements of Architecture," 111.

29. Semper, "Four Elements of Architecture," 107.

30. Semper, "Four Elements of Architecture," 102, 113.

31. Semper, "Four Elements of Architecture," 108.

32. Semper, "Four Elements of Architecture," 123.

33. Wolfgang Herrmann, *Gottfried Semper: In Search of Architecture* (Cambridge, MA: MIT Press, 1984), 139–52.

34. Carl Gottlieb Wilhelm Bötticher, "The Principles of Hellenic and Germanic Ways of Building with Regard to Their Application to Our Present Way of Building" (1846), repr. in *In What Style Should We Build? The German Debate on Architectural Style*, ed. Heinrich Hübsch (Santa Monica, CA: Getty Center, 1992), 147–68.

35. Bötticher, "Principles," 151–52; 164–66.

36. Bötticher, "Principles," 152.

37. See Michael Banton, *Racial Theories*, 12.

38. Schwarzer, *German Architectural Theory*, 182–89.

39. Bötticher used the term *Junkturen* to describe this aspect of his style theory. See Carl Gottlieb Wilhelm Bötticher, *Die Tektonik der Hellenen*, vol. 1 (Potsdam: Riegel, 1852), 76–78.

40. Schwarzer states, "Indeed, the *Sinnform* completes the architectural *Kunstform* by

sculpting out of the functional member symbols of a geometric, vegetative, or animalistic character. Unlike Bötticher, who described an earlier phase of historical tectonics, however, Heinzerling wrote of an ahistorical ornament, drawn from representation of nature." Schwarzer, *German Architectural Theory*, 187.

41. Herrmann, *Gottfried Semper*, 139–52.

42. The art historian Alois Riegl is most famously criticized for inaugurating a materialist interpretation of Semper's style theory. See Riegl, *Problems of Style: Foundations for a History of Ornament* (Princeton, NJ: Princeton University Press, 1992).

43. Semper, *Style*, 77.

44. Semper, *Style*, 77.

45. Semper, *Style*, 78.

46. Mallgrave, "Gustav Klemm and Gottfried Semper," 69–79.

47. Mallgrave, "Gustav Klemm and Gottfried Semper," 71–72.

48. For example, "Thus the features of eunuchs, staring through their wrinkles with haunting youth, remained an inherited trait of Chinese physiognomy." Semper, *Style*, 256.

49. See Fredrick Gregory, "Jacob Moleschott: 'Für das Volk,'" in *Scientific Materialism in Nineteenth Century Germany* (Dordrecht: D. Reidel, 1977), 88–93.

50. Gregory, *Scientific Materialism*, 88.

51. Mallgrave, "The Zurich Years: 1855–1869," in Mallgrave, *Gottfried Semper*, 284–85.

52. Mallgrave, "Zurich Years," 284–85.

53. Semper, *Style*, 467.

54. Semper, *Style*, 468.

55. Semper, *Style*, 469.

56. Semper, *Style*, 667.

57. Barbara Miller Lane traces the close relationship that existed between German and Scandinavian romantic myths during the nineteenth century in her text *National Romanticism and Modern Architecture in Germany and the Scandinavian Countries*.

58. Semper, *Style*, 674.

59. Semper, *Style*, 685.

60. See Rykwert, "Gottfried Semper," vii.

61. This literature has become vast, but the most representative examples have come from postcolonial theorists such as Frantz Fanon, Edward Said, Gayatri Spivak, Homi Bhabha, and Dipesh Chakrabarty. See Fanon, *Black Skin, White Masks* (New York: Grove, 1967); Said, *Orientalism* (London: Penguin, 1978); Spivak, *Can the Subaltern Speak?* (Basingstoke: Macmillan, 1988); Bhabha, *The Location of Culture* (New York: Routledge, 1993); and Chakrabarty, *Provincializing Europe: Postcolonial Thought and Historical Difference* (Princeton, NJ: Princeton University Press, 2000). See also Susan Buck-Morss, *Hegel, Haiti, and Universal History* (Pittsburgh: University of Pittsburgh Press, 2009).

62. Semper, *Style*, 665–710.

63. I use the term *organicism* here to indicate synthetic models of history that constructs a unified narrative of the past instead of a series of disconnected but parallel tendencies in cultural history. For a summary of the historical assumptions of German organicism, see Charles I. Armstrong, *Romantic Organicism: From Idealist Origins to Ambivalent Afterlife* (New York: Palgrave Macmillan, 2003).

64. Wilfried van der Will, "The Functions of '*Volkskultur*,' Mass Culture and Alternative Culture," in *The Cambridge Companion to Modern German Culture*, ed. Eva Kolinsky and Wilfried van der Will (Cambridge: Cambridge University Press, 1988), 153–60.

65. Ian Boyd White, "Modern German Architecture," in Kolinsky and van der Will, *Cambridge Companion to Modern German Culture*, 282–301.

66. Mallgrave, "Zurich Years," 100–105.

67. Andrei S. Markovits, Beth Simone Noveck, and Carolyn Hofig, "Jews in German Society," in Kolinsky and van der Will, *Cambridge Companion to Modern German Culture*, 88–89.

68. Helen Rosenau, "Gottfried Semper and German Synagogue Architecture," *Le Baeck Institute Yearbook* 22, no. 1 (1977): 237–44.

69. Semper, *Style*, 710.

70. Semper, *Style*, 668.

71. Semper, *Style*, 681.

72. Semper, *Style*, 709.

Chapter 3. The Search for an American Architecture

1. Lauren Weingarden credits Sherman Paul and Paul Sprague with starting the reassessment of Sullivan's work, as well as Robert Twombly, David Van Zanten, Claude Massu, and Richard Etlin for subsequent additions to Wright scholarship. See Lauren Weingarden, *Louis H. Sullivan and a 19th-Century Poetics of Naturalized Architecture* (Burlington, VT: Ashgate, 2009), 3–4.

2. See, for example, the work of Joanna Merwood-Salisbury, *Chicago 1890: The Skyscraper and the Modern City* (Chicago: University of Chicago Press, 2009), and "Western Architecture: Regionalism and Race in the Inland Architect," in *Chicago Architecture: Histories, Revisions, Alternatives*, ed. Charles Waldheim and Katerina Ruedi Ray (Chicago: University of Chicago Press, 2005), 3–14.

3. Patricia Morton uses the phrase "architectural physiognomy" to account for the ethnographic content of colonial pavilions and museum displays in the 1931 colonial exposition held in Paris, France. My use of this term extends her reading to Sullivan's attempts to develop an architectural expression for cultural nationalism outside of the immediate context of world's fairs and colonial expositions. See Patricia Morton, *Hybrid Modernities: Architecture and Representation at the 1931 Colonial Exposition, Paris* (Cambridge, MA: MIT Press, 2000).

4. The two most influential disciples of Sullivan's interpretation of democracy were Frank Lloyd Wright and Claude Bragdon. Their thoughts on the topic are recorded in Wright, *Genius and the Mobocracy* (New York: Horizon, 1971); and Bragdon, *Architecture and Democracy* (Freeport, NY: Books for Libraries, 1971). Robert Twombly and Narciso Menocal have also summarized democratic readings of Sullivan's architecture in *Louis Sullivan: The Poetry of Architecture* (New York: W. W. Norton, 2000).

5. There are many reference works on the importance of race science in the evolution of physiognomic theory in the nineteenth century. See, for example, Laurent Baridon and Martial Guédron, *Corps et arts: Physionomies et physiologies dans les arts visuels* (Paris: L'Harmattan, 1999); Martin S. Staum, *Labeling People: French Scholars on Society, Race, and Empire, 1815–1848* (Montreal: McGill-Queen's University Press, 2003); Martin Porter, *Windows of the Soul: Physiognomy in European Culture, 1470–1780* (New York: Oxford University Press, 2005); and Christopher J. Lukasik, *Discerning Characters: The Culture of Appearance in Early America* (Philadelphia: University of Pennsylvania Press, 2011).

6. Merwood-Salisbury, *Chicago 1890*, 15, 24–28.

7. This field of study is commonly known as whiteness studies, and it has been developing greater influence in academia since the first half of the 1990s. See, for example Noel Ignatiev, *How the Irish Became White* (New York: Routledge, 1995); David Roediger,

The Wages of Whiteness: Race and the Making of the American Working Class (London: Verso, 1991); and Matthew Frye Jacobson, *Whiteness of a Different Color: European Immigrants and the Alchemy of Race* (Cambridge, MA: Harvard University Press, 1998).

8. The most authoritative reference work on black life in Chicago remains St. Clair Drake and Horace Cayton, *Black Metropolis: A Study of Negro Life in a Northern City* (Harcourt, Brace, 1945). Follow-up studies include works such as Christopher Robert Reed, *The Rise of Chicago's Black Metropolis, 1920–1929* (Urbana: University of Illinois Press, 2014).

9. James B. Salazar, *Bodies of Reform: The Rhetoric of Character in Gilded Age America* (New York: New York University Press, 2010), 3.

10. Salazar, *Bodies of Reform*, 3.

11. See Sherman Paul, *Louis Sullivan: An Architect in American Thought* (Englewood Cliffs, NJ: Prentice-Hall, 1962); Narciso Menocal, *Architecture as Nature: The Transcendentalist Idea of Louis Sullivan* (Madison: University of Wisconsin Press, 1981); and Weingarden, *Louis H. Sullivan*. See also Twombly, *Louis Sullivan: His Life and Work* (Chicago: University of Chicago Press, 1987).

12. Lawrence Buell says of Emerson's thinking, "Still another strand of influence was republican-democratic political theory. This especially shaped Emerson's conviction that though everyone falls short of self-realization much of the time, everyone has self-transformative capacity. . . . Not that Emerson was an unqualified egalitarian. Like Jefferson, Adams, and other founding fathers, he believed in de facto natural aristocracy. He can sometimes sound like a patrician snob on the subjects of mobocracy and the benightedness of the mentally or socially unwashed." Buell, *Emerson* (Cambridge, MA: Harvard University Press, 2003), 62–63.

13. Twombly, *Louis Sullivan*, 40–41. See also Menocal, "Geometry and Ornamentation: Theory and Practice," in *Architecture as Nature*, 24. Menocal provides a brief chronological explanation for Sullivan's mature approach to architectural ornament. According to Menocal, Sullivan's initial approach to ornament was "picturesque" insofar as it was applied to the surfaces of buildings without being fully integrated into the underlying geometries of the building. This would include ornament applied to building surfaces and those contained within frames in interiors. A synthetic framework for integrating form and ornament did not emerge until Sullivan's application of Emanuel Swedenborg's theory of correspondences, which Menocal claims was most directly related to Sullivan through Emerson's lectures of the 1850s.

14. Michael J. Lewis, *Frank Furness: Architecture and the Violent Mind* (New York: W. W. Norton, 2001), 8–9, 14.

15. Twombly, *Louis Sullivan*, 79, 214.

16. Sullivan, letter to Whitman, February 3, 1887, cited in Paul, *Louis Sullivan*, 3–4. According to Weingarden, Sullivan owned the 1867 and 1881 editions of *Leaves of Grass*. See Weingarden, *Louis H. Sullivan*, 24. It is unclear whether he ever became aware of the earlier editions of this work.

17. Whitman's poetry is cited in Martin Klammer, *Whitman, Slavery, and the Emergence of* Leaves of Grass (University Park: Pennsylvania State University Press, 1995), 112.

18. Klammer, *Whitman, Slavery*, 1–5.

19. This quote first appeared in an editorial for the May 6, 1858, issue of the *Brooklyn Daily Times*. Cited in Klammer, *Whitman, Slavery*, 161.

20. "Now it is clear why and how the powerful and eminently unscrupulous few were growing richer, while the weaker but likewise unscrupulous many were passing into acquiescent slavery—for, historically, their black slavery was but the prophet of the present white serfdom." Louis Sullivan, *Democracy: A Man Search* (Westport, CT: Greenwood, 1973), 88.

21. Buell, *Emerson*, 242–87, examines the racial discourses operating within Emerson's political writings.

22. Fears of degeneration were widespread in the nineteenth century, with many scientists speculating on the destiny of European immigrants in the United States. For example, Robert Knox, *The Races of Men* (Philadelphia: Lea & Blanchard, 1850), speculates that European race types do not change upon geographical relocation. Knox states that "*races*, transplanted to the New World, would endeavour to carry out their destinies as they had done, and were now engaged with, in the Old World; and that *nationalities*, however strong, could never in the long run overcome the tendencies of race" (212). The belief in the immutable quality of racial characters over nationalism provides an important backdrop for considering Sullivan's critique of European immigrants on American soil, as Emerson directly cites Knox in *English Traits*. See Ralph Waldo Emerson, *English Traits*, ed. Howard Mumford Jones (1856; Cambridge, MA: Belknap Press of Harvard University Press, 1966), 213.

23. Philip Nicoloff, *Emerson on Race and History: An Examination of* English Traits (New York: Columbia University Press, 1961), 68–70.

24. Nicoloff, *Emerson on Race and History*, 68–70.

25. There are at least two book-length studies on Emerson's race theory and several chapters within books dedicated to other subjects. Most of the arguments hinge on interpretation of Emerson's *English Traits* and the longevity of the viewpoints expressed within this study. For studies on Emerson's elevation of a white, Anglo-Saxon, Protestant ideal for American democracy, see Nicoloff, *Emerson on Race and History*; and Nell Irvin Painter, *The History of White People* (New York: W. W. Norton, 2010), 151–89. These studies view Emerson's turn toward Anglo-Saxonism as a permanent aspect of his post-British travels. For a contrasting opinion, see Daniel Koch, *Ralph Waldo Emerson in Europe: Class, Race and Revolution in the Making of an American Thinker* (New York: I. B. Tauris, 2012), 167–78.

26. These included the writings of Robert Knox, Johann Friedrich Blumenbach, Samuel Morton, and the American anthropologists Josiah Nott and George Gliddon. See Koch, *Ralph Waldo Emerson in Europe*, 171.

27. In *English Traits*, he asserts: "It is race, is it not? that puts the hundred millions of India under the dominion of a remote island in the north of Europe. Race avails much, if that be true, which is alleged, that all Celts are Catholics, and all Saxons are Protestants, that Celts love unity of power, and Saxons the representative principle. Race is a controlling influence in the Jew, who, for two millenniums, under every climate, has preserved the same character and employments. Race in the negro is of appalling importance (30)." Emerson cites Robert Knox's 1850 study on race as a reference for his understanding of racial aptitudes; see 213n1.

28. For a discussion of Emerson's thoughts on poor, black citizens see Painter, *History of White People*, 184–89.

29. Sullivan was relatively positive in his assessments of ornamental motifs from the Far East compared to those found in Western European precedents. See Lauren Weingarden, "A Transcendentalist Discourse in the Poetics of Technology: Louis Sullivan's Transportation Building and Walt Whitman's Passage to India," *Word & Image: A Journal of Verbal/Visual Enquiry* 3, no. 2 (1987): 202–21.

30. Louis Sullivan, *The Autobiography of an Idea* (New York: Dover, 1956), 254.

31. Sullivan, *Autobiography*, 255.

32. Sullivan, *Democracy*, 261–337.

33. This was especially true for Irish immigrants, as they were considered to be "white negroes," or the social equivalent of blacks upon their arrival to the United States. However,

given their lack of value as a source of labor they were often derided by southerners with slaves. See Ignatiev, *How the Irish Became White*, 34–55.

34. Letter to Mr. C. H. Whitaker, dated January 14, 1922, box 1, folder 1.12, Sullivaniana Collection, 1780–2018, Ryerson and Burnham Archives, Ryerson and Burnham Libraries, Art Institute of Chicago.

35. Sullivan, *Autobiography*, 11.

36. Sullivan, *Autobiography*, 12.

37. See, for example, Michael Camille, *The Gargoyles of Notre-Dame: Medievalism and the Monsters of Modernity* (Chicago: University of Chicago Press, 2009), 119–33.

38. Sullivan, *Autobiography*, 14.

39. Timothy J. Meagher, *The Columbia Guide to Irish American History* (New York: Columbia University Press, 2005), 65, 77, 88.

40. Twombly, *Louis Sullivan*, 2–14.

41. Sullivan, *Autobiography*, 113.

42. Painter, *History of White People*, 185–89.

43. Investigations of the racial formation of whiteness in the United States are a common feature of whiteness studies. Ignatiev, Roediger, and Jacobson have pioneered work in this field since the mid-1990s.

44. These migrants called themselves "Scotch-Irish" to remain distinct from the subsequent waves of Irish Catholic immigrants coming into the United States during the 1840s. See Meagher, *Irish American History*, xx.

45. Ignatiev, *How the Irish Became White*, 62–89.

46. See Mari Hvattum's analysis of primitivism in Semper's writings in *Gottfried Semper and the Problem of Historicism* (Cambridge: University of Cambridge Press, 2004), 29–45.

47. See Jean-François Bédard, "The Measure of Expression: Physiognomy and Character in Lequeu's 'Nouvelle Méthode,'" in *Chora: Intervals in the Philosophy of Architecture*, ed. Alberto Pérez Gómez and Stephen Parcell, vol. 1 (Montreal: McGill-Queen's University Press, 1994), 35–56.

48. See Antoine Picon, *Ornament: The Politics of Architecture and Subjectivity* (Chichester, West Sussex, UK: Wiley, 2013), 59–62.

49. Sullivan's library contained many volumes of books on physiognomy. See *Catalogue at Auction at Our Salesrooms, No. 185 Wabash Avenue, Monday, Nov. 29, 10:30 am: Household effects, library, Oriental rugs, paintings, etc. of Mr. Louis Sullivan, the well-known Chicago architect, at unreserved sale* (Chicago: Williams, Barker & Severn, 1909), entries 18 and 27 under the subheading "Books."

50. Cover of *Journal Amusant*, no. 107, January 6, 1858, Bibliothèque Nationale de France.

51. Lombroso's racial anthropology has also been connected to the primitive theories of the Viennese architect Adolf Loos. See Jimena Canales and Andrew Hersher, "Criminal Skins: Tattoos and Modern Architecture in the Work of Adolf Loos," *Architectural History* 48 (2005): 235–56.

52. Alfred E. Willis, *Illustrated Physiognomy* (Chicago: Alfred E. Willis, 1879), 3.

53. Willis, *Illustrated Physiognomy*, 39.

54. Sullivan, *Autobiography*, 282.

55. Willis, *Illustrated Physiognomy*, 3.

56. Willis, *Illustrated Physiognomy*, 13.

57. Sullivan, *Autobiography*, 218.

58. This image, dated December 7, 1874, can be viewed at the Art Institute of Chicago. It has been reproduced in Twombly and Menocal, *Louis Sullivan*, 183.

59. For an example of Ruskin's romanticization of country life, see *The Poetry of Architecture: or the Architecture of the Nations of Europe Considered in Its Association with Natural Scenery and National Characteristics* (London: George Allen, 1893), 1–6.

60. Both illustrations have been published in catalogs of works held at the Art Institute of Chicago. See Twombly and Menocal, *Louis Sullivan*, 177, 213.

61. Louis Sullivan, "Characteristics and Tendencies of American Architecture," in *Louis Sullivan: The Public Papers*, ed. Robert Twombly (Chicago: University of Chicago Press, 1988), 2–7.

62. Louis Sullivan, *Kindergarten Chats* (1918; New York: Dover, 1979), 124.

63. Sullivan, *Kindergarten Chats*, 127.

64. The most typical reference to this division of labor is Dankmar Adler's letter to Montgomery Schuyler. "In the biographical notes with which he has favored me, and which are summarized above, Mr. Adler writes, that since the formation of the firm 'the pre-eminence in the artistic field of Mr. Sullivan' has relieved the senior partner from that branch of professional work, and left him free to devote himself to the engineering problems involved in the modern office building." Montgomery Schuyler, "A Critique (with illustrations) of the Works of Adler and Sullivan, D. H. Burnham & Co., Henry Ives Cobb," *Great American Architects Series: Architectural Record* 2 (February 1891), 15.

65. See Joseph Siry, *Beth Sholom Synagogue: Frank Lloyd Wright and Modern Religious Architecture* (Chicago: University of Chicago Press, 2012), 36.

66. Sullivan's comment, taken from an article in the *Chicago Tribune* titled "Church Spires Must Go," is cited in Sullivan, *Louis Sullivan*, 72–73.

67. Dana Evan Kaplan, *American Reform Judaism: An Introduction* (New Brunswick, NJ: Rutgers University Press, 2003), 6–26.

68. Reform theorists referred to this belief as ethical monotheism. See Kaplan, *American Reform Judaism*, 14–18.

69. The congregations of Jewish synagogues routinely formed *verein*, or social clubs, to precipitate all forms of self-improvement. See Alan Silverstein, *Alternatives to Assimilation: The Response of Reform Judaism to American Culture, 1840–1930* (Hanover: Brandeis University Press, 1994), 90.

70. "A typical plan of the older American synagogue was to have the worship hall as the major floor area of the structure. It was generally raised half a story above the street and designed to contain seating for the entire congregation. Its decoration was as elaborate as means allowed. Below was a large, low-ceilinged room, the 'vestry,' used for social functions, lectures, and the like. Flanking it were permanent and semi-permanent classrooms. The building was designed to serve a well-knit neighborhood, placed on a minimum-sized plot, often surrounded by commercial properties." Peter Blake, *The American Synagogue for Today and Tomorrow* (New York: Union of American Hebrew Congregations, 1954), 89.

71. Blake, *American Synagogue*, 89.

72. Jeanne Kilde, *When Church Became Theater: The Transformation of Evangelical Architecture and Worship in Nineteenth-Century America* (New York: Oxford University Press, 2002), 18–23; see 224n27.

73. According to Wise, "as the purest form of monotheistic religion, Judaism was therefore the strongest theological argument for ethical behavior. As such, it deserved to be taken seriously as a way of thought and a way of life by all individuals committed to finding a true understanding of God and God's place in the world. This allowed Reform leaders such as Wise to declare that Judaism was destined to become the faith of all humankind, or at least of all Americans who held liberal religious beliefs." Kaplan, *American Reform Judaism*, 16.

74. Siry notes this latter detail in his recent study of Jewish synagogues. Siry, *Beth Sholom Synagogue*, 46.

75. Schuyler, "Critique," 39–40. An equal amount of praise and criticism of the design can be found in response to Sullivan's designs for religious spaces. For example, complaints by congregants of Moody's Tabernacle were quelled only by a word from John Moody, the reverend of the church. "But a second reason was that when the frescoes went up, they caused a sensation within the congregation. Anticipating traditional religious motifs, several of Moody followers found Sullivan's offerings much too secular." Twombly, *Louis Sullivan*, 87–88. Siry also notes negative critiques. See Siry, *Beth Sholom Synagogue*, 38.

76. Schuyler's comments are typical of this opinion. See Schuyler, "Critique." His criticisms are echoed in Rachel Wischnitzer's survey of American synagogues: "The overall pattern used here by Louis Sullivan was the same as in Henry Hobson Richardson's Marshall Field warehouse in Chicago (1885); but if the formula was effective there because it provided a device for tying together the seven stories of a commercial building, here it produced an awkward monotony, not to speak of the unresolved problem of the treatment of the front." Wischnitzer, *Synagogue Architecture in the United States: History and Interpretation* (Philadelphia: Jewish Publication Society of America, 1955), 91.

77. Twombly, *Louis Sullivan*, 407–44.

78. One of the board members for this venture was Jesse Binga, a conservative black businessman who was president of the only black-owned bank in Chicago's South Side. Binga's real estate speculations made him familiar with the representational role of black civic structures in Chicago. His 1905 purchase of the Bates Building at 3635–3637 State Street initiated a gradual black in-migration to this block that began changing the racial demography of the neighborhood. According to the newspaper profile of his career, this expansion opened the way "for colored people to reside on every street and avenue from State Street east to Lake Michigan." "Mr. Jesse Binga, One of the Most Successful and Progressive Afro-American Bankers and Real Estate Brokers in the United States," *Broad Axe*, December 25, 1909, 1. He later placed a storefront bank in the same building in 1908, and marked the corner with a painted party wall sign advertising the presence of this black institution.

79. See "Plan Memorial to Booker T. Washington," *Broad Axe*, March 1, 1915, 1; and "Afro-American Cullings," *Kansas City Sun*, February 5, 1916.

80. Booker T. Washington, *Character Building* (1902; New Brunswick, NJ: Transaction, 2013), 24.

81. Washington, *Character Building*, 24.

82. Washington, *Character Building*, 153.

83. Washington, *Character Building*, 183.

84. "Plan Memorial to Booker T. Washington," 1.

85. Historical American Building Survey report of Kehilath Anshe Ma'ariv (HABS, 1965), 2.

86. See Michael W. Harris, *The Rise of Gospel Blues: The Music of Thomas Andrew Dorsey in the Urban Church* (New York: Oxford University Press, 1992).

87. See Harris, *The Rise of Gospel Blues*, 209–40; and Robert M. Marovich, *A City Called Heaven: Chicago and the Birth of Gospel Music* (Urbana: University of Illinois Press, 2015), 92–93, 112–31.

88. "To the right of the altar, a Christ clearly of African descent, displaying dark brown skin, a broad, flattened nose, and black, wavy hair, presided over the Last Supper and his disciples including the youthful John and the brooding Judas. Scott painted the disciples in

varying skin tones that ranged from light beige to medium brown." Kymberly Pinder, "Painting the Gospel Blues: Race, Empathy and Religion at Pilgrim Baptist Church," *American Art* 25, no. 3 (Fall 2011), 80.

Chapter 4. When Public Housing Was White

1. Henry-Russell Hitchcock and Philip Johnson, *The International Style* (1932; New York: W. W. Norton, 1996), 164–65.

2. See William Jordy's 1986 essay "William Lescaze Reconsidered," which was reprinted in *"Symbolic Essence" and Other Writings on Modern Architecture and American Culture*, ed. Joan Ockman (New Haven, CT: Yale University Press, 2005), 171–86.

3. Gaia Caramellino, *Europe Meets America: William Lescaze, Architect of Modern Housing* (Newcastle upon Tyne, UK: Cambridge Scholars, 2016).

4. Samuel Zipp and Nicholas Dagen Bloom, "Williamsburg Houses," in *Affordable Housing in New York: The People, Places and Policies That Transformed a City*, ed. Nicholas Dagen Bloom and Matthew Gordon Lasner (Princeton, NJ: Princeton University Press, 2016), 95.

5. "Lescaze's years in the United States, marked by his difficult status as an immigrant, overlap with various phases of the federal housing policies in New York." Caramellino, *Europe Meets America*, 5.

6. Interwar literature on Americanization theory were primarily concerned with outlining a set of principles for reforming the behavior of marginalized white ethnic immigrants arriving from Eastern and Southern Europe, as well as Catholic and Jewish congregants. The mission was to ensure that all new arrivals adopted the cultural norms of the first wave of Northern European immigrants to the States. See, for example, Isaac Baer Berkson, *Theories of Americanization: A Critical Study* (New York: Columbia University Teachers College, 1920), 55–57.

7. Berkson cites a passage from a 1909 pamphlet on education that reads: "Our task is to break up their groups or settlements, to assimilate and amalgamate these people as part of our American race, and to implant in their children, so far as can be done, the Anglo-Saxon conception of righteousness, law and order and popular government, and to awaken in them reverence for our democratic institutions and for those things in our national life which we as a people hold to be of abiding worth." Berkson, *Theories of Americanization*, 60.

8. See, for example, Douglas Massey and Nancy Denton, *American Apartheid: Segregation and the Making of the Underclass* (Cambridge, MA: Harvard University Press, 1996); and Katharine Bristol, "The Pruitt Igoe Myth," *Journal of Architectural Education* 44, no. 3 (1991), 163–71.

9. Martin Berger, *Sight Unseen: Whiteness and American Visual Culture* (Berkeley: University of California Press, 2005), 1–10. This critical approach has become most pervasive in studies of segregated white spaces, such as recent studies of the racial politics of the Levittown suburb. See, for example, Dianne Harris, *Second Suburb: Levittown, Pennsylvania* (Pittsburgh: University of Pittsburgh Press, 2010), and *Little White Houses: How the Postwar Home Constructed Race in America* (Minneapolis: University of Minnesota Press, 2012).

10. See Henry-Russell Hitchcock, "Introduction," in *Built in U.S.A.: Post-war Architecture*, by Hitchcock and Arthur Drexler (New York: Simon and Schuster, 1952), 16.

11. Berkson, *Theories of Americanization*, 55.

12. See David Roediger, *Working toward Whiteness: How America's Immigrants Became White: The Strange Journey from Ellis Island to the Suburbs* (New York: Basic Books, 2005).

13. Willard Van Dyke and Ralph Steiner, "The City," American Documentary Films, 1939. The film's narrative was constructed as a comparative analysis of tenement slums and modernist suburban housing estates. Lewis Mumford served as the narrator for this film.

14. William Lescaze, "New Deal Architecture," *New Republic*, July 26, 1933, 278–80.

15. The team of lawmakers and bureaucrats responsible for authoring the US Housing Act of 1937 overtly referenced their reliance on architectural studies that produced a careful analysis of the financial and technological standards of European social housing. See Nancy H. Kwak, "Planning Note: American Public Housing: Hardly a Domestic Affair," *Journal of the American Planning Association* 78, no. 4 (2012): 416–17.

16. Lewis Mumford, "Housing," in *Modern Architecture: International Exhibition, New York, Feb. 10 to March 23, 1932, Museum of Modern Art* (New York: Museum of Modern Art, 1932), 179–92.

17. "Still, the design of housing is probably closer than most other architectural activity to a long tradition in the United States of the social derivation of architectural form, with what has variously been called 'social functionalism' of the sort to which the pioneering research of Lewis Mumford has attested." Richard Plunz, *A History of Housing in New York City: Dwelling Type and Social Change in the American Metropolis* (New York: Columbia University Press, 1990), xxxv.

18. See Catherine Bauer, *Modern Housing* (Boston: Houghton Mifflin, 1934), 13; and Lewis Mumford, *The Culture of Cities* (New York: Harcourt, Brace, 1935), 236.

19. Plunz, *History of Housing*, 207–46.

20. Mumford, *Culture of Cities*, 220; Mumford cites Clarence Stein's design of Radburn, New Jersey (1929) as an example of an American housing settlement that was organically connected to American democratic values.

21. Caramellino, *Europe Meets America*, 13–23.

22. Lescaze, "New Deal Architecture," 280.

23. Lescaze, "New Deal Architecture," 280.

24. "So reads the testimony of the Secretary of the Prison Association of New York before a legislative committee appointed to investigate causes of the increase of crime in the State twenty-five years ago. . . . 'By far the largest part—eighty per cent. at least—of crimes against property and against the person are perpetrated by individuals who have either lost connection with home life, or never had any, or whose *homes had ceased to be sufficiently separate, decent, and desirable to afford what are regarded as ordinary wholesome influences of home and family*.'" Jacob August Riis, *How the Other Half Lives: Studies among the Tenements of New York* (New York: Charles Scribner's Sons, 1914), 1–2.

25. The practice of determining the racial character of a person from their physical outline dates back to historical studies of the criminal brain. These fields included physiognomy and phrenology in the nineteenth century and criminal anthropology in the twentieth century. See Richard T. Gray, *About Face: German Physiognomic Thought from Lavater to Auschwitz* (Detroit: Wayne State University Press, 2004); and Lucy Hartley, *Physiognomy and the Meaning of Expression in Nineteenth-Century Culture* (Cambridge: Cambridge University Press, 2001) for a general introduction.

26. Khalil Gibran Muhammad, *The Condemnation of Blackness: Race, Crime, and the Making of Modern Urban America* (Cambridge, MA: Harvard University Press, 2011).

27. Muhammad, *Condemnation of Blackness*, 1–14.

28. See Charles Abrams, *Race Bias in Housing*, cosponsored by the American Civil Liberties Union, National Association for the Advancement of Colored People, and the American Council on Race Relations (Detroit, MI: Department of Education, 1947), 7–13.

29. See Barry Parker and Raymond Unwin, *The Art of Building a Home: A Collection of Lectures and Illustrations* (London: Longmans, Green, 1901); and Raymond Unwin, *Town Planning in Practice: An Introduction to the Art of Designing Cities* (London: Adelphi Terrace, 1909).

30. This contributed to the popularity of Garden City planning principles among some bureaucrats. See Kwak, "American Public Housing," 416.

31. Riis, *How the Other Half Lives*, 1.

32. "The 'projects,' as public housing is commonly known, have since become associated with urban blight, crime, grime, and poverty. Yet they were initially intended for the 'submerged middle classes,' those 'worthy' of help, not the minority, unemployed, or 'untraditional' large, extended families." Arlene Dávila, *Barrio Dreams: Puerto Ricans, Latinos, and the Neoliberal City* (Berkeley: University of California Press, 2004), 31.

33. Van Dyke and Steiner, "City."

34. "Architecture Styled 'International': Its Principles Set Forth in Models Displayed in a New York Exhibition," *New York Times*, February 7, 1932, 11.

35. See David Huyssen, *Progressive Inequality: Rich and Poor in New York, 1890–1920* (Cambridge, MA: Harvard University Press, 2014); David W. Southern, *The Progressive Era and Race: Reaction and Reform, 1900–1917* (Wheeling, IL: H. Davidson, 2005); and Robert B. Fairbanks, "From Better Dwellings to Better Neighborhoods: The Rise and Fall of the First National Housing Movement," in *From Tenements to the Taylor Homes: In Search of an Urban Housing Policy*, ed. John F. Bauman, Roger Biles, and Kristin M. Szylvian (University Park: Pennsylvania State University Press, 2000), 21–29.

36. See Nicholas Dagen Bloom, *Public Housing That Worked: New York in the Twentieth Century* (Philadelphia: University of Pennsylvania Press, 2008), 54.

37. Abrams, *Race Bias in Housing*, 23.

38. See Nicholas Dagen Bloom, "Harlem River Houses," in Bloom and Lasner, *Affordable Housing in New York*, 92.

39. Lorraine Welling Lanmon, *William Lescaze, Architect* (Philadelphia: Art Alliance, 1987), 120–21.

40. Lescaze, "New Deal Architecture," 278.

41. See Mason B. Williams, *City of Ambition: FDR, La Guardia, and the Making of Modern New York* (New York: W. W. Norton, 2014), 29–37.

42. Howard Zinn, *LaGuardia in Congress* (Ithaca, NY: Fall Creek Books, 1958), 1–16.

43. *30 Years of Amalgamated Cooperative Housing, 1927–1957* (New York: Amalgamated Housing, 1958), 1–15.

44. *30 Years*, 1–15.

45. Peter G. Rowe, *Modernity and Housing* (Cambridge, MA: MIT Press, 1993), 75–170.

46. *30 Years*, 2.

47. *30 Years*, 1.

48. "North Brooklyn," in *New York City Guide* (New York: Random House with Works Progress Administration, 1939), 455.

49. John B. Manbeck, ed., *The Neighborhoods of Brooklyn* (New Haven, CT: Yale University Press, 1998), 209–10.

50. Bloom cites Mary Simkhovitch as saying, "We don't want to act in such a way and do this thing in such a way that it will deter white people from going into projects," and, "You may say it is up to the white population to receive the colored people in equal numbers everywhere because that is justice. But you know very well we haven't arrived at that condition of social justice that we should. And though we should do certain things, and the best things we can, we don't want to kick over the whole business of housing. We have to think first of housing." Bloom, *Public Housing That Worked*, 88.

51. Abrams, *Race Bias in Housing*, 21–23.

52. Le Corbusier's views on the cultural status of black Americans is most clearly outlined in *When the Cathedrals Were White: A Journey to the Country of Timid People* (New York: McGraw-Hill, 1964), 155–60. Social critiques of this text can be found in Mabel Wilson, "Black Bodies/White Cities: Le Corbusier in Harlem," *ANY: Architecture New York* 16 (1996): 35–39; and Darell Wayne Fields, *Architecture in Black* (London: Athlone, 2000), 5–16.

53. Janet Abu-Lughod, *Race, Space, and Riots in Chicago, New York, and Los Angeles* (New York: Oxford University Press, 2007), 129–58.

54. "The Negro in Harlem: A Report on Social and Economic Conditions Responsible for the Outbreak of March 19, 1935," Mayor's Commission on Conditions in Harlem, New York, 1935, 43–47.

55. Abu-Lughod, *Race, Space, and Riots*, 139.

56. See, for example, "Williamsburg Houses Queried," *New York Amsterdam News*, August 14, 1937, 12. This article tells of the Brooklyn Urban League's efforts to reverse Harold Ickes's decision that "only white tenants will occupy" Williamsburg Houses.

57. "Negroes Not Investigated," *New York Amsterdam News*, October 23, 1937, 10.

58. "City Ready to Start Huge Housing Plan," *New York Times*, March 3, 1945.

59. "$25,000,000 to Be Spent in Borough: Williamsburg Housing Only Beginning, Says Post at Celebration," *Brooklyn Daily Eagle*, September 30, 1937, 7.

60. "Fido's Locked Out of Uncle Sam's Williamsburg Houses," *Brooklyn Daily Eagle*, June 25, 1937, 1.

61. "Williamsburg Houses Queried," 12.

62. See Terence Riley, *The International Style: Exhibition 15 and the Museum of Modern Art* (New York: Rizzoli, 1992), 1–15.

63. Henry-Russell Hitchcock, *Modern Architecture: Romanticism and Reintegration* (New York: Hacker Art Books, 1970), xvi.

64. A conflict over these competing notions of organic architecture would arise again between Johnson, Hitchcock, and Mumford in the essay on housing for the catalog of MoMA's 1932 exhibition. See Mumford, "Housing."

65. Henry-Russell Hitchcock and Philip Johnson, *The International Style* (New York: W. W. Norton, 1995), 67.

66. Hitchcock and Johnson, *International Style*, 68.

67. For William Lescaze's role in the Americanization of the International Style, see Robert Bruce Dean, "European Modernism in an American Commercial Context," *William Lescaze: The Rise of Modern Design in America*, special issue, *Courier* 6, no. 1 (Spring 1984): 57–66; and Lorraine Welling Lanmon, "The Role of William E. Lescaze in the Introduction of the International Style in the United States" (PhD diss., University of Delaware, 1979). For references detailing the role of the Museum of Modern Art in the Americanization of the International Style, see Riley, *International Style*; and Sizheng Fan, "From 'Architecture and Allied Arts' to 'International Style': Architectural Exhibits in New York, 1925–1932," (PhD diss., Cornell University, 2000).

68. Mumford, *Culture of Cities*, 454.

69. After an initial run in the summer of 1932, the housing section of the MoMA exhibition was scheduled to tour across the entire country "so that our principal cities, North, South, East and West—all the way to Los Angeles—may have a chance to see what (we are told) we are coming to in the way of new housing accommodations. See Riley, *International Style*, 192.

70. "Architecture Styled 'International,'" 11.

71. Van Dyke and Steiner, "City."

72. Bauer, *Modern Housing*, 213–14.

73. Bauer, *Modern Housing*, 213–14.

74. William Lescaze, *On Being an Architect* (New York: G. T. Putnam's Sons, 1942), 76.

75. Lanmon "Role of William E. Lescaze," 23–48.

76. *William Lescaze: The Rise of Modern Design in America*, 57–66.

77. Lescaze, "New Deal Architecture," 278.

78. Lescaze, "New Deal Architecture," 279.

79. Lescaze, "New Deal Architecture," 280.

80. "Williamsburg Houses—Brooklyn NY," *Living New Deal*, accessed July 31, 2018, https://livingnewdeal.org/projects/williamsburg-houses-brooklyn-ny/. This website cites C. W. Short and R. Stanley-Brown, "Public Buildings: A Survey of Architecture of Projects Constructed by Federal and Other Governmental Bodies Between the Years 1933 and 1939 with the Assistance of the Public Works Administration" (1939).

81. "Williamsburg Houses." Landmarks Preservation Commission, June 24, 2003, Designation List 48, LP-2135, p. 5.

82. See Mary Mullen Cunningham, *Heinz Warneke (1895–1983): A Sculptor First and Last* (Newark: University of Delaware Press, 1994), 84–85.

83. Cunningham, *Heinz Warneke*, 83.

84. See Margaret Rose Vendryes, *Barthé: A Life in Sculpture* (Jackson: University Press of Mississippi, 2008), 81–87. Barthé's statue was relocated to the Kingsborough houses in Crown Heights, Brooklyn, in 1941.

85. Vendryes, *Barthé: A Life in Sculpture* (Jackson: University Press of Mississippi, 2008), 86. "Two of the males at the center of *Dance* sway at the waist, their lower bodies synchronized with the females at their sides. They reach toward each other with hand gestures eerily like the elaborate greetings performed by 1970s Black Power warriors."

86. "Green Pastures" also provided an alternative image of blackness to the ones represented at Harlem River Houses in 1937. Heinz Warneke, a German American sculptor and lead sculptor for Harlem River Houses, created a pair of sympathetic sculptures of a black laborer, titled *Man, the Provider* and a black woman, titled *Woman, the Mother and Housekeeper*, that ornament the brick piers of the first-floor courtyard. Warneke's work is animated by a love of organic form and a documented interest in primitivism. See Walter L. Nathan, "Living Forms: The Sculptor Heinz Warneke," *Parnassus* 13, no. 2 (1941): 58.

87. Dreck Spurlock Wilson, "John Louis Wilson, Jr.," in *African American Architects: A Biographical Dictionary, 1865–1945* (New York, Routledge, 2004).

88. "Fun for Housing Project Kids in New Kindergarten," *Brooklyn Daily Eagle*, March 20, 1938, 14.

89. Only one photocopy of the *Projector* magazine survives in the La Guardia and Wagner archive, although the existence of this newsletter is well documented. See, for example, "Williamsburg Houses," Landmarks Preservation Commission, June 24, 2003, Designation List 48, LP-2135, 7.

90. Bloom, *Public Housing That Worked*, 35–44.

91. Bloom, *Public Housing That Worked*, 35–44; and Plunz, *History of Housing*, 88–121.

Conclusion: Race, Nature, and Nation in Postwar American Architecture

1. See Jill Pearlman, *Inventing American Modernism: Joseph Hudnut, Walter Gropius and the Bauhaus Legacy at Harvard* (Charlottesville: University of Virginia Press, 2007).

2. George A. Dudley, *A Workshop for Peace: Designing the United Nations Headquarters* (Cambridge, MA: MIT Press, 1994), 328–43.

3. Amy Kaplan, *The Anarchy of Empire in the Making of U.S. Culture* (Cambridge, MA: Harvard University Press, 2002).

4. The literature on modern architecture in colonial and postcolonial contexts is quite extensive. A few canonical examples include Gwendolyn Wright, *The Politics of Design in French Colonial Urbanism* (Chicago: University of Chicago Press, 1991); Patricia Morton, *Hybrid Modernities: Architecture and Representation at the 1931 Colonial Exposition, Paris* (Cambridge, MA: MIT Press, 2000); Zeynep Çelik, *Empire, Architecture, and the City: French-Ottoman Encounters, 1830–1914* (Seattle: University of Washington Press, 2008), and *Displaying the Orient: Architecture of Islam at Nineteenth-Century World's Fairs* (Berkeley: University of California Press, 1992); and Vikramaditya Prakash, *Chandigarh's Le Corbusier: The Struggle for Modernity in Postcolonial India* (Seattle: University of Washington Press, 2002).

5. You can find democratic interpretations of Mies van der Rohe's architecture despite his use of similar spatial and tectonic strategies for creating Fascist and Socialist monuments in Europe. See, for example, Stanley Tigerman, "Mies van der Rohe: A Moral Modernist Model," *Perspecta* 22 (1986): 112–35; Richard Pommer, "Mies van der Rohe and the Political Ideology of the Modern Movement in Architecture," in *Mies van der Rohe: Critical Essays*, ed. Franz Schulze (Cambridge, MA: MIT Press, 1989), 134.

6. Public housing advocates in the United States such as Clarence Stein, Catherine Bauer, and Lewis Mumford had to quell the American public's suspicion of modernist social housing as a force for surreptitiously introducing socialist ideals to the working classes. This fear was fueled by the socialist rhetoric of some workers' unions as well as by negative critiques of German social housing experiments in the United States. See Nicholas Dagen Bloom, Fritz Umbach, and Lawrence J. Vale, eds., *Public Housing Myths: Perception, Reality, and Social Policy* (Ithaca, NY: Cornell University Press, 2015), 7–8.

7. The curator for *Built in USA: Post-war Architecture*, Arthur Drexler, noted later that Mock's historiography of American architecture was indeed a critical reaction to the purported European origins of the International Style. See Henry-Russell Hitchcock and Arthur Drexler, *Built in USA: Post-war Architecture* (New York: Simon and Schuster, 1952), 20–37.

8. All quotations included in this conclusion from Wright's *An Autobiography* are taken from the 1977 edition. Excerpts from this work can also be found in Henry-Russell Hitchcock, ed., *In the Nature of Materials, 1887–1942: The Buildings of Frank Lloyd Wright* (New York: Da Capo, 1942).

9. Wright, *Autobiography*, 75.

10. Wright, *Autobiography*, 118.

11. Wright, *Autobiography*, 117 (italics mine).

12. See Immanuel Kant's essay "On the Different Races of Man," 1775, repr. *Race and the Enlightenment: A Reader*, ed. Emmanuel Chuckwudi Eze (Malden, MA: Blackwell, 2000), 38–64.

13. Wright, *Autobiography*, 97.

14. Wright, *Autobiography*, 119.

15. Wright, *Autobiography*, 123.

16. Wright, *Autobiography*, 209. Wright also speaks poorly of Puerto Ricans. His negative depiction echoes the racist attitudes that Americans have today toward their fellow citizens: "Puerto Rico is beautiful but Puerto Ricans are pitiful. They seem small, fine-featured remains of a highly civilized race. Gentle, apathetic. Poor beyond belief. 'Americanos'

had already bought up the sugar-plantations. Most of them in the hands of capital from the States. Wages? Seventy cents a day, no raise in sight. It would affect the price of sugar" (300).

17. Wright, *Autobiography,* 206.

18. Wright, *Autobiography,* 148.

19. Wright, *Autobiography,* 148.

20. Claire Jean Kim, "The Racial Triangulation of Asian Americans," *Politics & Society* 27, no. 1 (March 1999): 105–38.

21. Wright, *Autobiography,* 221–23.

22. Wright, *Ausgeführte Bauten und Entwurfe von Frank Lloyd Wright,* ed. Ernst Wasmuth (Berlin: Ernst Wasmuth, 1910), 7 (italics mine).

23. Wright, *Autobiography,* 201.

24. Wright, *Autobiography,* 201.

25. Kevin Nute, *Frank Lloyd Wright and Japan* (New York: Van Nostrand Reinhold, 1993).

26. Alofsin, *Frank Lloyd Wright—The Lost Years, 1910–1922: A Study of Influence* (Chicago: University of Chicago Press, 1993).

27. Wright, *Autobiography,* 203–12.

28. Brown, *The Black Skyscraper: Architecture and the Perception of Race* (Baltimore: Johns Hopkins University Press, 2017).

29. Wright, *Autobiography,* 236.

30. Wright, *Autobiography,* 239.

31. Wright, *Autobiography,* 196, 346–47.

32. Wright, *Autobiography,* 241.

33. "Architectural ambition seems to have departed from the ranks of those architects who design large-scale public housing at just the point when Le Corbusier in France and younger men like Powell and Moyer in England (where little other building is permitted), have shown that a new and more vigorous sculptural expression can be as 'functional' as our barrack-like blocks of the pre-war period, which have aged into visual slums almost before their mortar dried." Henry-Russell Hitchcock, "Introduction," in Hitchcock and Drexler, *Built in USA: Post-war Architecture,* 14.

34. Hitchcock, "Introduction," 17.

35. Dudley, *Workshop for Peace,* xii.

36. Dudley, *Workshop for Peace,* 340; I am not sure that this suggests any particularly French motivation, as Le Corbusier was routinely maneuvering to surpass Harrison as the lead designer on the project.

37. Dudley, *Workshop for Peace,* 8–17.

38. "First U.N. Building to Open This Year," *New York Times,* January 20, 1950.

39. Dudley, *Workshop for Peace,* 340.

40. Hitchcock, "Introduction," 16 (italics mine).

41. Glaude, *In a Shade of Blue: Pragmatism and the Politics of Black America* (Chicago: University of Chicago Press, 2007), xiv–xviii.

42. Victoria Newhouse, *Wallace K. Harrison, Architect* (New York: Rizzoli, 1989), 97.

43. Richard Plunz, *A History of Housing in New York City: Dwelling Type and Social Change in the American Metropolis* (New York: Columbia University Press, 1990), 152–59.

BIBLIOGRAPHY

Primary Source Collections

Atkins Library. University of North Carolina, Charlotte
Bentley Historical Library. University of Michigan
Fine Arts Library. University of Pennsylvania
Fondazion Garbald. Castasegna, Switzerland
Gottscho, Samuel H. Photographs. Museum of the City of New York
Lescaze, William. Papers. WELA Special Collections Research Center. Syracuse University Library
LaGuardia and Wagner Archives. LaGuardia Community College
Base Mémoire. Archives Potographiques. Médiatheque de l'Architecture et du Patrimoine
Johnson, Phillip. Papers. Museum of Modern Art. New York City
Nickel, Richard. Photographs. Ryerson & Burnham Library
Park, Robert Ezra. Papers. University of Chicago Library
Sullivan, Louis. Papers. Ryerson & Burnham Libraries
Works Progress Administration Poster Collection. Library of Congress. Washington, DC
Yad Vashem Archives. Jerusalem

Primary Source Periodicals

Allgemeine Bauzeitung
Anthropological Review
Broad Axe
Brooklyn Daily Eagle
Inland Architect and Building News
Journal of the Society of Architectural Historians
Kansas City Star
New York Amsterdam News
New Republic
New York Times
Res: Anthropology and Aesthetics

Sources

Abrams, Charles. *Race Bias in Housing*. Cosponsored by the American Civil Liberties Union, National Association for the Advancement of Colored People, and the American Council on Race Relations. Detroit, MI: Department of Education, 1947.

Abu-Lughod, Janet. *Race, Space, and Riots in Chicago, New York, and Los Angeles*. New York: Oxford University Press, 2007.

Alofsin, Anthony. *Frank Lloyd Wright—The Lost Years, 1910–1922: A Study of Influence*. Chicago: University of Chicago Press, 1994.

Anderson, Benedict. *Imagined Communities: Reflections on the Origin and Spread of Nationalism*. New York: Verso, 1983.

Armstrong, Charles I. *Romantic Organicism: From Idealist Origins to Ambivalent Afterlife*. New York: Palgrave Macmillan, 2003.

Aronovici, Carol. *Housing and the Housing Problem*. Chicago: A. C. McClurg, 1920.

Banton, Michael. *Racial Theories*. New York: Cambridge University Press, 1998.

Baridon, Laurent, and Martial Guédron. *Corps et arts: Physionomies et physiologies dans les arts visuels*. Paris: L'Harmattan, 1999.

Bauer, Catherine. *Modern Housing*. Boston: Houghton Mifflin, 1934.

Berger, Martin. *Sight Unseen: Whiteness and American Visual Culture*. Berkeley: University of California Press, 2005.

Berkson, Isaac Baer. *Theories of Americanization: A Critical Study*. New York: Columbia University Teachers College, 1920.

Bernasconi, Robert, and Kristie Dotson, eds. *Race, Hybridity, and Miscegenation*. Bristol: Thoemmes, 2005.

Bernasconi, Robert, and Tommy Lott, eds. *The Idea of Race*. Indianapolis: Hackett, 2000.

Bhabha, Homi. *The Location of Culture*. New York: Routledge, 1993.

Blake, Peter. *The American Synagogue for Today and Tomorrow: A Guide Book to Synagogue Design and Construction*. New York: Union of American Hebrew Congregations, 1954.

Bloom, Nicholas Dagen. *Public Housing that Worked: New York in the Twentieth Century*. Philadelphia: University of Pennsylvania Press, 2008.

Bloom, Nicholas Dagen, and Matthew Gordon Lasner, eds. *Affordable Housing in New York: The People, Places, and Policies That Transformed a City*. Princeton, NJ: Princeton University Press, 2016.

Bloom, Nicholas Dagen, Fritz Umbach, and Lawrence J. Vale, eds. *Public Housing Myths: Perception, Reality, and Social Policy*. Ithaca, NY: Cornell University Press, 2015.

Blum, Edward J. *Reforging the White Republic: Race, Religion, and American Nationalism, 1865–1898*. Baton Rouge: Louisiana State University Press, 2005.

Blumenbach, Johann Friedrich. *The Anthropological Treatises of Johann Friedrich Blumenbach*. Edited by Thomas Bendyshe. London: Longman, Green, Longman, Roberts & Green, 1865.

Bragdon, Claude. *Architecture and Democracy*. Freeport, NY: Books for Libraries, 1971.

Bressani, Martin. "Notes on Viollet-le-Duc's Philosophy of History." *Journal of the Society of Architectural Historians* 48, no. 4 (December 1989): 327–50.

Bristol, Katharine. "The Pruitt Igoe Myth." *Journal of Architectural Education* 44, no. 3 (1991): 163–71.

Brown, Adrienne. *The Black Skyscraper: Architecture and the Perception of Race*. Baltimore: Johns Hopkins University Press, 2017.

Brulhart, Armand, and Pierre Frey, eds. *E. Viollet-le-Duc et le Massif du Mont Blanc, 1868–1879*. Lausanne: Payot, 1988.

Bryant, Edwin F., and Laurie L. Patton. *The Indo-Aryan Controversy: Evidence and Inference in Indian History*. New York: Routledge, 2005.

Buck-Morss, Susan. *Hegel, Haiti, and Universal History*. Pittsburgh: University of Pittsburgh Press, 2009.

Buell, Lawrence. *Emerson*. Cambridge, MA: Harvard University Press, 2003.

Camille, Michael. *The Gargoyles of Notre-Dame: Medievalism and the Monsters of Modernity*. Chicago: University of Chicago Press, 2009.

Campbell, James T., Matthew Pratt Guterl, and Robert G. Lee, eds. *Race, Nation and Empire in American History*. Chapel Hill: University of North Carolina Press, 2007.

Canales, Jimena, and Andrew Herscher. "Criminal Skins: Tattoos and Modern Architecture in the Work of Adolf Loos." *Architectural History* 48 (2005): 235–56.

Caramellino, Gaia. *Europe Meets America: William Lescaze, Architect of Modern Housing*. Newcastle upon Tyne, UK: Cambridge Scholars, 2016.

Carranza, Luis, and Fernando Luis Lara. *Modern Architecture in Latin America: Art, Technology, and Utopia*. Austin: University of Texas Press, 2014.

Catalogue at Auction at Our Salesrooms, No. 185 Wabash Avenue, Monday, Nov. 29, 10:30 am: Household effects, library, Oriental rugs, paintings, etc. of Mr. Louis Sullivan, the well-known Chicago architect, at unreserved sale. Chicago: Williams, Barker & Severn, 1909.

Çelik, Zeynep. *Displaying the Orient: Architecture of Islam at Nineteenth-Century World's Fairs*. Berkeley: University of California Press, 1992.

Çelik, Zeynep. *Empire, Architecture, and the City: French-Ottoman Encounters, 1830–1914*. Seattle: University of Washington Press, 2008.

Chakrabarty, Dipesh. *Provincializing Europe: Postcolonial Thought and Historical Difference*. Princeton, NJ: Princeton University Press, 2000.

Cheng, Anne. *Second Skin: Josephine Baker and the Modern Surface*. New York: Oxford University Press, 2011.

Cogdell, Christina. *Eugenic Design: Streamlining America in the 1930s*. Philadelphia: University of Pennsylvania Press, 2013.

Conrad, Sebastian. *German Colonialism: A Short History*. New York: Cambridge University Press, 2012.

Le Corbusier. *When the Cathedrals Were White: A Journey to the Country of Timid People*. New York: McGraw-Hill, 1964.

Cray, Clifton, and Pamela Scully. *Sara Baartman and the Hottentot Venus: A Ghost Story and a Biography*. Princeton, NJ: Princeton University Press, 2009.

Crinson, Mark. *Empire Building: Orientalism and Victorian Architecture*. New York: Routledge, 2013.

Cunningham, Mary Mullen. *Heinz Warneke (1895–1983): A Sculptor First and Last*. Newark: University of Delaware Press, 1994.

Dávila, Arlene. *Barrio Dreams: Puerto Ricans, Latinos, and the Neoliberal City*. Berkeley: University of California Press, 2004.

Drake, St. Clair, and Horace R. Cayton. *Black Metropolis: A Study of Negro Life in a Northern City*. New York: Harcourt, Brace, 1945.

Dudley, George A. *A Workshop for Peace: Designing the United Nations Headquarters*. Cambridge, MA: MIT Press, 1994.

Dyke, Willard Van, and Ralph Steiner. *The City*. American Documentary Films, 1939.

Eck, Caroline van. *Organicism in Nineteenth-Century Architecture: An Enquiry into Its Theoretical and Philosophical Background*. Amsterdam: Architectura and Natura Press, 1999.

Egbert, Donald Drew. *The Beaux-Arts Tradition in French Architecture*. Princeton, NJ: Princeton University Press, 1980.

Eigen, Sara, and Mark Larrimore, eds. *The German Invention of Race*. Albany: State University of New York Press, 2006.

Emerson, Ralph Waldo. *English Traits*. Edited by Howard Mumford Jones. 1856. Cambridge, MA: Belknap Press of Harvard University Press, 1966.

Erickson, Paul A., and Liam D. Murphy, eds. *Readings for a History of Anthropological Theory*. 5th ed. Toronto: University of Toronto Press, 2016.

Eze, Emmanuel Chukwudi. *Race and the Enlightenment: A Reader*. Malden, MA: Blackwell, 2000.

Fairbanks, Robert B. "From Better Dwellings to Better Neighborhoods: The Rise and Fall of the First National Housing Movement." In *From Tenements to the Taylor Homes: In Search of an Urban Housing Policy in Twentieth-Century America*, edited by John F. Bauman, Roger Biles, and Kristin M. Szylvian, 21–29. University Park: Pennsylvania State University Press, 2000.

Fan, Sizheng. "From 'Architecture and Allied Arts' to 'International Style': Architectural Exhibits in New York, 1925–1932." PhD diss., Cornell University, 2000.

Fanon, Frantz. *Black Skin, White Masks*. New York: Grove, 1967.

Fields, Darell Wayne. *Architecture in Black*. London: Athlone, 2000.

Glaude, Eddie S., Jr. *In a Shade of Blue: Pragmatism and the Politics of Black America*. Chicago: University of Chicago Press, 2007.

Gould, Stephen Jay. *The Mismeasure of Man*. New York: W. W. Norton, 2006.

Gray, Richard T. *About Face: German Physiognomic Thought from Lavater to Auschwitz*. Detroit: Wayne State University Press, 2004.

Gregory, Frederick. *Scientific Materialism in Nineteenth Century Germany*. Dordrecht: D. Reidel, 1977.

Gubler, Jacques. "In Search of the Primitive." In *Eugène Emmanuel Viollet-le-Duc, 1814–1879*, edited by Penelope Farrant, Brigitte Hermann, and Ian Latham, 80–83. Architectural Design Profiles. London: Academy Editions, 1980.

Gubler, Jacques. "Viollet-le-Duc et l'Architecture Rurale." In *Viollet-le-Duc. Centenaire de la mort à Lausanne*. Lausanne: Musée Historique de l'Ancien-Evêché, 1979.

Harris, Dianne. *Little White Houses: How the Postwar Home Constructed Race in America*. Minneapolis: University of Minnesota Press, 2012.

Harris, Dianne. *Second Suburb: Levittown, Pennsylvania*. Pittsburgh: University of Pittsburgh Press, 2010.

Harris, Michael W. *The Rise of Gospel Blues: The Music of Thomas Andrew Dorsey in the Urban Church*. New York: Oxford University Press, 1992.

Hartley, Lucy. *Physiognomy and the Meaning of Expression in Nineteenth-Century Culture*. Cambridge: Cambridge University Press, 2001.

Haywood, C. Robert. *Victorian West: Class and Culture in Kansas Cattle Towns*. Lawrence: University Press of Kansas, 1991.

Herrmann, Wolfgang. *Gottfried Semper: In Search of Architecture*. Cambridge, MA: MIT Press, 1984.

Hitchcock, Henry-Russell, ed. *In the Nature of Materials, 1887–1942: The Buildings of Frank Lloyd Wright*. New York: Da Capo, 1942.

Hitchcock, Henry-Russell. *Modern Architecture: Romanticism and Reintegration*. New York: Hacker Art Books, 1970.

Hitchcock, Henry-Russell, and Arthur Drexler. *Built in USA: Post-war Architecture*. New York: Simon and Schuster, 1952.

Hitchcock, Henry-Russell, and Philip Johnson. *The International Style: Architecture since 1922*. New York: W. W. Norton, 1932. Republished as *The International Style*, with a foreword by Philip Johnson. New York: W. W. Norton, 1995.

Horsman, Reginald. *Race and Manifest Destiny: The Origins of American Racial Anglo-Saxonism*. Cambridge, MA: Harvard University Press, 1986.

Hübsch, Heinrich, ed. *In What Style Should We Build? The German Debate on Architectural Style*. Santa Monica, CA: Getty Center, 1992.

Hugo, Victor. *En voyage, Alpes et Pyrénées*. Paris: Hetzel, 1890.

Huyssen, David. *Progressive Inequality: Rich and Poor in New York, 1890–1920*. Cambridge, MA: Harvard University Press, 2014.

Hvattum, Mari. *Gottfried Semper and the Problem of Historicism*. Cambridge: Cambridge University Press, 2004.

Ignatiev, Noel. *How the Irish Became White*. New York: Routledge, 1995.

Jacobson, Matthew Frye. *Whiteness of a Different Color: European Immigrants and the Alchemy of Race*. Cambridge, MA: Harvard University Press, 1998.

James, Cary. *Frank Lloyd Wright's Imperial Hotel*. New York: Dover, 1988.

Jordy, William. *"Symbolic Essence" and Other Writings on Modern Architecture and American Culture*. Edited by Joan Ockman. Buell Center/Columbia University Book on Architecture. New Haven, CT: Yale University Press, 2005.

Kant, Immanuel. "Of the Different Human Races." In *The Idea of Race*, edited by Robert Bernasconi and Tommy Lott, 8–22. Indianapolis: Hackett, 2000.

Kaplan, Amy. *The Anarchy of Empire in the Making of U.S. Culture*. Cambridge, MA: Harvard University Press, 2002.

Kaplan, Dana Evan. *American Reform Judaism: An Introduction*. New Brunswick, NJ: Rutgers University Press, 2003.

Kilde, Jeanne Halgren. *When Church Became Theater: The Transformation of Evangelical Architecture and Worship in Nineteenth-Century America*. New York: Oxford University Press, 2002.

Kim, Claire Jean. "The Racial Triangulation of Asian Americans." *Politics & Society*, 27, no. 1 (March 1999): 105–38.

Klammer, Martin. *Whitman, Slavery, and the Emergence of* Leaves of Grass. University Park: Pennsylvania State University Press, 1995.

Knox, Robert. *The Races of Men*. Philadelphia: Lea & Blanchard, 1850.

Koch, Daniel. *Ralph Waldo Emerson in Europe: Class, Race and Revolution in the Making of an American Thinker*. New York: I. B. Tauris, 2012.

Kolinsky, Eva, and Wilfried van der Will. *The Cambridge Companion to Modern German Culture*. Cambridge: Cambridge University Press, 1988.

Kwak, Nancy H. "Planning Note: American Public Housing: Hardly a Domestic Affair." *Journal of the American Planning Association* 78, no. 4 (2012): 416–17.

Lane, Barbara Miller. *Architecture and Politics in Germany, 1918–1945*. Cambridge, MA: Harvard University Press, 1985.

Lane, Barbara Miller. *National Romanticism and Modern Architecture in Germany and the Scandinavian Countries*. New York: Cambridge University Press, 2000.

Lanmon, Lorraine Welling. "The Role of William E. Lescaze in the Introduction of the International Style in the United States." PhD diss., University of Delaware, 1979.

Lanmon, Lorraine Welling. *William Lescaze, Architect*. Philadelphia: Art Alliance, 1987.

Lescaze, William. "New Deal Architecture." *New Republic*, July 26, 1933, 278–80.

Lescaze, William. *On Being an Architect*. New York: G. P. Putnam's Sons, 1942.

Lewis, Michael J. *Frank Furness: Architecture and the Violent Mind*. New York: W. W. Norton, 2001.

López-Durán, Fabiola. *Eugenics in the Garden: Transatlantic Architecture and the Crafting of Modernity*. Austin: University of Texas Press, 2018.

Love, Eric T. L. *Race over Empire: Racism and U.S. Imperialism, 1865–1900*. Chapel Hill: University of North Carolina Press, 2004.

Lukasik, Christopher J. *Discerning Characters: The Culture of Appearance in Early America*. Philadelphia: University of Pennsylvania Press, 2011.

Mallgrave, Harry Francis. *Gottfried Semper: Architect of the Nineteenth Century*. New Haven, CT: Yale University Press, 1996.

Mallgrave, Harry Francis. "Gustav Klemm and Gottfried Semper: The Meeting of Ethnological and Architectural Theory." *RES: Anthropology and Aesthetics* 9 (1985): 68–79.

Manbeck, John B., ed. *The Neighborhoods of Brooklyn*. New Haven, CT: Yale University Press, 1998.

Marovich, Robert M. *A City Called Heaven: Chicago and the Birth of Gospel Music*. Urbana: University of Illinois Press, 2015.

Massey, Douglas, and Nancy Denton. *American Apartheid: Segregation and the Making of the Underclass*. Cambridge, MA: Harvard University Press, 1996.

Meagher, Timothy J. *The Columbia Guide to Irish American History*. New York: Columbia University Press, 2005.

Menocal, Narciso. *Architecture as Nature: The Transcendentalist Idea of Louis Sullivan*. Madison: University of Wisconsin Press, 1981.

Merwood-Salisbury, Joanna. *Chicago 1890: The Skyscraper and the Modern City*. Chicago: University of Chicago Press, 2009.

Morton, Patricia A. *Hybrid Modernities: Architecture and Representation at the 1931 Colonial Exposition, Paris*. Cambridge, MA: MIT Press, 2000.

Muhammad, Khalil Gibran. *The Condemnation of Blackness: Race, Crime, and the Making of Modern Urban America*. Cambridge, MA: Harvard University Press, 2011.

Mumford, Lewis. *The Culture of Cities*. New York: Harcourt, Brace, 1938.

Mumford, Lewis. "Housing." In *Modern Architecture: International Exhibition, New York, Feb. 10 to March 23, 1932, Museum of Modern Art*, 179–92. New York: Museum of Modern Art, 1932.

Naranch, Bradley, and Geoff Eley, eds. *German Colonialism in a Global Age*. Durham, NC: Duke University Press, 2014.

Nathan, Walter L. "Living Forms: The Sculptor Heinz Warneke." *Parnassus* 13, no. 2 (1941): 55–59.

"The Negro in Harlem: A Report on Social and Economic Conditions Responsible for the Outbreak of March 19, 1935." Mayor's Commission on Conditions in Harlem, New York, 1935.

New York City Guide. New York: Random House with Works Progress Administration, 1939.

Newhouse, Victoria. *Wallace K. Harrison, Architect*. New York: Rizzoli, 1989.

Nicoloff, Philip. *Emerson on Race and History: An Examination of* English Traits. New York: Columbia University Press, 1961.

Norman, F. "'Indo-European' and 'Indo-Germanic.'" *Modern Language Review* 24, no. 3 (July 1929): 313–21.

Nott, Josiah, and L.-F.-Alfred Maury, eds. *Indigenous Races of the Earth, or New Chapters on Ethnological Inquiry*, volume 1, Philadelphia: J. B. Lippincott, 1857.

Nott, Josiah, and L.-F.-Alfred Maury, eds. *Indigenous Races of the Earth, or New Chapters on Ethnological Inquiry*, volume 2, Philadelphia: J. B. Lippincott, 1868.

Nute, Kevin. *Frank Lloyd Wright and Japan*. New York: Van Nostrand Reinhold, 1993.

O'Connell, Lauren. "A Rational, National Architecture: Viollet-le-Duc's Modest Proposal for Russia." *Journal of the Society of Architectural Historians* 52, no. 4 (December 1993): 436–52.

Osayimwese, Itohan. *Colonialism and Modern Architecture in Germany*. Pittsburgh: University of Pittsburgh Press, 2017.

Painter, Nell Irvin. *The History of White People*. New York: W. W. Norton, 2010.

Parker, Barry, and Raymond Unwin. *The Art of Building a Home: A Collection of Lectures and Illustrations*. London: Longmans, Green, 1901.

Paul, Sherman. *Louis Sullivan: An Architect in American Thought*. Englewood Cliffs, NJ: Prentice-Hall, 1962.

Pearlman, Jill. *Inventing American Modernism: Joseph Hudnut, Walter Gropius, and the Bauhaus Legacy at Harvard*. Charlottesville: University of Virginia Press, 2007.

Pérez Gómez, Alberto, and Stephen Parcell. *Chora: Intervals in the Philosophy of Architecture*. Vol. 1. Montreal: McGill-Queen's University Press, 1994.

Perraudin, Michael, and Jurgan Zimmer with Katy Heady, eds. *German Colonialism and National Identity*. New York: Routledge, 2013.

Picon, Antoine. *Ornament: The Politics of Architecture and Subjectivity*. Chichester, West Sussex, UK: Wiley, 2013.

"Pictet on the Aryan Race." *Anthropological Review* 1, no. 2 (1863): 232–46.

Pinder, Kymberly. "Painting the Gospel Blues: Race, Empathy, and Religion at Pilgrim Baptist Church." *American Art* 25, no. 3 (Fall 2011): 76–99.

Pink, Louis. *The New Day in Housing*. New York: John Day, 1928.

Plunz, Richard. *A History of Housing in New York City: Dwelling Type and Social Change in the American Metropolis*. New York: Columbia University Press, 1990.

Porter, Martin. *Windows of the Soul: Physiognomy in European Culture, 1470–1780*. New York: Oxford University Press, 2005.

Prakash, Vikramaditya. *Chandigarh's Le Corbusier: The Struggle for Modernity in Postcolonial India*. Seattle: University of Washington Press, 2002.

Quetelet, Adolphe. *Anthropométrie, ou mesure des différentes facultés de l'homme*. Brussels: C. Muquardt, 1870.

Reed, Christopher Robert. *The Rise of Chicago's Black Metropolis, 1920–1929*. Urbana: University of Illinois Press, 2014.

Riegl, Alois. *Problems of Style: Foundations for a History of Ornament*. Princeton, NJ: Princeton University Press, 1992.

Riis, Jacob August. *How the Other Half Lives: Studies among the Tenements of New York*. New York: Charles Scribner's Sons, 1914.

Riley, Terence. *The International Style: Exhibition 15 and the Museum of Modern Art*. New York: Rizzoli, 1992.

Roediger, David R. *The Wages of Whiteness: Race and the Making of the American Working Class*. London: Verso, 1991.

Roediger, David R. *Working toward Whiteness: How America's Immigrants Became White: The Strange Journey from Ellis Island to the Suburbs*. New York: Basic Books, 2005.

Rosenau, Helen. "Gottfried Semper and German Synagogue Architecture." *Le Baeck Institute Yearbook* 22, no. 1 (1977): 237–44.

Rowe, Peter G. *Modernity and Housing.* Cambridge, MA: MIT Press, 1993.

Ruskin, John. *The Poetry of Architecture: or the Architecture of the Nations of Europe Considered in Its Association with Natural Scenery and National Characteristics.* London: George Allen, 1893.

Rykwert, Joseph. *The Dancing Column: On Order in Architecture.* Cambridge, MA: MIT Press, 1998.

Rykwert, Joseph. *The Idea of a Town: The Anthropology of Urban Form in Rome, Italy and the Ancient World.* Princeton, NJ: Princeton University Press, 1976.

Rykwert, Joseph. *On Adam's House in Paradise: The Idea of the Primitive Hut in Architectural History.* Cambridge, MA: MIT Press, 1981.

Said, Edward. *Orientalism.* London: Penguin, 1978.

Salazar, James B. *Bodies of Reform: The Rhetoric of Character in Gilded Age America.* New York: New York University Press, 2010.

Schulze, Franz, ed. *Mies van der Rohe: Critical Essays.* Cambridge, MA: MIT Press, 1989.

Schuyler, Montgomery. "A Critique (with illustrations) of the Works of Adler and Sullivan, D. H. Burnham & Co., Henry Ives Cobb." *Great American Architects Series: Architectural Record* 2 (February 1891), 15.

Schwarzer, Mitchell. *German Architectural Theory and the Search for Modern Identity.* Cambridge: Cambridge University Press, 1995.

Semper, Gottfried. *The Four Elements of Architecture and Other Writings.* Translated by Harry Francis Mallgrave and Wolfgang Herrmann. Cambridge: Cambridge University Press, 1989.

Semper, Gottfried. *Style in the Technical and Tectonic Arts; or, Practical Aesthetics.* Translated by Harry Francis Mallgrave and Michael Robinson. Los Angeles: Getty Research Institute, 2004.

Sharpley-Whiting, T. Denean. *Black Venus: Sexualized Savages, Primal Fears, and Primitive Narratives in French.* Durham, NC: Duke University Press, 1999.

Shelley, Percy. *History of a Six Weeks' Tour through a Part of France, Switzerland, Germany and Holland.* London: T. Hookham, 1817.

Silverstein, Alan. *Alternatives to Assimilation: The Response of Reform Judaism to American Culture, 1840–1930.* Hanover: Brandeis University Press, 1994.

Siry, Joseph. *Beth Sholom Synagogue: Frank Lloyd Wright and Modern Religious Architecture.* Chicago: University of Chicago Press, 2012.

Southern, David W. *The Progressive Era and Race: Reaction and Reform, 1900–1917.* Wheeling, IL: H. Davidson, 2005.

Spivak, Gayatri. *Can the Subaltern Speak?* Basingstoke: Macmillan, 1988.

Staum, Martin S. *Labeling People: French Scholars on Society, Race, and Empire, 1815–1848.* Montreal: McGill-Queen's University Press, 2003.

Stephanson, Anders. *Manifest Destiny: American Expansion and the Empire of Right.* New York: Farrar, Straus and Giroux, 1996.

Sullivan, Louis. *The Autobiography of an Idea.* New York: Dover, 1956.

Sullivan, Louis. *Democracy: A Man Search.* Westport, CT: Greenwood, 1973.

Sullivan, Louis. *Kindergarten Chats.* 1918. New York: Dover, 1979.

Sullivan, Louis. *Louis Sullivan: The Public Papers.* Edited by Robert Twombly. Chicago: University of Chicago Press, 1988.

30 Years of Amalgamated Cooperative Housing, 1927–1957. New York: Amalgamated Housing, 1958.

Tigerman, Stanley. "Mies van der Rohe: A Moral Modernist Model." *Perspecta* 22 (1986): 112–135.

Twombly, Robert. *Louis Sullivan: His Life and Work*. Chicago: University of Chicago Press, 1987.

Twombly, Robert, and Narciso Menocal. *Louis Sullivan: The Poetry of Architecture*. New York: W. W. Norton, 2000.

Unwin, Raymond. *Town Planning in Practice: An Introduction to the Art of Designing Cities*. London: Adelphi Terrace, 1909.

Vendryes, Margaret Rose. *Barthé: A Life in Sculpture*. Jackson: University Press of Mississippi, 2008.

Vidler, Anthony. *The Writing of the Walls: Architectural Theory in the Late Enlightenment*. New York: Princeton Architectural Press, 1987.

Viollet-le-Duc au Chateau d'Eu, 1874–1879. Eu, France: Musée Louis-Philippe, 1979.

Viollet-le-Duc, Eugène Emmanuel. *The Foundations of Architecture: Selections from the Dictionnaire Raisonné*. Introduction by Barry Bergdoll, Translation by Kenneth D. Whitehead. New York: George Braziller, 1990.

Viollet-le-Duc, Eugène Emmanuel. *Habitations of Man in All Ages*. Translated by Benjamin Bucknall. London: James R. Osgood, 1876.

Viollet-le-Duc, Eugène Emmanuel. *Histoire d'un dessinateur*. Paris: J. Hetzel, 1879.

Waldheim, Charles, and Katerina Ruedi Ray. *Chicago Architecture: Histories, Revisions, Alternatives*. Chicago: University of Chicago Press, 2005.

Washington, Booker T. *Character Building*. 1902. New Brunswick, NJ: Transaction, 2013.

Weingarden, Lauren S. *Louis H. Sullivan and a 19th-Century Poetics of Naturalized Architecture*. Burlington, VT: Ashgate, 2009.

Weingarden, Lauren. "A Transcendentalist Discourse in the Poetics of Technology: Louis Sullivan's Transportation Building and Walt Whitman's Passage to India." *Word & Image* 3, no. 2 (1987): 202–21.

William Lescaze: The Rise of Modern Design in America. Special issue, *Courier* 6, no. 1 (Spring 1984): 57–66.

Williams, Mason B. *City of Ambition: FDR, La Guardia, and the Making of Modern New York*. New York: W. W. Norton, 2014.

Willis, Alfred E. *Illustrated Physiognomy*. Chicago: Alfred E. Willis, 1879.

"Williamsburg Houses." Landmarks Preservation Commission, June 24, 2003, Designation List 48, LP-2135.

Wilson, Dreck Spurlock, ed. *African-American Architects: A Biographical Dictionary, 1865–1945*. New York, Routledge, 2004.

Wilson, Mabel. "Black Bodies/White Cities: Le Corbusier in Harlem." *ANY: Architecture New York* 16 (1996): 35–39.

Wischnitzer, Rachel. *Synagogue Architecture in the United States: History and Interpretation*. Philadelphia: Jewish Publication Society of America, 1955.

Wood, Edith Elmer. *Housing Progress in Western Europe*. New York: E. P. Dutton, 1923.

Wright, Frank Lloyd. *Ausgeführte Bauten und Entwurfe von Frank Lloyd Wright*. Edited by Ernst Wasmuth. Berlin: Ernst Wasmuth, 1910.

Wright, Frank Lloyd. *An Autobiography*. 1932. New York: Horizon, 1977.

Wright, Frank Lloyd. *Genius and the Mobocracy*. New York: Horizon, 1971.

Wright, Gwendolyn. *The Politics of Design in French Colonial Urbanism*. Chicago: University of Chicago Press, 1991.

Zantop, Susanne. *Colonial Fantasies: Conquest, Family, and Nation in Precolonial Germany, 1770–1870*. Durham, NC: Duke University Press, 1997.

Zimmerman, Andrew. *Anthropology and Antihumanism in Imperial Germany*. Chicago: University of Chicago Press, 2001.

Zinn, Howard. *LaGuardia in Congress*. Ithaca, NY: Fall Creek Books, 1958.

Zipp, Samuel, and Nicholas Dagen Bloom. "Williamsburg Houses." In *Affordable Housing in New York: The People, Places and Policies That Transformed a City*, edited by Nicholas Dagen Bloom and Matthew Gordon Lasner, 94–99. Princeton, NJ: Princeton University Press, 2016.

INDEX

Note: Page numbers in *italics* refer to figures.